Sharing the World

Sustainable Living and Global Equity in the 21st Century

Michael Carley
and
Philippe Spapens

Earthscan Publications Ltd, London

First published in the UK 1998 by
Earthscan Publications Limited

A catalogue record for this book is available from the British Library

ISBN: 1 85383 463 7 (paperback)
ISBN: 1 85383 464 5 (hardback)

Typesetting and page design by PCS Mapping & DTP, Newcastle upon Tyne

Printed and bound by Biddles Ltd, Guildford and Kings Lynn

Cover design by Declan Buckley

Illustrations by Jim Lewis except figures 1.2, 1.3 and 1.9 by Meinte Strikwerda

All royalties from this publication will be paid to Friends of the Earth Netherlands (Vereniging Milieudefensie)

For a full list of publications please contact:
Earthscan Publications Limited
120 Pentonville Road
London N1 9JN
Tel. (0171) 278 0433
Fax: (0171) 278 1142
Email: earthinfo@earthscan.co.uk
WWW: http://www.earthscan.co.uk

Earthscan is an editorially independent subsidiary of Kogan Page Limited and publishes in association with WWF-UK and the International Institute for Environment and Development.

Sharing the World

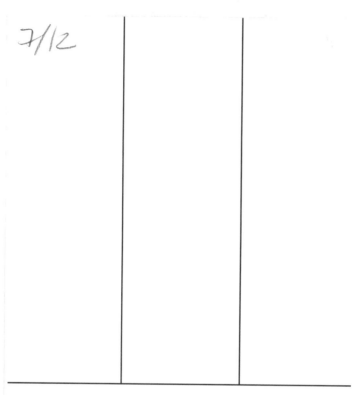

7/12

Please renew or return items by the date shown on your receipt

www.hertsdirect.org/libraries

Renewals and enquiries: 0300 123 4049

Textphone for hearing or 0300 123 4041
speech impaired users:

L32

Hertfordshire

Dedicated to Nicholas, Thea, Pieter and Oliver
and all the members of the next generation
who might put these ideas into practice.

The best book yet on sustainable consumption.
ED MAYO, DIRECTOR, NEW ECONOMICS FOUNDATION

Sharing the World is compulsory for everyone who wants to contribute to the world as a better place for all. It shows what we need to do and how to do it, but also that we have no time to lose. It is an unprecedented, exciting challenge.
JOHN HONTELEZ, SECRETARY GENERAL, EUROPEAN ENVIRONMENTAL BUREAU

Scientific findings justify precautionary action to save our Earth. *Sharing the World* anticipates trends in resource consumption, highlights the challenges of materialism, and shows that, apart from different starting points, both developed and developing countries need to rethink their development paths.
PROFESSOR MUHAMMAD YUNUS, MANAGING DIRECTOR, GRAMEEN BANK, BANGLADESH

A pessimist, they say, is simply a well-informed optimist. Certainly the global environmental problems facing us are enough to take the wind out of the sails of even the best of optimists. How does one solve the problems of over-consumption in the North, gnawing poverty in the South, progress in some newly-industrialized countries, and face the challenges created by the globalization of the market economy? *Sharing the World*, with its emphasis on a sophisticated, equitable and ecologically-sound development framework, is a valuable guide to help us envision and thus undertake the necessary change. What is more, because environmental problems will be solved by action at all levels – government, corporate, and individual – this volume has outlined steps for each.

We emerge from *Sharing the World* as optimists. Some optimists are pessimists who have seen the way the world is heading and have decided that the best way to market difficult changes is to show people what is in it for them, whether they are operating as investors, consumers, managers, employees or even ordinairy citizens. This is the message of *Sharing the World*.
ELIZABETH DOWDESWELL, EXECUTIVE DIRECTOR, UNITED NATIONS ENVIRONMENT PROGRAMME

Sharing the World is for any business person wishing to learn about innovative approaches to global sustainable development.
BJOERN STIGSON, EXECUTIVE DIRECTOR, WORLD BUSINESS COUNCIL FOR SUSTAINABLE DEVELOPMENT

As a result of Rio+5, held in New York in June 1997, we now know that far too little has been done about achieving equitable, sustainable development. *Sharing the World* shows what could have been done, what should have been done and hence what is to be done. Let's start now, as the 21st century begins.
PROFESSOR HANS OPSHOOR, FORMER CHAIRMAN, THE NATIONAL COUNCIL ON ENVIRONMENTAL AND NATURE RESEARCH, THE NETHERLANDS

Contents

List of Figures, Tables, Boxes and Guest Essays

Figures

Tables

Boxes

Guest Essays

List of Acronyms and Abbreviations

AIDS   acquired immune deficiency syndrome
ASEAN   Association of South-East Asian Nations
ATM   automatic teller machine
BAT   best available technology
BUND   Friends of the Earth, Germany
CBI   Confederation of British Industries
CFC   chlorofluorocarbon
CHDI   Corporate Human Development Index
CIA   US Central Intelligence Agency
CO_2 carbon dioxide
CPRE   Commission for the Protection of Rural England
CSD   United Nations Commission on Sustainable Development
CSE   Centre for Science and Environment
DoE   Department of the Environment, UK
EDP   environmentally adjusted net domestic product
EJ   exajoule (10^{18})
EU   European Union
FAO   United Nations Food and Agriculture Organisation
FoE   Friends of the Earth
GATT   General Agreement on Tariffs and Trade
GDP   gross domestic product
GEF   Global Environmental Facility
GJ   gigajoule (10^9)
GNP   gross national product
HCFC   hydro-chlorofluorocarbon
HDI   Human Development Index
IEEA   Integrated Environmental and Economic Accounting
IIED   International Institute for Environment and Development
ILO   International Labour Organization
IMF   International Monetary Fund
IPCC   Intergovernmental Panel on Climate Change
IPPC   Integrated Pollution Prevention Control
IPTES   Intergovernmental Panel on Trade, Environment and Sustainability

ISEW	Index of Sustainable Economic Welfare
IUCN	International Union for the Conservation of Nature
kmph	kilometres per hour
kWh	kilowatt hours
LCA	life-cycle assessment
MAI	Multilateral Agreement on Investment
MIPS	material intensity per product or service unit
mph	miles per hour
MW	megawatt (one million watts, or 10^6W)
NAFTA	North American Free Trade Association
NGO	non-governmental organisation
NIC	newly industrialising country
NSDS	national sustainable development strategy
OECD	Organisation for Economic Cooperation and Development
PCB	polychlorinated biphenyl
ppb	parts per billion
ppm	parts per million
ppmv	parts per million volume
SAP	Structural Adjustment Programme
SDR	Special Drawing Rights
SEI	Stockholm Environment Institute
SO_2	sulphur dioxide
UNCED	United Nations Conference on Environment and Development
UNCTAD	United Nations Commission on Trade and Development
UNDP	United Nations Development Programme
UNEP	United Nations Environment Programme
VCR	video cassette recorder
WHO	World Health Organisation
WMO	World Meteorological Organisation
WRI	World Resources Institute
WTO	World Trade Organisation
WWF	World Wide Fund For Nature/World Wildlife Fund

Preface

This book is a contribution to global sustainable development from the Sustainable Europe Campaign of Friends of the Earth – an international organisation with associated member groups in 63 countries around the world. The campaign is an intellectually stimulating, action–research process bringing together organisations and kindred groups from 30 countries of greater Europe. A parallel North–South project brought a further eight countries from Asia, Africa and South America into the framework of dialogue and analysis.

The purpose of the Sustainable Europe Campaign, begun in 1992, is to assess what sustainable development means in practical terms, and how it can be achieved. To do this we use the concept of fair shares in environmental space, based on three principles: the need for measurable progress toward sustainable production and consumption; balanced opportunities for development among all countries; and total quality of life rather than just materialism as a guiding force in public policy and values.

The lessons of the campaign are relevant to a worldwide audience. This book is intended to reach out to that wider audience, both in the other consumer societies of the North (such as in North America or Japan), the societies of the South, and Central and Eastern Europe and the former Soviet Union, which have an equally important and influential stake in sustainable development in the 21st century.

The term 'environmental' space was first applied to the sustainability debate by Hans Opschoor in 1987. The environmental space approach as developed by Friends of the Earth has its origins in the pioneering *Action Plan Sustainable Netherlands* published by Friends of the Earth Netherlands (Vereniging Milieudefensie), as a contribution to the United Nations Conference on Environment and Development (UNCED) in Rio de Janeiro in 1992. The *Action Plan* maintained that sustainability can only be achieved if the use of natural resources is limited and more equally distributed throughout the world.

Sustainable Europe is a project of Friends of the Earth Europe, whose headquarters are in Brussels, with Vereniging Milieudefensie in Amsterdam as the coordinating group. Scientific analysis and method-ological development was carried out by the Wuppertal Institute for Climate, Environment and Energy in Germany. An international steering committee of sustainable development experts from the various regions of Europe met regularly to serve as a think tank for the project, considering both scientific content and policy impact. The message of environmental space is now spreading globally through the new Sustainable Societies Programme of Friends of the Earth International, which links member organisations on every populated continent.

Of course, any approach to global sustainable development raises a host of political, ethical, social, economic and scientific issues. We have not tried to deal with all of these, as this would have resulted in a book of daunting size, if it had been possible at all. Rather we have tried to explain the environmental space approach in a relatively straightforward and succinct manner. For a more technical analysis of environmental space, the reader is referred to the many references throughout this book to the work of the Wuppertal Institute, other research organisations from around the world, and the national Friends of the Earth organisations, each of which analysed and published reports on the environmental space available to their own country. Most of the references here are to documents in English, but the reader should note that material on environmental space is available in 26 languages including French, Spanish, Portuguese, German, Italian, Dutch, Greek, Polish, Russian, Norwegian, Japanese, Mandarin and many others. Readers who prefer material in languages other than English should get in touch with Vereniging Milieudefensie, or any of the national teams whose addresses are to be found in Appendix B. National environmental space studies referred to in the text are not separately footnoted. Instead these are all listed in Appendix A.

Finally, we should note that throughout the book we use the shorthand terms North and South. The term North refers mainly to the high-consuming member countries of the Organisation for Economic Cooperation and Development (OECD). The term South is less specific. Obviously it refers to the world's subsistence economies, but also to former communist economies in transition. The newly industrialising countries (NICs) of Asia are also included here, but with recognition that their economic stature on the world stage means their economic development levels are bypassing those of some current OECD members, and that they too will join the club. Perhaps a better reason for using the terms North and South is that the distinction reflects the current balance of power in world politics. As Friends of the Earth in London says, 'the North controls the global institutions that set the framework for international relations, Northern companies control the vast majority of world trade, and Northern consumer lifestyles, reinforced by advertising, set the global culture'.

We would like to conclude by thanking the many people who assisted in the Sustainable Europe Campaign, the North–South Project and in the preparation of this book. The members of the 38 action–research teams are far too numerous to mention, but their reports, discussions in meetings in Brussels, and in regional meetings around Europe, have been the inspiration for this book.

We are particularly grateful to our eminent guest authors, whose contributions appear as short essays throughout the text. They broaden the perspective of the environmental space approach and provide insightful commentary on our work. They are: Lester Brown, President of the Worldwatch Institute, Washington; Josefa Rizalina M Bautista, Vice President, Development Academy of the Philippines; Svend Auken, Minister for Environment and Energy of Denmark; Jacqueline Aloisi de Larderel, Director, UNEP Industry and Environment; Anil Agarwal, Director and Sunita Narain, Deputy Director, Centre for Science and Environment, New Delhi; Claude Fussler, Vice President, Dow Europe SA; Claude Martin, Director General, World Wide Fund for Nature; Alan Durning, Executive Director, Northwest Environment Watch, Seattle; Ernst Ulrich von Weizsäcker, President, Wuppertal Institute; Izaak LG Van Melle, Managing Director, Van Melle International; and Joachim Spangenberg and Odile Bonniot of the Wuppertal Institute.

Friends of the Earth Europe gratefully acknowledges the sponsorship of the Sustainable Europe Campaign by the Commission of the European Communities, Directorate General of Environment, Nuclear Safety and Civil Protection (DG XI); the Dutch Ministry of Housing, Spatial Planning and the Environment; the Government of Norway; Gesellschaft für Technische Zusammenarbeit (GTZ); the Wuppertal Institute; the United Nations Environment Programme (UNEP) and many other organisations which provided help in cash and in kind.

We would also like to thank members of the campaign who made particular contributions to this book: Joachim Spangenberg, Wuppertal Institute; Dag Hareide and John Hille, Friends of the Earth Norway; Kim Ejlertsen, NOAH – Friends of the Earth Denmark; Robert Kaspar, Friends of the Earth Austria; Duncan McLaren, Friends of the Earth England, Wales and Northern Ireland; Chris Revie, Friends of the Earth Scotland; Daniel Mittler, Bund – Friends of the Earth Germany; and Maria Buitenkamp, Vereniging Milieudefensie. However, the ideas presented in this book are ours, and do not necessarily reflect the opinions of these individuals, campaign members or Friends of the Earth. Most importantly, we would like to thank our families for their patience and commitment to the future.

Michael Carley
Chair, Sustainable Societies Programme,
Friends of the Earth International,
Steering Group, Sustainable Europe Campaign
Professor of Planning and Housing,
Centre for Environment and Human Settlements,
Heriot-Watt University, Edinburgh

Philippe Spapens
Campaigner, Sustainable Europe Campaign
Vereniging Milieudefensie, Amsterdam

Autumn, 1997

1

A New Approach to Global Development

Introduction

Looking to the new century, and the world we bequeath to our children and grandchildren, there are causes for optimism but also major challenges. On the positive side, globalisation is bringing to the fore a common agenda for sustainable development, balancing economic progress with social and environmental concerns. Exciting partnerships and networks are linking North and South, and innovation is reflected in local action on Agenda 21 and fledgling political commitment at the international level. Action networks are enabled by the communications revolution which breaks down isolation and allows rapid exchanges of information and views. For example, indigenous tribes in the South American rainforest are linked via satellite to health centres and support groups all over the world. They can now campaign for their own, and the global, future. New means of communication could also support the spread of opportunities for lifelong education which can foster, in turn, a trend towards more widespread democratic freedom and personal liberty. Another positive development is triggered by the end of the Cold War – giving relief from polarised political thinking and global alliances. This creates the opportunity to rethink development processes and embed the global market economy in a social context, so that we can secure its positive benefits without so many of the negative impacts.

On the other side of the coin, the challenges include the long-term damage to the planet caused by pollution; the ecological and cultural dislocations caused by an infatuation with material goods in wealthy countries and enclaves; and the impacts of poverty and unemployment, which flow through generations.

The challenges are complicated by a number of factors. Firstly, the production and consumption processes which underpin the highly attractive global consumer lifestyle are unsustainable. They are taking us past critical thresholds in the planet's ability to absorb waste and pollution, and in the use of scarce resources, including the air itself. Secondly, there is an unequal distribution of the benefits of industrialisation compared to the costs. Most of the benefits accrue to a small number of wealthy nations, which are vastly overconsuming the planet's resources when assessed on a per capita basis. Conversely, a disproportionate amount of the costs are borne by people and countries which do not share the benefits. This serious imbalance, roughly along North–South lines, is foreclosing future development opportunities for Southern countries. It also means that current favoured models of national development fail to provide realistic guidance for the next century.

Although the inequality caused by overconsumption is glaring and morally unjustifiable, the intent of the overconsumers is hardly malicious. The short-term benefits of consumerism are many, and its lure is powerful and seductive. Many people in lower income countries would like nothing better than to emulate the lifestyles common in the advanced industrial economies. Overconsumption is part of a process of modernisation in which most of humankind would willingly participate. Progress towards sustainability is also hampered by the tendency of governments and political and business leaders to take a short-term, rather than a much needed long-term view of the relationship between people and the planet. And our approach to managing the human–environment interaction is also short-term, being mainly too little, too late.

The underlying problem is that, however much we talk about sustainable development, the sheer volumes of resource consumption and pollution embodied in our ever-expanding consumer lifestyles means that these problems are out of control. They cannot be resolved without major changes in the efficiency of production and consumption systems to reduce their material intensiveness, coupled to fundamental changes in the values that underpin consumerism. Because these challenges affect the prospect of everyone on Earth and their descendants, they cannot be resolved except by a common global effort linking North and South, East and West.

In spite of the magnitude of the challenge, this book argues that it is well within human competence to achieve harmonious, sustainable development by the year 2050. We propose a practical, gradual approach to fundamentally alter industrial processes and the values that drive consumption, so that the world shifts to clean, sustainable and satisfying modes of living within the boundaries of what we call environmental space. The rest of this introductory chapter examines the challenges of development to be overcome and introduces the concept of environmental space.

The Poisonous Legacy of Our Industrial Age

A first challenge is the restoration of ecological balance, globally and locally. This has been disturbed by industrial pollution, and by a dramatic rise in consumption of global resources, such as the decimation of the world's fish stocks, the cutting of one fifth of the world's forests and the exhaustion of underground freshwater supplies. About 40 per cent of natural ecosystems are biologically degraded. The atmosphere itself is under threat from global warming, which can no longer be denied or ignored. Coastal regions, polar ice and island states may disappear, as could their ecosystems, plants and animals, such as the polar bear, walrus and the narwhal. Ozone holes in both hemispheres continue to grow, making it increasingly dangerous for humans to venture into the sunshine without protection in countries such as Canada, the USA, Australia and Argentina.

Concern for climate change extends to global change, which means that pollution and resource consumption, such as deforestation, are negatively affecting fundamental interactions between the earth's atmosphere, biosphere and oceans. There is also disturbing evidence of the endemic effects of

Figure 1.1
Yo! Amigo!!

the more than 50,000 industrial chemicals in everyday use – for example, organochlorines which disrupt human hormone systems and damage human fertility. Urban air pollution has a growing impact on health in the huge city regions emerging around the world, and even retards agricultural production in rural areas. Dangerous chemicals and pollutants are now found in every part of the planet, including in the peoples and landscape of the Arctic at high concentrations. In each case, safe thresholds are being exceeded which define the planet's and our bodies' abilities to absorb pollution.

The Challenge of Too Much in the Wealthy Countries

The related challenge is the overconsumption which characterises the Western consumer lifestyle. This way of life has caused consumption since 1950 to equal that of all previous human history. This causes two problems. Firstly, much of the damage to the planet's global commons is the result of consumption by the consumer societies of the developed countries. For example, the 20 per cent of the world's population which lives in the richest countries have generated almost three-quarters of the cumulative carbon dioxide emissions which are a primary cause of global warming. Many other global resources, from metals to timber, are consumed in about the same proportion, with a fifth of the world's population consuming four-fifths of all resources consumed annually, many of which are non-renewable. On a global basis, overconsumption by some countries means a reduced resource base for the development of others. The gap between the world's rich and poor is constantly widening with the richest one fifth now having 85 per cent of the world's income. This is the result of a development model which overvalues economic growth without considering the social and environmental impacts. It is no longer obvious that the benefits of high consumption outweigh the costs – not even to the high consumers themselves who are fouling their own nests. These high rates of unsustainable consumption are overwhelming the modest ecoefficiency savings being achieved by methods such as recycling.

Figure 1.2

Current patterns of global resource consumption are unsustainable – ecologically and socially

Secondly, within these consumer societies many people feel they are locked into a dispiriting and stressful cycle of work and spend, to 'keep up with the Joneses'. This emphasis on material goods to give meaning to life diminishes the quality of family and community life and erodes traditional cultural values. An incipient movement against overconsumption has been started in the USA, called 'downshifting' to a saner, less materialistic lifestyle. However, overconsumption in the wealthy countries is taking place even while around 100 million people in those countries are marginalised by poverty, unemployment and low pay. Poverty damages family life and the prospects of children and can destabilise communities by fostering crime and violence. An emphasis in industry on substituting technology for people, making unemployment endemic, means that much economic growth has become jobless growth. During the 1980s, 35 million people in the wealthy countries suffered unemployment, but even this enormous sum is small compared with the problems of lack of employment and household income in the poor countries of the world. Even where employment appears to be created by economic growth, the quality of the employment is changing. In advanced economies there is less opportunity for full-time, permanent work and increasing emphasis on short-term, part-time work to reduce employers' wage bills. This insecurity of income contributes to family stress, and the result can be an underclass of working poor.

The Challenge of the World's Poor

A third vital challenge is to alleviate poverty in the low-income countries, as well as in the industrialised countries. In 2010 there will still be more than 800 million chronically undernourished people in the developing world while, perversely, obesity causing ill-health is becoming endemic in the wealthy countries. Poverty is both a cause and effect of environmental degradation. It is indicated by lack of basic needs such as food, water, shelter and access to primary education and health services. Absolute poverty is incompatible with sustainable development, which seeks to balance economic, social and environmental goals. As Svend Auken, the Danish Minister for Environment and Energy, says: 'Wealth creates overconsumption, but poverty also destroys nature due to the fact that too many have too little to share.' The grinding effects of poverty extend even to many people in work in the developing world, such as child labourers in Asian factories earning ten cents an hour making sporting goods, or in the *maquiladoras* in Mexico – foreign-owned factories where workers assemble consumer goods for Northern markets for poverty level wages. On a global scale, the problems of insufficient income extend to about one fifth of the world's population, a growing number of which are concentrated in the exploding megacities of ten million persons or more in the developing world.

It is essential to avoid a two-track global economy in which only industrialised countries and a small number of newly industrialising countries sustain widespread technological and economic progress. This could marginalise the development potential of the majority of countries in Africa, Asia and Latin America by making it difficult for them to access the resources needed for development.

The Challenge of a Development Leapfrog by the NICs

Following dramatic economic growth in Asia's export-led tiger economies, we are now likely to see the emergence of another round of newly industrialised economies, or NICs, in key countries in Asia and South America. In countries such as China and India, growth can be based on the vast size of the internal market. Including China and India, these NICs will encompass more than a third of the world's population. Economic growth in these countries is obviously a key to the vital amelioration of poverty and to a broader opportunity to enjoy the fruits of the global economy.

Nevertheless, the major challenge is for the NICs to realise their legitimate aspirations for development in a way which does not cause yet more ecological destruction. As in the North, many material benefits will flow from industrialisation, including the meeting of basic needs and the provision of necessary infrastructure. But careful management of the process is important to avoid ecological damage, and the social and cultural dislocations of overconsumption. If the NICs go down the same highly polluting route to industrialisation as the Northern countries, ecological imbalances will pass critical thresholds even more quickly. The massive forest fires and air pollution over South East Asia in 1997 may be an example. The rainforest was being cleared for the planting of wood pulp, palm oil and rubber plantations – much of this for Northern consumption. In spite of this, NICs are suspicious of the agenda of sustainable development, which they fear is a ploy to protect Northern markets by slowing their well-earned rush to industrialisation. Given that Northern lifestyles caused many of the world's environmental problems, the NICs feel that the North has no moral authority to deny them the opportunity to make full use of their natural resource base, just as the North does.

Similar opportunities and risks beckon in the transition economies of Central and Eastern Europe, including Russia. On the one hand, they use resources inefficiently and are heavily polluted; on the other they are among the world's richest sources of biodiversity. In their cities, they have excellent public transport systems and low levels of car use. But they are being encouraged to rush into the unsustainable Western development model, in part because the ideal of democracy has been confused with an unleashed and unregulated winner-take-all market economy.

Figure 1.3

Equitable consumption levels are not necessarily sustainable

The Challenge of Governance and Participation

The accelerating pace of change, and the cumulative interactions between humans and the environment, is taxing the ability of political leaders everywhere to comprehend the future and to manage it for the benefit of coming generations. Most politicians are locked into short-term perspectives and a perceived need to foster economic growth at almost any cost. Although many are open to the idea of sustainable development, they have yet to bring forward practical ways of addressing the long-term needs for development, either in their own countries or in the increasingly interconnected global economy.

It is also clear that no government, or any level of government, acting on its own can address these challenges. Partnership between government, business and citizens' organisations is the key – as are creative, enabling linkages between top-down and bottom-up initiatives, tying together the levels in between. New means of forging partnerships in action networks to accomplish and monitor practical development tasks is a new and positive way of working. This implies a rethink of organisational relationships within the market framework, a basic level of embedded human rights and the empowerment of local communities and regions within the national structure.

Rethinking the Market Economy

Finally, to achieve sustainable development we need to overcome a dilemma. On the one hand, with the demise of the failed experiments of socialism every country recognises the need to compete in the emerging knowledge-based, technology-driven marketplace which defines the global economy. Economic development is vital to the amelioration of poverty in large parts of the world. Competition is a key to securing the advantages of the market, whose material benefits are appreciated by much of the world's population. Markets, although far from perfect, are the most efficient means for building critical feedback into production and consumption systems.

On the other hand, the roots of many global and local problems can be found in the limitations of markets as currently organised. The origins of these problems are found in:

- the failure of the market to encompass socially disruptive and ecologically destructive impacts (or externalities) in prices;
- the short-term perspective of the market, which undervalues (or discounts) the prospects of future generations;
- the promotion of excessive individualism and materialistic values as opposed to public or community values and the common good; and
- the market's tendency to concentrate power and wealth in the hands of the few rather than the many.

In terms of consumption, a serious problem is the market's inability to distinguish behaviour which appears rational to the individual consumer (one family driving a car) from the cumulative aspects of individual behaviour which is irrational from a societal perspective (massive traffic jams and air pollution), or a longer-term global perspective (the impacts of climate change).

A challenge for governments, and for civil society, is to understand better how to reap the benefits of the market economy without suffering so many of the costs, and without passing these costs on to other countries, to other generations, or just dumping them in the environment. The market economy has proved resilient and attractive but it is not a metaphor for democracy, and its workings do not guarantee a high quality of life. On the contrary, in too many cases economic growth has become unhinged from genuine progress. For example, global trade liberalisation brings cheaper products and other benefits – but at social and environmental costs which are being ignored in the rush to secure short-term economic gains.

The market economy therefore, may be necessary but not sufficient to generate a high quality of life in the societies of the 21st century. A major challenge is creative adjustment of the processes of capitalism to encompass the need for environmental quality and social justice.

Environmental Space: Living Comfortably within Global Means

Given their interrelated nature, it is obvious that the planet's major challenges as we move into the 21st century are not just about pollution and natural resource consumption per se. Rather they are about unsustainable processes of production and consumption, and how we manage our societies to ensure that a high quality of life, rather than just more and more money and material goods, is the outcome.

The answer to these environmental and developmental challenges will not come from what we will call business as usual, that is mild environmental policies and disjointed regulations nibbling at the edge of big problems, or from radical 'deep green' perspectives which ignore the fascinating lure and the benefits of a global market economy. Rather the answer can only come from a *sophisticated, equitable and ecologically sound development framework* which generates prosperity without environmental degradation or social marginalisation. This must encompass the diverse economic and social needs of South and North in a common framework for development, amelioration of poverty and concern for the health

Figure 1.4

Sharing the world – the only way to realise ecologically and socially sustainable development

of societies. Otherwise the poorest countries will remain poor, while NICs will follow the OECD countries' unsustainable industrial path.

Environmental space is a tool to help us understand and meet these enormous challenges for the 21st century. The environmental space approach encourages us, on a country-by-country basis, to combine enhanced efficiency in production, and thus decreased consumption of non-renewable resources whose use taxes the earth's capacity to absorb pollution, with a new understanding of sufficiency in consumption based on a more sophisticated understanding of the meaning and the dimensions of genuine quality of life in modern societies.

Environmental space means simultaneously using maximum human ingenuity within the market system, and the best available technology for development, while altering our perceptions, as societies and individuals, of the definition of human development. Environmental space is a flexible philosophy of sustainable living and an approach to the management of planetary resources. It is also, in a more specific way, a means of assessing and measuring how much we can afford to produce and consume without damaging the planet, or the opportunities of our children and grandchildren.

Principles of Environmental Space

Environmental space is based on three straightforward principles. The first is that global and national sustainability can only be achieved if the throughput of natural resources in modern economic processes is reduced to manageable, ecologically sound levels. These are dictated by the earth's carrying capacity, the availability and renewability of resources and the recuperative power of natural systems.

This approach recognises that controlling end-of-pipe pollution through regulation will never be sufficient – because economic growth means the volumes of pollution and numbers of individual pollutants

Box 1.1 Environmental space

Environmental space is the total amount of energy, non-renewable resources, land, water, wood and other resources which can be used globally or regionally:

- without environmental damage;
- without impinging on the rights of future generations; and
- within the context of equal rights to resource consumption and concern for the quality of life of all peoples of the world.

The environmental space approach is based on a quantitative and qualitative assessment of sustainable resource use at the national level compared to the national 'fair share' calculated on a global or regional basis, and policies and value changes to accommodate development based on that fair share without loss of quality of life.

increase faster than our ability to understand and manage their cumulative impacts. Under current arrangements we lose at both ends of production processes: resources are used at unsustainable rates, and the industrial transformation of those resources requires energy consumption and polluting outputs which are seriously damaging to our health and that of the planet.

The first principle implies that environmental space is limited. Environmental space analysis helps us to understand the magnitude of those limits, and it is sufficiently quantifiable to provide valuable policy guidance. These limits can and must be assessed, and we will demonstrate the means for doing so. Later chapters give examples of national targets and suggestions for global action around sustainable production and consumption.

The second principle is that there is a need for equitable global development, as opposed to selfish, greedy development. This means that all countries should have equal access to the world's resources, but also equal responsibility for the management of those resources. This equity principle means a lower resource use per capita than is currently the case in developed countries, and the opportunity for a rise in consumption of resources to a sustainable level for developing countries, to give a balanced pattern by the middle of the 21st century. Although there are good moral reasons for taking this approach, it is also a matter of increasing political urgency.

The third principle is that production and consumption should serve to enhance quality of life rather than degrade it. We therefore need to redefine the objectives of development North and South so that vital aspects of living, such as the need for health, work, family and community, and cultural and spiritual life, are balanced against the short-term benefits of material consumption. The benefits and costs of consumption beyond basic needs is considered in a broader perspective of the objectives of development. Figure 1.5 shows in a simple way how the world's environmental space can support many different sustainable lifestyles.

Figure 1.5

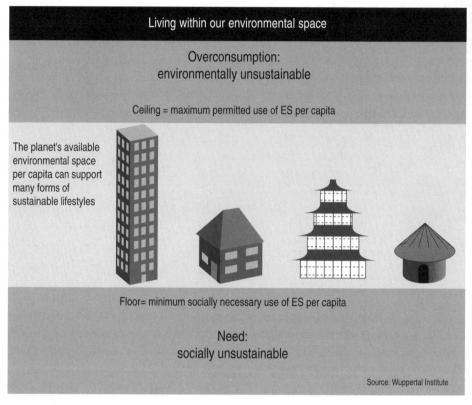

Source: Wuppertal Institute

Organisation of this Book

Chapter 2 looks at three areas in which current production and consumption patterns are causing us to cross dangerous thresholds in development in a global, full-world economy where there is no room left for dangerous pollution and waste. These are indicative of a broader range of challenges, and help us grasp the complexity of the issues and the need for fundamental rather than just superficial responses. Such challenges include atmospheric damage, urban sprawl and motor vehicle use, and the chemical pollution of our bodies.

    Readers familiar with these issues can jump to Chapter 3 which looks at developments in national and international economies, North–South relations and environmental space in more detail. Here, by way of example, we discuss the two most powerful superpowers, North and South: America and the American dream, whose influence affects us all; and China, home to almost one quarter of the world's population and a country with a staggering rate of economic growth. These countries, and their main trading partners, will have a profound effect on global development patterns and values in the next century.

    Chapter 4 discusses in more detail why reorganisation of production and consumption according to the three principles of environmental space is so important to our future. Chapter 5 looks at how, and why, environmental space is assessed in five vital resource sectors: energy, non-renewable resources, land, wood and freshwater. Consumption is measured by a small number of key indicators which, taken together, can help us to understand the impacts of around 90 per cent of resource flows in the global economy. These indicators explain how we can reduce consumption to sustainable levels. The environmental space approach argues the best way to do this is to simultaneously pursue initiatives to achieve both ecoefficiency and sufficiency, which can be thought of as living better on less.

Chapter 6 examines ways to promote sustainable production through ecoefficiency, concentrating particularly on the role of innovation and entrepreneurialism in business. Chapter 7 looks at ways to promote sustainable consumption through the concept of sufficiency and changing values, beginning with an examination of the lure of overconsumption and its damaging impact on modern lifestyles. The chapter also argues for a renaissance of public local places and community life, a review of the dubious benefits of the acceleration of time and the shrinkage of space in the modern economy, a better balance between public life and private consumption, a re-evaluation of the nature of work, and a concern for the damaging effects of income inequality.

Chapter 8 concludes by examining the basic institutional requirements to promote a new world order in sustainable production and consumption. This must be based on networks linking top-down and bottom-up initiatives supported by innovation at all levels. Firstly, improvements to the multilateral framework are considered. The roles of key organisations such as the United Nations (UN), World Bank, International Monetary Fund (IMF) and World Trade Organisation (WTO) are discussed. Secondly, the role of the nation state in enabling sustainable production and consumption is considered. The importance of national sustainable development strategies is stressed, including the key guidance role environmental space analysis can play in developing national and international policies.

CHAPTER **2**

The Global Commons: Wild Frontier to Full World

Introduction

A dramatic change in just the last half of the 20th century is that truly wild places on earth no longer exist: humankind, in an endless search for resources to exploit and places to store pollution, now impacts every bit of the planet. The recent discovery of high levels of poisonous industrial chemicals in the Arctic peoples and their visually pristine environment is a striking example and is discussed later.

   This situation requires a shift in perception from that of a world of apparently unlimited resources for industrial conversion to one where we must make wise use of rapidly diminishing options or face a growing range of environmental and social crises. This aptly has been called the transition from the frontier to the full world economy.[1] In the frontier economy, there are always more resources over the next hill, more trees to cut, more minerals to mine, more rural land to urbanise, more clean air and fresh-water, and more countryside to escape to – if not nearby then in the next state or on the next continent. Suddenly we find ourselves in the final throes of this all-too-brief period of industrialised human history: the oceans are being vacuumed of fish and the great primeval forests which girdled the earth are reduced to one twentieth of their original size. There is not even a boundless resource of clean air or clean water, which we have taken for granted during all of human history. Man, and man-made pollution, has altered the entire planet, its oceans, its land, even its deserts and polar regions. The frontier is gone and we are in the age of 'the man-made future':

1 Daly, H E
*Steady State
Economics*
second edition,
London:
Earthscan, 1992

2 Dator, J 'It's
only a paper
moon' *Futures*
December,
1990,
pp1084–1102

> *We must understand that we already live in a largely, and increasingly, and irreversibly, artificial world. Nature and the natural world (in the sense of an environment uninfluenced by human activity) scarcely exist anywhere.[2]*

Industrialism beyond Our Control

In this chapter we look at a few of the endemic effects of industrialism, and the relentless commodification of natural and even human resources for economic gain. This is the culmination of the 250 years of industrial production which began in England, and which was spread worldwide by colonialism. Although many benefits have been achieved, this technological revolution initiated a dynamic process which threatens to escape beyond our control – unless we act firmly and promptly to live within the environmental space made available to us by the planet.

The task now of all responsible people, is nothing less than planetary stewardship. The situation cannot continue: global industrialisation is untenable in its current form. For example, if the entire world were to have the same patterns of consumption as the current industrialised countries (meaning the richest 20 per cent of the population), total global industrial output would need to rise by four to tenfold depending on future population levels. The result could be unimaginable pollution levels. Even if we just look at the proportion of the world's population, mainly in Asia, who are likely to achieve a higher income status by the year 2025, and even if we project a favourable downward trend in energy use per unit of gross domestic product (GDP), their industrial achievements could increase carbon dioxide emissions fivefold using current energy sources. This would make resolution of global warming an impossibility. On the other hand, because of the poverty of the poorest one fifth of the world's population, there remains a desperate need for continued economic development and the promise of a better life it can offer to those with insufficient incomes to sustain their livlihoods and enjoy life. When one considers the ecological limits to business-as-usual, we need a new model of sustainable 'eco-industrialism', which is less energy- and resource-intensive. The environmental space approach outlined in the rest of this book offers a base on which to develop this model.

A further problem is that our market economies, although a reasonably good system for producing and trading goods and services, are still grounded in the era of frontier economics. Such economics assume that man-made capital, such as a house or a ring road, are appropriate substitutes for natural capital, such as a forest, and that development is primarily limited by a lack of man-made capital. However, today we have entered an era in which there are no substitutes for critical natural capital, such as the ozone layer. Sustainable development therefore requires that the overall stock of existing natural

Box 2.1 Welcome to the man-made future

Even though the air is thick with predictions of new global post-industrial civilisation, we seem unable – or afraid – to grasp the truth of how the world has changed. Evolution no longer follows the Darwinian rules. That vision is as obsolete as its first cousin, Newton's clockwork cosmos. Today the driving force in evolution is human intelligence. The world has changed, and the human species, which has wrought the change, is now being required to change in response to the conditions we have created. The change calls for a massive reappraisal of basic ideas. We are talking about a transition in the evolution of the planet itself.

W T Anderson[3]

3 Anderson, W T *To Govern Evolution* Dallas: Harcourt Brace Jovanovich, 1987

Global trends affecting natural capital		
Issue	Trend	Remarks
Population	+1.7% p.a.	For instance, +34% globally by 2010, +5.2% in Europe
Fertile soil	−2.5% p.a.	Data probably underestimates the problem as current estimates rarely take into account nutrient loss and the resulting decrease in fertility 1000 times faster than at natural rates
Biodiversity	decreasing	Significantly faster than expected; ozone hole will not be closed before 2050
Stratospheric ozone	−3% p.a.	Causing forest decline and human health problems
Tropospheric ozone	+1% p.a.	New trace gases causing serious concern: CF_4, C_2F_6 are 'eternal' risks; C_2F_6 is emitted from aluminium processing plants
Greenhouse gases	+1% CO_2 – equivalent	Disturbs radiation balance More than twice the geological rate
Aerosols	+1% sulphur p.a.	
Material flows	increasing	

Source: *Towards Sustainable Europe: The Handbook*

4 For a discussion of natural capital, see Hinterberger, F, Luks, F and Schmidt-Bleek, F 'Material flows vs. "natural capital": What makes an economy sustainable?' *Ecological Economies* forthcoming

* Both the British/American ton (2000 lbs, a 'short' ton) and the metric tonne (1000 kg) are used in this book, depending on the original source. A ton is 0.907 of a tonne.

capital should remain intact, with critical resources maintained in working order for future generations.[4] Aspects of the challenge are set out in Table 2.1.

Lingering Frontier Mentality

Of course, for most of us, the frontier mentality lingers; it is almost impossible to shake off, either in terms of personal consumption or in terms of the global industrial systems which cater to, and influence, our consumption patterns. At a personal level, an obvious case is tourism, now the world's largest industry, which sees a vast number of people use every last wild refuge for temporary enjoyment and often defilement. Legions of backpackers leave their rubbish in the Himalayas and cause the meagre forest to be denuded for heat and fuel, causing soil erosion; the number of trekkers in Nepal is growing by 17 per cent per year. Large cruise ships in increasing numbers penetrate isolated island cultures, such as in the Moluccas, and even the polar regions. They dump 3.6 million tons of raw sewage into the oceans every year.* The cruise industry now carries six million holidaymakers, and their numbers are growing by 8 per cent per year. At the same time, millions of tourists on Mediterranean, Balinese and Mexican beaches overload water and sewerage systems and turn fishing villages into huge touristic city regions dominated by pavements, traffic jams and fast food. Such places are then branded as spoiled, causing the tourists

5 Quoted in
*National
Geographic*, vol
187, April 1995,
p63

Box 2.2 The last frontier?

With the loosening of state controls and the end of the trade embargo, entrepreneurs are pouring money and merchandise into Vietnam. 'Ho Chi Minh City will grow, grow, grow', says the manager of the new Coca Cola franchise. 'This is one of the last frontiers in the business world.'

Source: *The National Geographic*[5]

---

to venture yet further afield in a fruitless search for the remote holiday experience with all the modern conveniences.

The tourism industry is growing 23 per cent faster than the world economy – international tourist arrivals will double to 937 million by the year 2010. As result, air transport, with a long-term growth trend of 6 per cent per annum, is a fast-growing source of greenhouse gas emissions. The exhaust fumes of high-flying, long-haul aircraft produce sulphur trioxide, which interacts with other pollutants from aerosols and fire retardants to accelerate the destruction of the ozone layer. In 1996, 14,000 aircraft carried two billion passengers: 500 million international tourists and another 1.5 billion domestic travellers. It is not uncommon for people from the UK to travel to Prague for a few hours' shopping, returning the same day, to New York or even Hong Kong, for a weekend break, or to Costa Rica for a week's holiday. By the first decade of the next century there will be three billion people in transit every year: a mass movement without parallel.

There are, of course, numerous examples of the full world economy, as it affects us personally, and the planet itself. In the rest of this chapter, we look at three areas where we have crossed vital thresholds: damaging the atmosphere which encompasses us; sprawling our suburbs over the now finite resource of the once-rural countryside; and allowing chemicals to pollute our bodies and those of our

---

Box 2.3 Global sustainable development

Today almost the entire planet is one huge building site, fuel depot and waste repository. Great quantities of valuable things are extracted from nature. This primary production process already leads to enormous quantities of waste. The extracted materials are processed with a huge, mainly fossil fuel, energy input into goods which, after use, are discarded into the environment as valueless, where they impair, damage or even destroy ecological processes.

This type of economy is not sustainable, particularly if we consider that many Southern countries are only at the beginning of their industrialisation. If they copy the patterns of the North, global environmental collapse is inevitable. The fact that the economic subsystem is threatening to destroy society and ecology calls for new forms of economy and management. This cannot happen in opposition to industry and economic institutions, but only with them. They must be an active part of the transformation process.

Source: *Sustainable Germany: a Contribution to Global Sustainable Development*

children. These give a sense of the scale and complexity of the problem, and the urgent need to do something genuinely constructive.

Passing Safe Thresholds 1:
What Have We Done to Our Atmosphere?

Global Warming

6 Houghton, J et al (eds) *Climate Change: The Science of Climate Change*; Watson, R T (ed) *Climate Change: Impacts, Adaptations and Mitigation*; Bruce, J *Climate Change: Economic and Social Dimensions*, IPCC, 1995

The warming of the earth's atmosphere is now substantiated by the authoritative source of information in this field, the Intergovernmental Panel on Climate Change (IPCC).[6] The causes are greenhouse gases emitted by the burning of fossil fuels, especially the main greenhouse gas, carbon dioxide, and intensive agriculture, which releases methane. The global concentration of greenhouse gases has already risen by 25 per cent since the 19th century. Over the next decades temperatures will change more rapidly than at any time since the last ice age, 10,000 years ago.

The implications are well documented: climatic disruption, including severe storms; disruption of ocean currents, vegetation and agriculture; and sea level rise resulting in the flooding of the world's low-lying areas, including entire island countries, such as the Maldives. Asia is particularly vulnerable to this flooding because many of its sandy coastlines are backed by densely populated, low-lying plains. As much as 20,000 square kilometres could be overwhelmed, including some of the region's most economically productive land. A similar amount of land in North America is also under threat.

The UN World Glacier Monitoring Service reports glacial recession all over the earth – for example, a 50 per cent reduction in volume and a 40 per cent in surface area of the glaciers in the European Alps, with similar reports in Central Asia, New Zealand and South America. As mountain glaciers melt, rivers will be subject to increased flooding. Of all the continents on earth, those with ice-clad polar regions will be most affected by global warming as winter temperatures increase by about 10°C and summer temper-

Figure 2.1

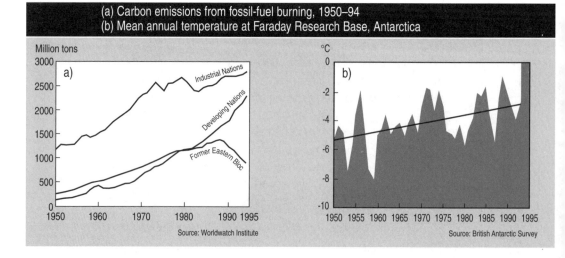

(a) Carbon emissions from fossil-fuel burning, 1950–94
(b) Mean annual temperature at Faraday Research Base, Antarctica

Figure 2.2

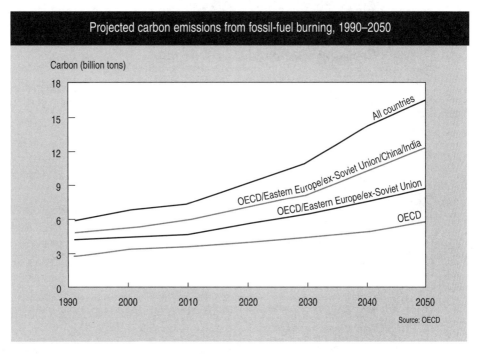

Projected carbon emissions from fossil-fuel burning, 1990–2050

Carbon (billion tons)

All countries

OECD/Eastern Europe/ex-Soviet Union/China/India

OECD/Eastern Europe/ex-Soviet Union

OECD

Source: OECD

atures by about 5°C. Already the British Antarctic Survey reports a warming of 2.5°C over the past 40 years at their Faraday Research Base.

Unless urgent action is taken, atmospheric carbon dioxide levels are likely to continue rising at around 1 per cent per year well into the 21st century. The International Energy Agency forecasts a rise of over 10 per cent between 1990 and 2000, and a doubling by the year 2050. By contrast, a global reduction of more than half is necessary just to stabilise worldwide atmospheric concentrations and to avoid catastrophic consequences. Even if emissions are held at their current level, something most countries agreed to at the Rio Earth Summit in 1992 and very few countries are managing to achieve, concentrations will rise by about 40 per cent over the next 100 years.

The reason for our failure to tackle global warming policies is lack of political will and the fact that greenhouse gas emissions are difficult to control. Large point sources such as power stations are amenable to pollution control regimes; however, increasingly the causes of global warming are multitudinous sources, for instance emissions from houses and motor vehicles. Even apparently 'clean' sources of energy cause additional warming. For example, hydroelectric dams which flood land covered by thick vegetation which subsequently begins to decompose can cause large releases of methane and carbon dioxide into the atmosphere. The methane is particularly problematic because in the long term it causes more heat trapping per unit emitted than does carbon dioxide. Some hydroelectric projects cause global warming at a rate similar to that of a coal-fired power station generating the same amount of electricity.[7]

One of the first visible impacts of global warming will be a substantial increase in heat stress deaths in hot summers in major cities around the world. Victims of heat stress tend to be poor and elderly people living in substandard housing. Some North American cities, such as Chicago, propose air conditioned shelters for people who cannot afford home air conditioning, but with no recognition on the part of city officials that air conditioning machinery is a growing cause of increased CO_2 emissions. In some

7 Canadian
Geographic
May/June 1992

GUEST ESSAY 2.1

Lester R Brown

Crossing Thresholds

When a sustainable yield threshold is crossed, it signals a fundamental change in the relationship between the consumer and that which is being consumed. The demands of our generation now exceed the income (the sustained yield) of the earth's ecological endowment. It is difficult, if not impossible, to find a developing country that is not losing tree cover. Every major food-producing country is suffering heavy topsoil losses from erosion by wind and water. In every country in Africa, rangeland is being degraded by overgrazing. Forests all over Europe are suffering from air pollution and acid rain.

By 1989, all oceanic fisheries were being fished at or beyond capacity. Water use is exceeding the sustainable yield of aquifers in much of the world. Underground water tables are falling in the south-western United States, the American Great Plains, several states in India (including the Punjab, the country's breadbasket), in much of northern China, across northern Africa, in southern Europe and throughout the Middle East. Claims on rivers are also becoming excessive, draining some rivers dry before they reach the sea, such as China's Huang He (Yellow River), the Colorado River in the United States, and the Amu Dar'ya, which originates in the northern Himalayas and once fed the Aral Sea.

The demand for firewood, lumber and paper is overwhelming the sustainable yield of forests in many countries. Forests are receding from villages in country after country as the demand for firewood climbs apace with population rise. The wholesale deforestation of South-East Asia to supply lumber to Europe and North-East Asia is now spreading into Africa and the Amazon basin.

With the earth's capacity to fix atmospheric carbon dioxide (CO_2) more or less unchanged, the rise in fossil fuel use and carbon emissions has upset the natural balance, pushing CO_2 levels higher each year. As this happens, average temperatures are also rising, altering the earth's climate, and leading to increased storm intensity. Threshold crossings often trigger a chain of events that affect the course and pace of history. For example, as the excessive demand for forest products leads to deforestation, the soil is left unprotected. Rainfall runoff increases, leaving less water to percolate downwards to recharge aquifers. The increased runoff carries topsoil with it, reducing land fertility and silting rivers and reservoirs. As firewood becomes scarce, villagers turn to cow dung and crop residues for fuel, depriving their fields of organic matter and nutrients. The situation in Ethiopia illustrates this cascading series of events. The country was half covered by forests at the turn of the century, but today trees cover less than 3 per cent of the land. The resulting erosion, chronic food shortages and periodic famine are all part of the same package.

Evolution has prepared us to compete with other species, to survive and to mulitply. But it has not equipped us well to either understand or deal with the threat we pose to ourselves with the uncontrolled growth in our numbers and in our consumption per person. In short, we have not yet learned to stabilise our demands within the sustainable boundaries of the earth's ecosystems.

Lester R Brown is President of the Worldwatch Institute in Washington, which authors the annual *State of the World: Report on Progress Toward a Sustainable Society.*

countries, air conditioning is the fastest growing, energy-using part of the economy. A vicious cycle is underway.

Depleting the Ozone Layer

A second, dramatic form of industrial pollution is the chemical diminishing of the upper atmosphere's protective ozone layer. This is the result of the release of chlorofluorocarbons (CFCs) – developed by scientists in the 1930s for use in refrigeration, foam packaging, aerosol propellants and cleaning solvents – and methyl bromide, used in crop storage and horticulture. Until recently, these chemicals were thought to be inert, while all the while they were, and are, destroying the atomic structure of ozone molecules in the upper atmosphere in a chain reaction. This occurs particularly during the coldest part of winter in the Arctic and Antarctic. In the latter, the ozone has been reduced to about 40 per cent of its level in the 1970s, indicating the rapidity of the destruction. Overall, 10 per cent of the earth's ozone shield has been destroyed. The ozone layer forms a fragile but protective shield in the stratosphere. Without the ozone layer, most life on earth would receive a lethal dose of solar radiation in about one hour.

1995 saw record depletion of the ozone layer over both northern and southern hemispheres. In autumn 1995 the Antarctic ozone hole, now three times the size of the continental United States, was larger and expanding faster than ever. In the same year, record falls of between 20 and 30 per cent took place in the protective ozone layer above North America, Europe and Russia. In 1996, the situation worsened: radiation alerts have been issued in Argentina and the World Meteorological Organisation (WMO) reported that the ozone layer had been 'nearly completely annihilated' in an area of the southern hemisphere twice as big as Europe from the Urals to the Atlantic. In 1996, an ozone hole, representing a 50 per cent depletion, opened up in the northern hemisphere.

In spite of serious chemical disruption, there is some progress. A ban on chlorofluorocarbons (controlled by the Montreal Protocol on Substances that Deplete the Ozone Layer, to give the treaty its full name), is gradually taking effect. However the ozone layer will not be fully restored until late in the 21st century because of the continuing activity of existing CFCs, halons, bromine, fluorine and methyl bromide. At a minimum, this chemical disruption will increase the global rate of skin cancer by around 25%, with fair-skinned people living in the temperate zones, such as the USA, Europe and Australia, particularly susceptible. The British Government already expects an additional 8000 skin cancer cases per year in future among people who are now children. The higher levels of ultraviolet radiation will also weaken resistance to AIDS, other cancers, tuberculosis and herpes. It will cause additional cataracts and blindness, with an extra 150,000 cases of blindness predicted each year for every 1 per cent decrease in ozone.[8] Ozone depletion could also shrink the world's food supply by reducing soil fertility and crop yields, and by disrupting the ocean's food chain by killing phytoplankton and krill.

At best, the ozone holes could close around the year 2050, assuming smuggling of stockpiled CFCs can be controlled. This is not the biggest threat to recovery, however. Two others are more significant. Firstly, developing countries do not need to phase out CFCs until 2010, and their rate of consumption is on the rise. Secondly, substitute chemicals, such as hydrofluorocarbons (HCFCs), are also harmful, albeit at a lower rate. Under current provisions, HCFCs will be in use until 2040. There is real risk that, as the economies of booming Asian countries expand, the danger to the ozone layer will be greater than before

8 Lean, G
'Holding our
breath' *The
Independent on
Sunday* London,
31 December
1995

9 Lean, op cit

10 'Ultraviolet damaging fish DNA' *The Scotsman* 18 April 1997

11 'Ozone blamed for shorter crops' *The Times Higher Educational Supplement* 7 July 1995

12 *Equinox*, 5/6,92, no 63, 1993

the treaty was agreed.[9] A final concern is emerging evidence that the increased levels of radiation pouring through the ozone holes is causing not only immediate impacts but may actually be damaging the DNA of plants and animals, thereby affecting the entire food chain.[10] The implications of ozone depletion may extend well beyond the time when chemical disruption is brought under control.

Air Pollution at Ground Level

It is not only in the upper atmosphere that we are storing a legacy of dangerous pollutants which will continue to harm our children and future generations. At ground level, ozone is a serious problem, most common in photochemical smog created by sunlight reacting with nitrogen oxides and hydrocarbons in automobile exhaust. It can damage field crops at low concentrations, stunting crop growth by 40%.[11] One component in particular, nitrogen dioxide, is a highly poisonous gas that attacks the respiratory system, and is especially dangerous for the young and the elderly. When inhaled it attacks the mucous lining of the lungs, causing or exacerbating asthma, bronchitis and emphysema. It is also linked to deaths from cardiovascular disease.

A likely consequence is the rise in the incidence of respiratory disease, such as asthma. In the USA, for example, the rate of severe cases of asthma requiring hospitalisation rose by 43 per cent during the 1980s. Over the same period, the asthma mortality rate has grown by over 50 per cent in the USA, Canada, Great Britain, Sweden and New Zealand for patients between the ages of 15 and 34.[12] Although the exact reasons for this escalating death are uncertain, there is widespread agreement among scientists that the culprit is air pollution, particularly from vehicle exhausts and from fumes and vapours generated by chemical emissions to the atmosphere. Studies of inflamatory responses show that the airways of asthmatics are very vulnerable to sulphur dioxide, sulphuric acid and ground-level ozone.

Ground-level ozone pollution increases dramatically during hot, sunny weather, suggesting that, as a result of global warming, asthma will be a major illness of the next century . An asthma specialist from Ottawa's Civic Hospital in Canada says, 'the environment may be literally taking our breath away'. But ozone is not the only danger. Another cause for concern is the emission of fine particulates, which recent American research suggests may be prematurely ending the life of 35,000 Americans and 9000 British every year. Particulate concentrations are even higher in many of the emerging megacities of the Third World, from Mexico City to Manila to Mumbai. Sadly, the car is a killer, although you would not know it from a recent ad for a motor car interior air filter – implying that in the city of the future only those who can afford to travel in a vehicle, itself the cause of pollution, will be able to breathe clean air.

Passing Safe Thresholds 2:
Automobility and Urban Sprawl in the City Region

By 2050 two-thirds of the world's population will live in urban areas. A growing crisis of 'automobility' and urban sprawl is affecting city regions the world over. This is a function of modernisation and rising disposable income, coupled with urban migration. As vehicle numbers grow, living with traffic congestion and dirty air becomes a main fact of urban life. Urban functions such as housing, employment and shopping

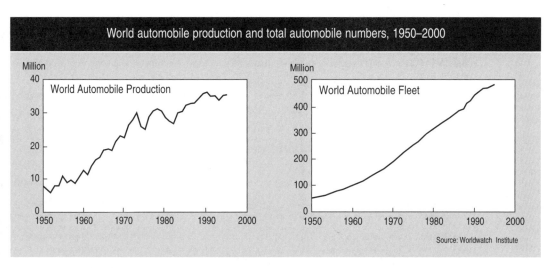

Source: Worldwatch Institute

Figure 2.3

'sprawl' out over the countryside, generating a range of negative impacts which may be impossible to undo, and which will constrain sustainable development in the next century. Urban sprawl diminishes the scarce rural land resource and frequently gobbles up the most productive farmland.

For most city regions around the world without strict land-use planning, the problems will get worse. Already, in the past 40 years, the number of vehicles has increased almost tenfold, and modern societies have quickly reorganised most aspects of daily life around the motor car. World vehicle sales will grow by 25 per cent to 59 million units by 2001. It is likely that the number of vehicles will double to 1000 million by the year 2010, and treble to the 1500 million point by 2035. The industry market analysis *World Vehicle Market Strategic Review* predicts that, worldwide, motor vehicle sales will increase by more than 50 per cent in the next 20 years to 75 million vehicles per year, up from current production of 33 million.

One third of this growth will be in Asian NICs, which could purchase 500 million new vehicles by 2020. Strong growth in car ownership is also forecast for Eastern Europe. By 2010 more than a third of all vehicle sales will be in less-developed countries. Already, cities such as São Paulo, Cairo, Lagos, Mexico, Bombay and Jakarta are overwhelmed by automobility, air pollution and urban sprawl. In São Paulo, for example, a fleet of five million vehicles is growing by 250,000 per year and contributes an estimated 90 per cent of polluting gases and particulates deposited into the air every year. Even small 'island paradises' such as Mauritius or Bali are caught up in the relentless drive to automobility and urban sprawl.

The extent to which automobility, coupled to rising income levels, might be taken up is indicated by ownership of 700 vehicles per 1000 people in the USA, and levels in Europe of around 450 vehicles per 1000 persons. The purchase of more and more automobiles, however, is only part of the problem. The evidence is that as soon as families acquire their first car, their overall number of journeys increases threefold. As people become more mobile, their homes, jobs, shops and recreational locations sprawl out across a suburban landscape, creating the need for yet more car travel. Similarly, as incomes rise, many people prefer a suburban lifestyle, requiring substantial land for a single family dwelling. These patterns may be replicated in many prosperous city regions of the world, even in countries which are not prospering at the national level.

13 Confeder-
ation of British
Industry *Moving
Forward: A
Business
Strategy for
Transport*
London: CBI,
1995

14 Steinzor, N
'Healthy Cities in
the Making',
unpublished
paper from
Environmental
Studies
Discussion List,
1995

15 1000
Friends of
Oregon,
Landmark, May
1966; Hell's
Canyon Tracking
Group, 1996

As cities sprawl into the countryside, and in the absence of strong land-use planning, people and businesses enter into a vicious cycle of attempting to escape congestion by relocating to rural areas on the urban fringe. This situation is already the norm in city regions such as Houston, Bangkok and Mexico City. In Thailand, new factories are built further and further from congested Bangkok, including a new US$750 million plant, building General Motors cars for export to other Asian countries. Unfortunately, relatively few countries have the strict land-use controls necessary to manage the situation in any benefi- cial manner.

The world's fleet of 500 million motor vehicles is already the largest single source of global air pollu- tion, accounting for 17 per cent of the main greenhouse gas, CO_2, released from fossil fuels, and around 30 per cent of emissions in the industrialised countries. For the overall mix of air pollutants in the average urban area, road vehicles account for anywhere from 40 to 80 per cent of the total. The approx- imate contribution of road transport to environmental problems is estimated as: ground-level ozone and carcinogenic particulates causing lung diseases, and damage to plant growth and buildings, 70%; acidi- fication, 20%; lead pollution, 50 to 85%; and noise pollution, 60%. There are related problems, such as the fact that 25 million people have died in motor vehicle accidents in the 20th century. Do we envision another 25 million dead in the next? The current rate of 250,000 deaths per year from traffic accidents and many millions of serious injuries to road users and pedestrians suggests we do. This toll is likely to rise further. In many countries, road accidents are the leading cause of death.

On the social side, the spread of congestion and air pollution and the increase in accidents tend to seriously decrease the quality of life for those who do not have the resources to purchase a vehicle. In many of the world's megacities these households are in the majority. An unbreakable cycle is created where a reasonable lifestyle only appears possible by vehicle purchase, thereby contributing to the problem and marginalising households on low incomes. Congestion rapidly diminishes the advantages of bus transport, and makes it less cost-effective, adding to the vicious cycle of congestion as more people switch to the personal vehicle. As automobility grows, sustainable modes such as cycling and walking are then discouraged. Already bicycles and bicycle rickshaws are banned in Jakarta and New Delhi as old- fashioned, and Calcutta's tram network may be dismembered to build motorways for the 1 per cent of the population with cars. In Shanghai, city officials have recently announced plans to reduce the three million cyclists by two-thirds to allow more room for automobiles!

Another problem is the economic cost of congestion, which wastes billions of dollars annually, and the erosion of the rural land base. Funds could be devoted to business investment or other development objectives. In Greater London, for example, the cost of road congestion is estimated by the Confederation of British Industry (CBI) at around UK£19 billion per year.[13] In Chicago, during 1975 to 1995, population grew by 4 per cent but the take-up of farm land for residential purposes increased by 46%.[14] Around 1.3 million acres of land are paved over annually in the USA, and the term rural sprawl has recently been used to describe the steady conversion of American farmland to low-density suburban residential use, and the incursion of motorised traffic into many of the last lowland vestiges of the American wilderness.[15]

Although automobile congestion problems can conceivably be solved, it is in the land use pattern that a threshold is crossed. Once low-density suburbanisation is established, it is very difficult to revert to a more sustainable pattern of concentrated, nodal density. As urban life penetrates further into the countryside, political pressure grows for yet more road building. In the Washington–Baltimore Metropolitan area in the USA, for example, the last piece of rural land disappeared in the 1980s, and development

16 Grant, K 'Test tube bodies' *The Scotsman*, 24 February 1997

Reference on page 24

17 Toppari, J et al 'Male Reproductive Health and Environmental Xenoestrogens' *Environmental Health Perspectives* vol. 104 supplement 4 (August 1996), pp741–803. This new report is a revised and abridged version of a report originally commissioned by the Danish Environmental Protection Agency in Copenhagen; also Schettler, T Solomon, G Burns, P and Valenti, M *Generations At Risk: How Environmental Toxins May Affect Reproductive Health In Massachusetts* Cambridge, Massachusetts: Greater Boston Physicians for Social Responsibility, 1996

pressure is spreading further afield to adjacent farming regions. Similarly, in developing countries, along with the purchase of automobiles, road building is seen as crucial for development, taking up a disproportionate share of national development resources. With a few exceptions in Europe and in the city states of Asia, suburban sprawl onto the diminishing land resource represents an unsustainable pattern of development.

A related environmental pressure is the use of aggregates, which are currently consumed at a rate of about 8 to 10 tons per capita per year in developed countries. Aggregates are sand, gravel and crushed stone, the latter bedrock blasted loose at quarries. Aggregates can be mixed with water and a small amount of cement, itself manufactured from quarried limestone, to create concrete, or with a tar-like liquid called bitumen to make asphalt for road paving. About 10,000 tonnes of aggregates are required for each kilometre of two-lane highway, and about 31,500 tonnes for each kilometre of motorway. Environmental battles rage over proposed sites for new quarries, as recycling currently meets only 3 per cent of demand. Aggregates are currently shipped, for example, from superquarries (sites which produce more than five million tons of aggregate per year) in Scotland and as far afield as Germany and even Texas. Mining companies have set their sights on many mountainous regions in Europe for superquarries, which can remove whole mountains in the course of their lifetime.

Automobility and urban sprawl are just one trend which causes us to pass critical thresholds in our environmental management of the planet. This trend is not surprising, given widespread attitudes shared by most of us that car ownership is both an indicator of modernisation and a major aspect of personal life fulfilment. The spread of global advertising on satellite television reinforces such attitudes. These trends and their implications are a classic case of Fred Hirsch's 'social limits to growth', in which the car is seen as a positional social good, and where individual rationality is at odds with what is rational at the societal level or for the earth as a whole. These social limits are discussed again in Chapter 7.

Passing Safe Thresholds 3: Organochlorines and the Human Body

Chlorine combines with anything that has carbon in it, such as petroleum, sugar and carbohydrates, to form organochlorine. Some organochlorines are key components of pesticides or consumer products, such as household solvents. Others are by-products of industrial processes, such as dioxins, which are produced at pulp mills when paper is bleached with chlorine. Some organochlorines are released into the atmosphere when plastic rubbish is incinerated. We now know that some plastics used as packaging are not inert, but leach gases into foodstuffs. This reflects a growing trend where toxic wastes enter the biosphere and our bodies, not from end-of-pipe emissions but from products that have exited the factory gates. The process has been called 'a global experiment to find out how man-made chemicals affect human health and reproduction'.[16]

When ingested, organochlorines can disrupt the workings of the human endocrine system. The endocrine system uses hormones as messengers to control the workings of our bodies in areas such as cell regeneration and the functioning of internal organs. There are 51 synthetic chemicals known to disrupt human hormones, such as polychlorinated biphenyls (PCBs), furans, DDT, hexachlorobenzene, dieldrin, mirex and dioxins. Many of these disruptors are organochlorines. Some mimic and some disrupt estrogen, the main female hormone. Some block testosterone, the main male hormone. The use of

18 Reported in
The Scotsman
3 January 1997.
Finnish studies
cited as
published in the
*British Medical
Journal* by J
Pajarinen et al

19 Fein, G at al
'Prenatal
exposure to
polychlorinated
biphenyls:
Effects on birth
size and
gestational age'
*The Journal Of
Pediatrics* vol
105 (1984)
pp315–320

20 Jacobson, J
and Jacobson, S
'Intellectual
Impairment in
Children
Exposed to
Polychlorinated
Biphenyls in
Utero' *New
England Journal
Of Medicine* vol.
335, no 11
(1996),
pp783–789.
Jacobson, J L
and Jacobson, S
W 'Dose-
Response in
Perinatal
Exposure to
Polychlorinated
Biphenyls
(PCBs): The
Michigan and
North Carolina
Cohort Studies'
*Toxicology and
Industrial Health*
vol 12, no 3/4
(1996),
pp435–445

*See over for
references 21
and 22*

industrial organochlorines only became widespread after the Second World War, and the consequences are only now apparent. Recent research suggests that hormone disruption caused by chemicals is leading to increased rates of birth deformity, breast cancer and testicular cancer, and a drop in sperm production rates of up to 50 per cent in some industrialised countries.[17] Finnish studies show an increase of the number of men with no healthy sperm as rising from 8 to 20 per cent, and the UK's Medical Research Council Reproductive Biology Unit reports that men born in 1970s produce on average 25 per cent fewer sperm than those born in the 1950s. They suggest that if the annual decline continues at this rate, boys born in the 2050s could be infertile.[18] Incidences of birth defects of the penis and undescended testicles are also increasing. Research also suggests that organochlorines may be responsible for learning and behavourial problems in young children which disrupt their normal patterns of socialisation and education.

There are reproductive problems occurring in wildlife species. For example, alligators in pesticide-contaminated lakes in Florida have such small penises that they are sexually incompetent – a result of exposure to hormone-disrupting pesticides. Florida panthers, which get a large dose of hormone-disrupting chemicals by eating racoons (who ingest these chemicals from the fish they eat), are reported to have undescended testicles, poor sperm production and other reproductive problems.[19] Another example of the problem is the Great Lakes Basin of North America – the largest body of freshwater in the world and home to 40 million people. Recently the Great Lakes Science Advisory Board of the International Joint Commission of Canada and the USA has found the persistent presence of more than 200 toxic substances, especially PCBs and other organochlorines. High PCB concentrations have been detected in the breast milk of mothers living in the region. This exposure produces 'statistically significant neurobehavioural defects in children' and poor memory.

The latest study, published in the *New England Journal of Medicine* in 1996, confirms that children exposed to low levels of PCBs in the womb suffer reduced birth weight and grow up with lower IQs, impaired learning ability, poor reading comprehension, difficulty paying attention and short-term memory problems.[20] This latest study describes a group of 11-year-old children whose mothers ate two to three meals per month of fish from Lake Michigan for at least six years before giving birth. The children's mental and physical growth have been followed since birth. The greatest mental deficits have occurred in the 11 per cent of children whose mothers ate the most fish. Scientists speculate that the mechanism of harm is PCB interference with thyroid hormones, which are essential for the development of the brain. These findings have been mirrored in studies of Taiwanese children exposed to high levels of PCBs.[21]

Humans are not the only affected species. Downstream in the St Lawrence River, which links the Great Lakes to the Atlantic, the few remaining Beluga whales from a once large population are so polluted with organochlorines that carcasses washed ashore are classified as toxic waste. Upstream, healthy ducks released by the Canadian Wildlife Service into the St Clair River, which divides the US and Canada, and in Hamilton Harbour on Lake Ontario, were found after just one month in the wild to have accummulated dangerous levels of 12 toxic chemicals, including PCBs, mirex, hexachlorobenzene and dieldrin.[22] There have been many press reports that frogs in the Great Lakes' watersheds have an alarming number of birth defects. Commitments to detoxify and clean up the Great Lakes Basin are proving difficult to implement due to seepage from polluted groundwater and ageing chemical dumps, such as the infamous Love Canal, which is just one of the 15,000 hazardous waste landfills and 80,000 contaminated lagoons in the USA alone.

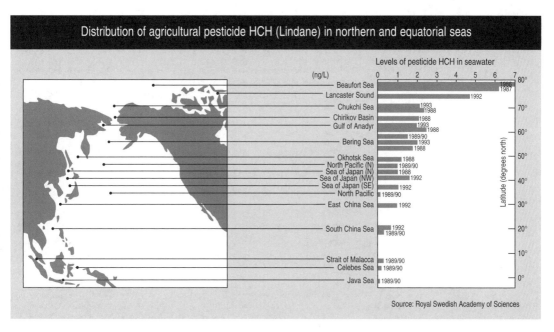

Distribution of agricultural pesticide HCH (Lindane) in northern and equatorial seas

Levels of pesticide HCH in seawater

Source: Royal Swedish Academy of Sciences

Figure 2.4

References on page 24

21 Guo, Yueliang L et al 'Growth Abnormalities in the Population Exposed in Utero and Early Postnatally to Polychlorinated Biphenyls and Dibenzofurans' *Environmental Health Perspectives*, vol 103 supplement 6 (1995), pp117–122

22 *Equinox*, vol 9/10, 1992

23 Brown, L et al *Vital Signs 1996–1997* London: Earthscan, 1996 p20

The problems in the Great Lakes are mirrored all over the world. Every seal sampled in Europe's North Sea is contaminated by a large variety of industrial chemicals, ranging from organic solvents to PCBs. Fish in the Mersey Estuary have been found to contain over 300 chemicals, many of which are unregulated. In the high Arctic, virtually pristine at the start of the 20th century, a heavy chemical load, including PCBs and other organochlorines, is found in every part of the food chain, at similar or even greater levels than present in southern industrial areas. These have been carried thousands of kilometres through the atmosphere from European and Asian industrial and agricultural areas, with the sad result that the people of Arctic Canada, Greenland, Europe and Russia, who have never used these chemicals, are their victims. In 1988 scientists working near Hudson's Bay in Canada experienced a 'brown snowfall' of around 4000 tonnes of soil which had been lifted in a storm in China five days previously. Among other things, the soil was contaminated with Lindane, a dangerous organochlorine pesticide, known to cause serious health defects in Britain. Figure 2.4 shows the distribution of Lindane (HCH) in the seas of the Northern hemisphere. Overall, the World Health Organisation (WHO) estimates there are around 20,000 pesticide-related deaths annually.[23]

There are two main problems in terms of environmental control of organochlorines. The first is that they remain in circulation for long periods of time, up to centuries. They can linger in our bodies for five to ten years, but even when excreted, they are simply recycled into the air, the water, the soil and thus the food we eat. There is no place on earth, and no human being, that is not already contaminated. Second, there may be no safe dose of such hormone disruptors, and we have little understanding of the synergistic effects of different chemicals acting together. Of course, there are many related problems of chemical pollution, such as the use of organophorous pesticides which have long-term impacts on human health and damage central nervous systems. In 1975, 137 species of insects had become resistant to one or more chemical pesticides. By 1992, that figure had risen to over 500. The latest form

Table 2.2

Summary of issues in global sustainable development
◆   Global pollution of atmosphere, land and water; the North–South equity of the impacts of pollutants, especially national consumption patterns of fossil fuels contributing to climate change and sea-level rise; freshwater pollution; soil degradation and erosion, chemical pollution from excessive use of fertilisers and pesticides, and soil salinisation from improper irrigation.
◆   Concern about intergenerational flows of natural and man-made capital in a full world where natural capital is the limiting factor of production; loss of biodiversity, fresh water supplies and degradation of ecosystems by deforestation, fuel wood collection, erosion and urbanisation; loss of genetic diversity in modern farming systems; the equity of trends to commoditise virtually all remaining exploitable natural resources, even genetic material and genetically altered organisms, for onward sale.
◆   An increasing inequality between the world's rich and poor, and the urgent need to address poverty and basic needs on a global scale; the needs of 800 million undernourished people; to secure world food supply in face of rising population; the breakdown of traditional, ecologically sound systems of resource management by commercial and population pressure; and displacement by economic processes of the resource-poor to agriculture on marginal lands or to underemployment in rapidly growing cities.
◆   Concern about powerful trends which may contribute to unsustainable development: industrialisation and integration of finance, marketing and advertising in a global marketplace; the rapid spread of aspirations to Western-style consumption patterns fuelled by satellite television; suburbanisation in land use patterns and growing motor vehicle numbers.
◆   Issues of governance in development and the need for long-term, holistic planning; for reconciling market mechanisms and short-term political objectives with longer-term development needs; concern for international equity among nations as recompense for past unsustainable resource extraction and pollution; and for developing national policies, human resources, management systems and mechanisms of participation which define sustainable processes of development.

Source: Carley

24 *Canadian Geographic*, vol 11/12, 1992

25 *Rachel's Environment and Health Weekly* no 519, 7 November 1996

26 Carley, M *Policy Management Systems and Methods of Analysis for Sustainable Agriculture and Rural Development* Rome: UN-FAO and International Institute for Environment and Development, 1995

of resistence to emerge is herbicide-resistent weeds. None of this was expected when modern pesticides were developed at the end of the Second World War. At the time, the American magazine *Popular Science* proclaimed that 'science has found the weapons for total victory on the insect front'. *Science News Letter* predicted that DDT 'would send malaria mosquitoes to join the dodo and the dinosaur in the limbo of extinct species'.[24]

And what of risk assessments and governmental controls over chemicals in the environment? We seem to have it backwards. Instead of defining a societally acceptable risk to humans from ingesting contaminants, and then apportioning allowable risk to each contaminant and discharge, we grant each chemical a risk level, and do not even make the effort of calculating the cumulative risk of all chemicals to humans. If the latter is impossible, it is an argument for zero-discharge industries.[25]

Conclusion

This chapter has documented just a few areas in which current patterns of production and consumption are threatening quality and even viability of human life. This gives no more than a flavour of a broad range of serious issues, which are outlined in Table 2.2.[26] In spite of the passing of safe thresholds, a few of which were discussed in this chapter, there is only modest progress among the world's countries to move to more sustainable patterns of production and consumption which could begin to reduce the dramatic physical impacts discussed here. On the positive side, the Montreal Protocol, and discussion around control of CO_2 emissions at the national level, have initiated steps in the right direction. Against this must be set the concern that, as long as the developed countries continue to consume resources at grossly unsustainable rates, there is no logical reason or moral imperative for the NICs to do otherwise than continue to increase consumption to Western levels. In that case, history will repeat itself, with the exception that an overloaded planet will suffer the stress – as threshold after threshold crumbles under the industrial onslaught.

There must be a better, more sophisticated alternative, which holds promise for coming generations. The next five chapters explore such an alternative, which is to begin a creative process of restructuring production and consumption around the principles of environmental space.

Managing the Global Commons – North and South, One World?

Introduction

Understanding the complexity of existing problems is not enough. We also need to get a feel for how things might develop in the next century, in terms of consumption patterns in the North, spreading industrialisation in the South and the relationship of South and North. In the first part of this chapter, we look briefly at economic growth and consumption patterns of the most influential superpowers, North and South, at the turn of the century: the USA and China. Along with Europe, the superpower of the 19th century, they represent the emerging pattern of major tri-polar trading blocks: North America, and an expanding North American Free Trade Association (NAFTA); an expanding European Union (EU), now 15 countries and 369 million citizens and likely to grow further to encompass Central and Eastern Europe; and Asia, with a huge population base, a growing number of NICs and, by 2010, one third of the world's productive capacity.

This chapter then goes on to examine the global impact of Northern consumption, the emergence of the newly industrialising countries, and the current, unbalanced relationship of North to South. Given our past record in environmental management, the chapter suggests how the environmental space approach provides a means of bringing the impacts of industrialism under control and explains how to resolve the unbalances inherent in the North–South relationship over the first half of the next century.

1 Commission
of the European
Community
*White Paper on
Growth,
Competitiveness
and Employment*
Brussels:
COM(93)700,
1993

2 Chandler, W U
*The Changing
Role of the
Market in
National
Economies*
Washington:
Worldwatch,
1986, Paper
72; Hittle, A
'The Dutch
Challenge: How
the United
States'
Consumption
Must Change to
Achieve Global
Sustainability'
Washington:
Friends of the
Earth, 1994

3 Brown, L 'The
Acceleration of
History' in *State
of the World
1996*, Brown, L
et al (eds)
London:
Earthscan, 1996

> ## Box 3.1: Consumption
>
> Extrapolating current industrial consumption and production patterns to the entire world would require about ten times the existing resources, which illustrates the scope for possible distribution tensions and ecological problems at a global level if current tendencies are not curbed.
>
> European Commission: *White Paper on Growth, Competitiveness and Employment*[1]

Thresholds to the American Dream and the Chinese Reality in a Full World Century

If the crossing of safe environmental thresholds is a profound reason to be concerned about the prospects for our children and grandchildren, current patterns of socio-economic development reinforce these concerns. Here, for better or worse, the USA and China are likely to be among the most influential super-powers shaping the direction of global development in the next century. Their cases are instructive, and we discuss them here to raise issues that are important for all of us, whatever our country. We cannot remain immune to the physical and cultural influences of these giants.

More than almost any country on the planet, America epitomises the successful capitalist, democratic state. America is the world's largest unitary investment market and is still the world's most important producer of manufactured goods. It is the world's most privatised, market-oriented economic power, with the highest proportion of production means in private hands. It is also the largest consumer nation on earth, on both a per capita and a collective basis.[2] For a century or more, it has been a focus of immigration from every corner of the world and a leader in technological achievement, such as putting the first man on the moon. America is particularly important in this analysis because of the tremendous influence of the American Dream. This is the promise of a life of economic prosperity fuelled by technological advancement, giving almost unlimited access to consumer goods and services. The consumption patterns represented by the American dream, encouraged by global marketing, television and advertising, condition social and economic aspirations of people and households around the world.

If Europe was dominant in the 19th century, and America in the 20th, the 21st century is commonly held to be Asia's, with around 58 per cent of the world's population and many of its fastest growing economies. Here the role of China is pivotal, not only because it has 22 per cent of the world's population, but because it is the biggest economy in one of the world's most dynamic regions. China is transforming itself from a developing country to the world's most powerful newly industrialising country. During 1991 to 1995, average growth was 10.5 per cent and the economy grew by 57 per cent, raising the income per person by more than half.[3] According to the World Bank, China's economy is doubling in size every eight years. It will overtake Japan, and then the USA, to become the world's largest economy probably by the second decade of the 21st century.

In terms of economic impact and cultural influence, China may be the leading superpower of the next century. Shanghai is tipped by *The Economist* to emerge as a major centre for marketing and advertising services. The country as a whole will not only dramatically influence global production and consumption patterns, but will play a much more prominent role in international organisations and deliberations. As such, it may hold one of the keys to unlocking the challenge of sustainable production and consumption.

The American Dream

Since the Second World War, the American dream has exerted a powerful influence on the countries and cultures of the world. The dream is the promise of a brighter future for the family, not only in terms of goods and services, but in the sense of improving quality of life as a result of personal initiative, unburdened by class distinctions and traditional social structures. The dream includes not only material prosperity, but the opportunity to rise in status – the feeling that every American could be president one day. The American dream has inspired many people labouring in poverty or under oppressive regimes, and rightly so, since the majority of Americans enjoy levels of material possession and personal freedom which exceed those of most countries of the world. And at the macro-economic level, the American model of managing the national economy, with a commitment to free trade, flexible labour markets and a democratic state, is influential everywhere, including in Europe.

Nevertheless, there is a growing downside to the American dream, of which we all need to be aware. This occurs for two reasons. Firstly, the consumption patterns which the model represents fuel pollution problems around the world, both globally and locally. Secondly, because many Americans feel their quality of life is declining due to the effects of overconsumption, there is a loss of community spirit, and a growing rift between rich and poor. Declining quality of life in America and other developed countries is borne out by analysis, taken up again in Chapter 7.

Consumption patterns are creating major pollution problems for the 268 million Americans and for the rest of the world. For example, North America has the highest levels of per capita CO_2 emissions in the world and is a major agent of global warming. The USA emitted 16 tons of CO_2 per capita in 1950 and around 19.8 tons in 1995. This compares to current emissions of 12 tons in Germany, 9 in Japan and 2.6 in China. More than half of the electricity made in the United States is from coal-fired power stations. The US also has a booming public relations sector hired by the oil, gas, automobile and chemical industries to argue that global warming is non-existent and that the Intergovernmental Panel on Climate Change (IPCC) is unscientific.[4] Overall, four primary production industries – paper, plastics, chemicals and metals – account for 71 per cent of all toxic emissions from manufacturing in the USA.[5]

America's love-affair with the car, a major source of CO_2 emissions, shows little sign of abatement since the heyday of huge tailfinned cars, when Americans owned three-quarters of all the cars in the world. Americans still own by far the highest number of motor vehicles per capita, at around 700 per 1000 people. The average American household owns two cars, with three or four cars per household not uncommon. This car dependency, combined with suburbanisation as a way of life, virtually precludes any sizeable shift to more sustainable modes. In the greater Washington area, for example, 78 per cent of all journeys to work are now to suburban destinations which cannot be served effectively by public transport. The public transport share of the market is 2 per cent and falling, in spite of investment in a new $7 billion Washington metro.

Beyond this, the average American in his or her lifetime accounts for the consumption of 540 tons

4 *Rachel's Environment and Health Weekly* no 522, 28 November 1996

5 Young, J E and Sachs, A *The Next Efficiency Revolution: Creating a Sustainable Materials Economy* Washington: Worldwatch Paper 121, 1994

Table 3.1

The USA and China at a glance		
(1995 unless indicated)	*USA*	*China*
Population (growth rate)	269 million persons (1%)	1,240 million persons (0.8%)
Labour force	131 million	647 million
GDP (1993)	$6,259,899 million	$425,611 million
GDP per head (1993)	$24,279	$361
Exports/Imports (1994)	$513b./$664 billion	$121b./$115.7 billion
Agriculture	2% of GDP	29% of GDP
Life expectancy	76 years	68 years
Infant mortality	7.88 per 1000 live births	52.1 per 1000 live births
Surface area	9,370 million sq.km	9,320 million sq.km
Kilometres of paved road	3,600,000 km	170,000 km
Annual automobile production	6.6 million	239,000
Telephones per 1000 persons	500	33
Electricity consumption per capita	11,236 kwh/year	593 kwh/year

$ = US dollars

Source: World Resources Institute, US Central Intelligence Agency

6 ibid

7 Schor, J *The Overworked American: The Unexpected Decline of Leisure* New York: Basic Books, 1991

8 Young and Sachs, op cit p 18

9 Schor, op cit p108

10 On assessment of body-mass index in *National Health and Nutritional Examination Survey* 1996

of construction materials, 18 tons of paper, 23 tons of wood, 16 tons of metal and 32 tons of organic chemicals.[6] In crude terms, this is the equivalent in material weight to the consumption of about eight automobiles each year over a 75 year lifespan. The main point, however, is that the American rate of consumption of finished products has increased dramatically during the 20th century. In just the five years between 1983 and 1987, for example, 180 million adult Americans purchased 85 million colour televisions, 51 million microwaves, 48 million video cassette recorders (VCRs), 44 million washers and dryers and 36 million refrigerators.[7] Given this rate of consumption, it is not surprising that consumption of raw materials in the USA increased 17-fold between 1900 and 1990 – while population only tripled (see Figure 3.1). The transformation of these vast amounts of materials into goods by extractive and industrial processes, in America and in the rest of the world, causes a range of serious pollution problems. US industries are estimated to produce 180 million tons of hazardous waste every year.[8]

What of the influence of a culture of consumption on the body and mind? Consumption has become a way of life in what has been described by Juliet Schor of Harvard University as 'what may be the most consumer-oriented society in history'. She suggests that Americans spend on average three to four times as many hours per week shopping as their counterparts in Europe.[9] Physically, about half of all Americans consider themselves overweight, and more than one third are clinically so.[10] On present trends, 75 per cent of Americans will be obese by 2050. Paediatric obesity rates are climbing rapidly. The main cause is

Figure 3.1

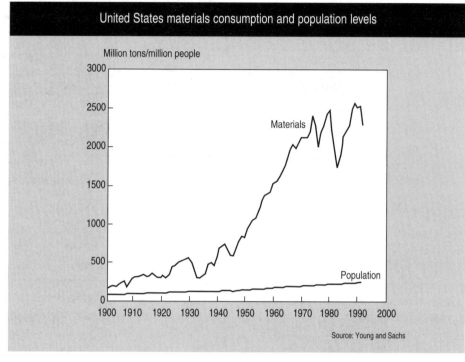

United States materials consumption and population levels

Million tons/million people

Source: Young and Sachs

11 *Financial Times* 15 March 1997

12 *Yes – A Journal of Positive Futures*, Spring/Summer 1996

13 United Nations Development Programme *Human Development Report 1996* p59, New York and Oxford: Oxford University Press, 1996

14 *New York Times* 8 March 1997

15 At the World Economic Forum, Davo, 1997 quoted in *The Independent*, 10 February 1997

16 *The Economist*, 19 October 1996

Reference from p 33

17 *The Economist* 'The World in 1997' p 60

takeaway foods, especially hamburgers, the biggest source of fat in the American diet, and one of the most exported icons of American popular culture.[11] America's GDP includes the billions of dollars Americans spend on food they wish they had not eaten – but also the 32 billion more dollars they spend each year on diet and weight-loss cures, in a desperate effort to rid themselves of the effects of fast food consumption.[12]

On the psychological side, Americans spend 40 per cent of their free time watching television and see, on average, around 25,000 television commercials each year.[13] A child born today will have watched around 1.75 million commercials when he or she arrives at the age of 75. America's homes receive on average almost eight hours of television per day.[14] One result is that Americans are concerned about what they call a 'dumbing down' of intelligence. The American dream, however, does not extend to the entire population. One out of every 20 Americans is too poor to afford a nutritious diet. Without cars they cannot travel from the inner cities to new jobs in the suburbs. The extreme effects of American poverty were described by a US government official, Deputy Treasury Secretary Larry Summers.

A child born in New York today is less likely to live to the age of five than a child born in Shanghai. A child born in Bangladesh has a better life expectancy than a child born in Harlem. We have to find a more equal society.[15]

Around 23 million Americans rely on emergency food programmes and soup kitchens, and a total of 60 million are in insecure, low-paid work. Among this group, real wages have declined continuously since 1973.[16] The top fifth of American households took 49 per cent of the nation's income in 1995; the

18 Miringoff, M L 1995 *Index of Social Health; Monitoring the Social Well Being of the Nation*; Tarrytown, NY: Institute for Innovation in Social Policy, Fordham Graduate Center, 1995

19 Miringoff, M L 'Toward a National Standard of Social Health: The Need for Progress in Social Indicators' *American Journal Of Ortho-psychiatry* vol 65, no 4 (October 1995), pp462–67 See also Miringoff and Miringoff, 'America's Social Health: The Nation's Need to Know' *Challenge* September/ October 1995 pp19–24

20 The gains were seen in infant mortality; drug abuse; high-school dropouts; poverty among those over 65; and food-stamp coverage. The indicators that worsened over the same period were children in poverty; child abuse; teen suicide; unemployment; average weekly wages; health insurance coverage; out-of-pocket health costs for those over 65; homicide;

bottom fifth received just 3.6 per cent – a historic record for inequitable distribution of income in America. Money is even more concentrated among the top 5%, who owned 16 per cent of America's wealth in 1975 and 21 per cent today.[17]

While American GDP continues to rise, many indicators of American quality of life are falling. A good example is the *Index of Social Health*, published each year by Fordham University in New York. This measures 16 indicators of well-being during different stages of life. The data goes back to 1970. For children, the index includes reports of infant mortality and household poverty. For youth, it reports teenage suicides, drug use and the high-school dropout rate. For adults, it reports unemployment, average weekly earnings and health insurance coverage among those under age 65. For those aged 65 and over, it reports poverty and out-of-pocket health-care costs. For people of all ages, it reports homicides; alcohol-related highway deaths; free food given to welfare recipients; access to affordable housing; and the gap between rich and poor.[18] These measures are not assessed against an absolute standard, such as zero poverty or 100 per cent health insurance coverage, which might reflect the research team's value judgements. Instead they are taken against the best that the USA has achieved in each category since 1970 as a model year. Each year's performance is then expressed as a proportion of the model year. As well, all 16 measures are combined into a single numerical index.[19]

The *Index of Social Health* has steadily declined. Since 1970, America's social health (represented by the 16 measures) has declined from 73.8 out of a possible 100 in 1970 to 40.6 in 1993, a fall of more than 45%. During this time, 11 measures declined and five rose.[20] In 1993, the most recent year for which data is available, the Fordham Index declined two points from 1992, down to 40.6 out of a possible 100. In 1993, six of the indicators – children in poverty; child abuse; health insurance coverage; average weekly earnings; out-of-pocket health costs for those over 65; and the gap between rich and poor – reached their worst recorded levels. Americans are aware that they are working harder and harder to less benefit. For example, since 1948 the average productivity of the American worker has doubled and the amount of household consumption has also doubled, but the American worker has less free time than in 1948. Juliet Schor in *The Overworked American* notes that:

> The American standard of living embodies a level of material comfort unprece-
> dented in human history. On the other hand, the 'market' for free time hardly even
> exists. Nationwide, people report their leisure time has declined by as much as one
> third since the early 1970s. Predictably, they are spending less time on the basics,
> such as eating and sleeping. Parents are devoting less attention to their children.
> Stress is on the rise, partly owing to the balancing act of reconciling the demands of
> work and family life. Stress-related diseases have exploded.[21]

There is a growing sense of disquiet, not only with the stress of having to work harder, but with the lifestyle of 'too much stuff', as revealed in a recent survey of American households for the Merck Family Fund.[22] However, most Americans also feel locked into a treadmill of consumption. As long as the neighbours are chasing more and more goods, they cannot stop even if they want to, because of the 'keeping up with the Joneses' syndrome. Some are downshifting in attempt to break out of the situation. These issues are discussed in more detail in Chapter 7.

alcohol-related
highway deaths;
housing; and the
gap between
rich and poor.

*References from
p 33*

21 Schor, J op
cit

22 Merck Family
Fund *Redefining
the American
Dream: The
Search for
Sustainable
Consumption*,
Conference
Report, 1995

23 Simai, M *The
Future of Global
Governance:
Managing Risk
and Change in
the Global
System*
Washington: The
United States
Institute of
Peace, 1994

24 UNDP, op cit
p94

25 Wallace, B
'China's tricky
balancing act of
economic
change'
Scotsman 6
November 1996

26 *Financial
Times*, 26 April
1997

27 Simai, M ibid
p160

28 *The
Economist* 'The

The Chinese Reality

China demonstrated its development potential by its rapid increase in agricultural output since the 1970s, which has resolved its food supply problems. Since the early 1980s it has made major changes to its economic systems in pursuit of economic efficiency and the expansion of manufacture and trade. The proportion of enterprises owned by the state is decreasing steadily: down from three-quarters in 1980 to half in 1992, stimulating much needed innovation.[23] During this period, Chinese exports rose fivefold from US$10 to US$52 billion. Under stable circumstances, China's economic and political role will increase substantially at a regional and global level.

China's population soon will reach 1.3 billion. Its natural resources are also immense. The country is the world's largest coal producer and has substantial oil and iron ore reserves. It also has large areas of fertile soil, although this comprises only 7 per cent of the world's farmland to feed 20 per cent of the world's population. Its active working age population is 647 million strong, and its industrial work force is growing rapidly. In the 1980s, China created 100 million new jobs in modern and small-scale industries. Urban employment increased by 3.5 per cent per year from 1978 to 1993, and rural employment by 2.5%. This reflects the government's employment-led growth strategy. The results are that the share of labour-intensive manufactures rose from 36 per cent in 1975 to 74 per cent in 1990.[24] China is now a major exporter of labour-intensive products.

On the whole, the economic reform programme initiated by the late Deng Xiaoping in 1978 has been enormously successful, and for the past 15 years China has had the fastest growing economy in the world.[25] More than half its annual wealth is now created by the private sector, and the country's gross domestic product has more than quadrupled; its industrial and service sectors have increased fivefold. China's economy is now the world's seventh biggest in imports and ranks eighth on exports. Between 1979 and 1997, China attracted about one quarter of the world's foreign investment. Around 200 of the world's 500 largest transnational corporations have established a presence in China since 1990. The special economic zones in southern China are said to be near saturation point in terms of inward investment, which is now spreading into the interior of the country.[26]

> To get rich is glorious.
>
> The late Deng Xiaoping

This spread of inward investment can be seen in Taiwan – increasingly encompassed by a 'Chinese economic area'. Within 20 years, this area will account for 12 per cent of global GDP and 20 per cent of world trade, with high-tech commodities, electrical equipment, chemicals and textiles among the exports.[27] The area of influence could also extend to Malaysia, Indonesia and Singapore. In 1993, China's economic growth peaked at 13.5 per cent but in 1995 economic growth still surpassed 10 per cent. The increase of purchasing power for a small minority in south-eastern China, but for an increasingly larger group within the coming decade, will be enormous. In 1995, urban incomes grew by 4.9 per cent in real terms, and the gap between the richest and poorest 10 per cent increased fourfold.[28]

Already economic growth has seen China switch, in 1995, from being a net exporter of grain to being

Figure 3.2

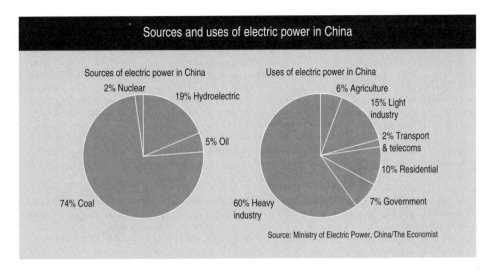

Sources and uses of electric power in China

Sources of electric power in China
- 2% Nuclear
- 19% Hydroelectric
- 5% Oil
- 74% Coal

Uses of electric power in China
- 6% Agriculture
- 15% Light industry
- 2% Transport & telecoms
- 10% Residential
- 7% Government
- 60% Heavy industry

Source: Ministry of Electric Power, China/The Economist

29 Brown, L op cit p 8

30 Brown, L Who Will Feed China? Wake-Up Call for a Small Planet Washington: Worldwatch, 1995

31 Central Intelligence Agency, http://www.odci.gov/cia/index.html, 1996

32 The Independent 8 November, 1996

33 The World Resources Institute et al World Resources 1996–1997 New York: Oxford University Press, 1996

the world's second highest importer, contributing to global stock decline and rising prices.[29] One reason is the rapid conversion of agricultural land to urban, industrial and infrastructural uses: 1 per cent of grainland is converted every year. Lester Brown estimates that one million factories will need to be built in China just to provide employment for the 100 million workers who have left the countryside for the cities.[30] Most of these factories, with associated roads and warehouses, will be on productive cropland. The US Central Intelligence Agency (CIA) estimates that as much as one fifth of China's agricultural land has been lost to soil erosion or urbanisation since 1957.[31] The CIA concludes that 'one of the most severe long-term threats to continued economic growth in China is environmental deterioration, notably air pollution, soil erosion and the steady fall in the water table'.

With one fifth of the Earth's population, the impact of Chinese economic growth on global resource consumption will be equally dramatic. For example, current Chinese primary energy consumption is around 23 gigajoules (GJ) per capita, which is only 7 per cent of the American consumption rate of 320 GJ per capita. Much of China's electricity is produced by the burning of mainly high-sulphur coal, which provides three quarters of the country's electricity (see Figure 3.2). Coal is the fossil fuel which produces most carbon dioxide per unit of useful energy, so the potential for an increasing rate of global warming is substantial, alongside continued problems with acid rain. Coal consumption is currently 420 million tonnes a year. This is forecast to double by 2010 and to triple by 2030, in line with increases in energy demand (see Figure 3.3).[32] However, China also has the world's largest hydropower potential at around 2.2 million megawatts (MW) of exploitable potential.[33] Massive hydroelectric projects at Three Gorges and Xiaolangdi, displacing one million and 170,000 persons respectively, attest to the commitment to exploit this resource.

Industrialisation is driving economic development. In 1996, China became the world's largest crude steel producer, outstripping Japan for the first time. The USA ranks third. Asian steel production, at 292 million tons, exceeds that of Europe at 270 million tons, with China's production at 100 million tons (see Table 3.4). As part of its modernisation strategy, the Chinese Government has identified automobile manufacturing, petrochemicals, telecommunications and computers as key development sectors. For example, annual vehicle sales are expected to grow to three million per year by 2000.

Given that car ownership in the neighbouring tiger economy of South Korea is expanding at 20 per

Figure 3.3

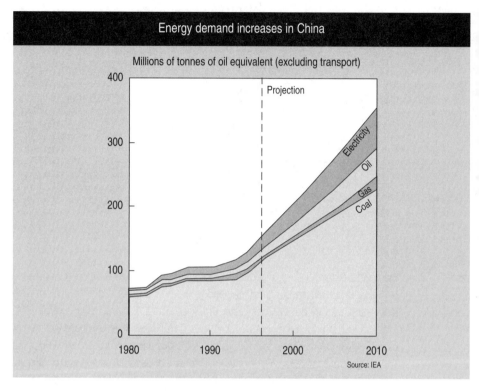

Energy demand increases in China

Millions of tonnes of oil equivalent (excluding transport)

Projection

Electricity
Oil
Gas
Coal

Source: IEA

cent per year, it is possible that car ownership in China will grow to UK per capita levels by 2030, which are as yet relatively low compared to, say, American ownership levels. This will mean an increase in the global fleet of almost 400 million cars, almost doubling the number of motor vehicles on earth, even assuming no growth in any other country. Of course, many other countries, such as India and Brazil, will also be consuming many more vehicles. On the other side of the coin, China produces 43 million bicycles per year, making it a world leader in this highly efficient form of sustainable transport.

Unless there is a transformation in automobile technology, Chinese motor vehicle consumption will increase global iron-ore consumption by 50 per cent in the next two decades, and will require large imports of petroleum products. And with the growth in vehicle numbers will come substantial increases in air pollution and CO_2 emissions that contribute to climate change. The Chinese currently emit 2.2 tonnes of CO_2 per capita per year. Compared to the developed countries, this is still a relatively modest contribution, but China is already the third largest emitter of total CO_2, accounting for about 11 per cent of global emissions. Without a shift in policy or practice, the situation could change substantially given the size of the Chinese population, the potential domestic economy and the widespread use of coal-fired power stations. If the Chinese reach the current OECD average level of emissions by 2050, then China alone will be emitting twice the sustainable level of emissions.

Other areas of consumption and emissions must also be of concern. The consumption of energy-intensive aluminium has already increased by 11 per cent a year between 1977 and 1991. China's aluminium consumption is now around 1.1 kilogrammes per capita compared with US consumption of 16 kilogrammes per capita. If the growth of aluminium consumption continues to be around 10 per cent,

34 The World
Resources
Institute et al,
*World Resources
1994–1995*
New York: Oxford
University Press,
1994

35 *The
Independent* 20
February, 1997

36 McRae, H
'China's
Challenge: value
thy neighbours'
*The Independent
on Sunday* 23
February 1997

then within the coming 15 years China's consumption will grow by over three million metric tons. The per capita consumption level will then exceed environmental space boundaries – although it will still be four times lower than the current consumption level in the European Union.

Industrial pollution in China has also reached record levels, a combination of ageing and dirty heavy industry and rapid economic development. As China modernises, the nature of the problems may shift, but the overall effect will still be staggering. Pollution by cadmium, arsenic and lead (the three wastes) from the metal industry is a major problem. China's share of metals consumption is around 5 per cent of the global total except for iron ore and steel consumption, which stands at 10 per cent. The consumption of cadmium, zinc and tin has doubled since 1977. Other major pollutants from the metal industry include sulphur dioxide, industrial dust and smog, fluoride, waste water containing heavy metal ions, and hazardous solid wastes which are generally called five-hazards. The World Resources Institute notes that in China 'water supplies in the North are dwindling, while most of the nation's rivers, especially in urban areas, are seriously polluted'.[34]

All areas of consumption will increase rapidly. The Chinese market for new commercial aircraft will account for a tenth of all the world's deliveries of single-aisle aircraft in the first five years of the next century. All the major Chinese cities have towering skylines, over 140 high-rise buildings are under construction in Shanghai alone – which intends to be a global financial centre by 2010. In these towns, 89 per cent of households already have washing machines and 66 per cent have refrigerators, although in the countryside the statistics are 17 and 5 per cent respectively. Average per capita income in the countryside is only two-fifths of the urban level, suggesting that growth potential is enormous. China's trade surplus with America is of the order of US$40 billion already, so additional reciprocal trading arrangements are likely.

China's Growth Imperative

Many labour market challenges remain for China. There is a reported floating population of around 100 million people released by economic reform and seeking work. It is estimated that 40 million of 147 million urban workers are at risk of unemployment, and even the Chinese Ministry of Labour speaks of the possibility of 286 million jobless at the turn of the millennium. Approximately 350 million Chinese, mainly in rural areas, live below China's poverty line and have inadequate nutrition.[35] They too may decide to join the massive migration to China's cities. All have aspirations for a better life.

These kinds of pressures mean that China's leaders have to maintain a high rate of economic growth, at least at 7 to 8%, if they are to continue to manage the country's social and economic challenges, such as the influx of migrants from the countryside and the need to close down subsidy-gobbling state indus-tries. If growth falls too much, even to 5%, or if pressures rise for jobless economic development as in the North, the social consequences and the risk of civil unrest could be unmanageable.

There is every possibility that China can maintain this pace. While average growth in the first half of the 1990s was 10.5 per cent, consumption grew at between 4 and 6 per cent, indicating that while people have become richer, only half that growth was absorbed in consumption, leaving ample scope for investment to underpin future growth.[36] Figure 3.4 summarises the situation, showing growth of indus-trial production, which only dipped below zero once in 14 years, mapped against fixed-asset investment

Figure 3.4

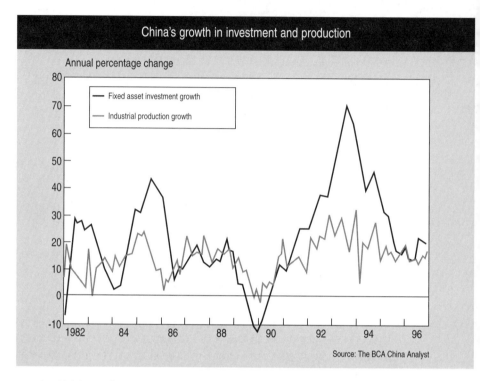

China's growth in investment and production

Annual percentage change

- Fixed asset investment growth
- Industrial production growth

Source: The BCA China Analyst

growth, which is equally impressive. The economic motor for this growth has been exports, and these will continue to play a key role, if only to pay for energy imports such as those pertaing to the motor vehicle sector. Many of these exports will be to the South-East Asian region, firmly placing China's prospects for stable economic growth in the context of prosperity and continued economic growth in Asia.

The Impact of Consumption Patterns

Northern Consumption and Ecological Debt

With regard to China's willingness to control CO_2 emissions, the World Resources Institute notes that:

> *Its expressed willingness to work with the global community in reducing carbon emissions not withstanding, China remains adamant that economic development at home should not suffer to solve a problem it regards as largely created by the industrialised world.*[37]

The Chinese have a strong case because many global ecological problems are largely the result of historic economic processes which have taken place in, and benefited, the Northern developed countries over the past century. This was achieved through the industrial transformation of an enormous proportion of the Earth's resources into goods and services, and the North's take-up of the planet's limited absorp-

37 ibid p70

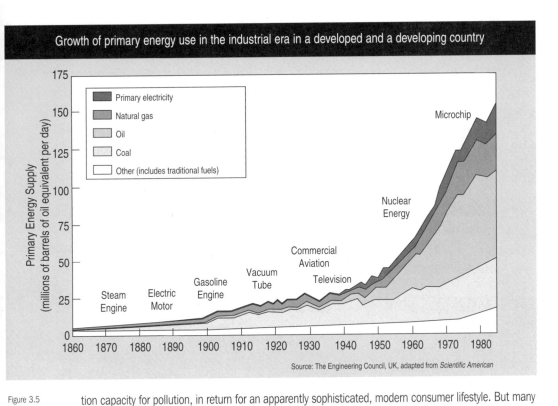

Growth of primary energy use in the industrial era in a developed and a developing country

Source: The Engineering Council, UK, adapted from *Scientific American*

Figure 3.5

tion capacity for pollution, in return for an apparently sophisticated, modern consumer lifestyle. But many of the environmental impacts of pollution and resource consumption have been cumulative, building up what many developing countries see as an ecological debt on the part of the North. For example, the beginnings of increased levels of CO_2 in the atmosphere can be traced back more than a century to the early industrial revolution. The Chinese would certainly argue that their current and future levels of emissions, presently just one ninth of the American per capita level, should be balanced against this historic fact. Conversely, China could be compensated for the North's ecological debt by financial and technological transfers to abate the problem without damaging Chinese economic prospects.

Around 80 per cent of total global pollution is the responsibility of the industrialised countries. Figure 3.5 shows the dramatic effect of industrial technology, and population growth, on primary energy use from about 1860 to the present. It is the consumption of fossil fuels such as coal, gas and oil which is the main cause of global warming. Figure 3.6 shows the consumption patterns of a typical Northern country, Germany, compared to Egypt, the Philippines or Argentina. The difference is stark: Germany uses seven times more energy per capita than does Egypt, 14 times more aluminium than does Argentina and 130 times more steel than does the Philippines. And yet Germany's per capita consumption rates are generally still less than those of the USA. The average North American, for example, uses as much energy per capita as 525 Ethiopians, highlighting the grossly disproportionate burden on the planet's ecology.

Southern countries, without yet acquiring many of the benefits of the modern high-consumption lifestyle, suffer the consequences. Northern patterns of resource consumption affect their living conditions locally (for example, mining pollution in Papua New Guinea), regionally (Bhopal) and nationally (climate change). To compound the inequity, the world's resource transfers are organised to flow mainly

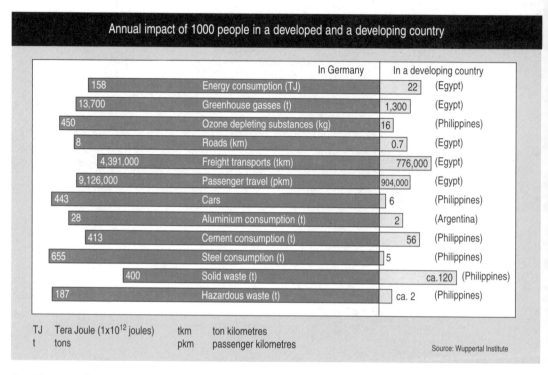

	In Germany		In a developing country
Energy consumption (TJ)	158	22	(Egypt)
Greenhouse gasses (t)	13,700	1,300	(Egypt)
Ozone depleting substances (kg)	450	16	(Philippines)
Roads (km)	8	0.7	(Egypt)
Freight transports (tkm)	4,391,000	776,000	(Egypt)
Passenger travel (pkm)	9,126,000	904,000	(Egypt)
Cars	443	6	(Philippines)
Aluminium consumption (t)	28	2	(Argentina)
Cement consumption (t)	413	56	(Philippines)
Steel consumption (t)	655	5	(Philippines)
Solid waste (t)	400	ca.120	(Philippines)
Hazardous waste (t)	187	ca. 2	(Philippines)

Annual impact of 1000 people in a developed and a developing country

TJ Tera Joule (1x10^{12} joules)   tkm ton kilometres
t   tons   pkm passenger kilometres

Source: Wuppertal Institute

Figure 3.6

from South to North in terms of raw materials and funds for debt servicing. The need to make hard-currency interest payments on debt encourages the production and export of agricultural products from land better used for domestic food production.

In other cases, such as corn grown in the American mid-west, heavily subsidised agricultural products from North America and Europe undercut local markets and rural economies, such as corn grown in Mindanao in the Philippines.[38] The North, while preaching the advantages of free trade, has more than enough resources to subsidise predatory pricing of agricultural products from tax revenues. Northern use of resources also diminishes the abilities of Southern countries to access, in the future, their own easily exploitable resources, which will have been exported northwards to build up the very industrial infrastructures which are undermining the planet's ecological viability.

The entire world has served as a resource base for the development of the 25 or so industrialised countries, which have between them just 20 per cent of the world's population. Wood consumption provides an example, since these 20 per cent consume 76 per cent of the world's harvested timber and 81 per cent of the world's paper every year. Since 1950, one fifth of the earth's forested area has been cleared.[39] In North America, clear-cut logging and road construction have broken the continuity of once vast sweeps of forest into little islands, resulting in winter flooding, summer drought, soil erosion and the destruction of salmon breeding streams. In Canada, the great boreal forest is being sold off for pulp at unprecedented rates – some Can$13 billion worth of new pulp mills are scheduled to turn one million hectares of forest cover into industrial products annually.[40] Under threat in Ontario is the last 1 per cent of ancient red and white pine ecosystems in North America. Aside from the loss of the carbon sink, which would have reduced global warming, the natural environment suffers – 75 per cent of North America's forest songbird species are in decline. North American environmentalists are battling logging companies

38 Oxfam, *Trade Liberalisation as a Threat to Livelihoods* London, 1996

39 Young and Sachs, op cit

40 Worldwatch Institute *Vital Signs 1996* Washington, 1996

over the remaining original forest, which stands at just 6 per cent of ground cover. The only continent where the situation is worse is Europe, where only 1 per cent of the original forest remains.

However, the North's voracious resource consumption is not confined to northern continents. The tropical forests are disappearing at a rate of 15 million hectares per year, in part because of the North's appetite for foodstuffs such as coffee, tea, palm oil, rubber and bananas and other exotic fruits. In the forests of Asia, Africa and South America, some of the finest hardwood on the planet is being gobbled up for Japanese and European markets for conversion to low-cost, single-use items such as pallets, packing crates, concrete building frames and disposable chopsticks – though reusable substitutes are readily available. In Thailand, for example, forest cover declined from 55 per cent to 28 per cent in the previous three decades. To supply consumption in the North, the habitats and food sources of forest dwellers have been destroyed, their watersheds polluted and the world's greatest source of biodiversity partly eliminated. Even where pollution might be controlled in Northern countries, the destruction of landscapes and pollution in Southern countries, where resources are imported is increasing.

Where Do We Stand?

Sustainable development on a global basis requires attention to both absolute consumption rates of limited resources and the available sink capacity for pollution, including distributional impacts of consumption. Any national economic burden on the ecosystems which underpin it is a function of:

- average consumption;
- the size of population; and
- the broad set of technologies which the economy uses to provide goods and services.

41 Durning, A
How Much is
Enough? The
Consumer
Society and the
Future of the
Earth New York:
WW Norton for
Worldwatch
Environmental
Series, 1992

42 Linz, M
'Sustainable
Economy:
Implications for
the South'
Report on
International
Conference on
Sustainable
Economy for the
North –
Implications for
the South Berlin:
Carl Duisberg
Gesellschaft,
1995

The challenge of sustainable development in a world where the fortunate consume vast amounts of resources while others subsist on almost nothing can be understood from Table 3.2.

Worldwide, since 1950, the per capita consumption of copper, energy, steel and wood has doubled, cement consumption has quadrupled and aluminium consumption grown sevenfold. This increase in consumption is attributed to the 1.1 billion persons in the consumer class who use, for example, around three-quarters of all steel and aluminum produced each year. By comparison, the consumption rate of the middle income group has grown much more slowly, and that of the low income group has remained virtually unchanged since the Second World War.[41]

The fact that around 40 countries out of approximately 175 in the world account for 96 per cent of all world trade indicates the current concentration of production and consumption.[42] Nor has the situation been static. Between 1960 and 1990, for example, the industrialised North was able to use its greater financial resources to treble the ratio of GNP per capita compared to the South from 20:1 to 60:1. Continuing this unequal distribution of resources in an expanding world populace could give rise to conflict.

These disparities in production and consumption rates give rise to regional disparities and national disparities. Figure 3.7, for example, shows energy consumption rates on a regional basis, and Table 3.3 gives examples of CO_2 emissions which reflect, in part, these disparities. The latter also shows, however, that countries with similar per capita incomes and lifestyles, such as the USA and Japan, can vary considerably in the efficiency with which they transform resources to income and prosperity. This suggests

Table 3.2

Sharing the world: distribution of financial and industrial resources at the beginning of the 21st century			
	Consumer group: the OECD countries	Middle income group	Low income group
Current population	1.1 billion persons	3.4 billion persons	1.2 billion persons
Percentage of world population	19%	60%	21%
Percentage of world GNP	82.7%	15.9%	1.4%
Percentage of world trade	81.2%	17.8%	1.0%
Percentage of commercial lending	94.6%	5.2%	0.2%
Consumption of foodstuffs/fertilizer	50% of global grain production and 60% of artificial fertilisers	Around 30%–40% of world foodstuffs	500–800 million chronically undernourished; limited access to fresh water
Transport and household technologies	92% of private cars	2 billion persons with no household electricity or telephone	
Consumption of energy and industrial production per year	75% of energy use; 80% of iron and steel; 81% of paper; 85% of chemical production and 86% of copper and aluminium	Around 10%–15% of world energy and industrial production	Mainly meeting energy needs by cutting fuelwood at higher than replacement levels; 100 million without adequate fuel

Source: UNDP, World Resources Institute, Worldwatch Institute

options for improving the situation and is discussed again in subsequent chapters.

To summarise, there is no doubt that for historical reasons industrialised countries have imposed a disproportionate share of global environmental burdens on the planet. This whole question of ecological debt must be addressed if sustainable production and consumption patterns are to be achieved on a global, balanced basis. However, the situation is further complicated by the fact that, without drastic action by the North, the per capita imbalances will continue for some time to come, as is indicated by Figure 3.8.

The Growth of Industrialisation in the South

As the Chinese example has shown, the rapidity of industrialisation in NICs, which is occurring over the space of as little as two generations, should not be underestimated. The ten newly industrialised countries

Figure 3.7

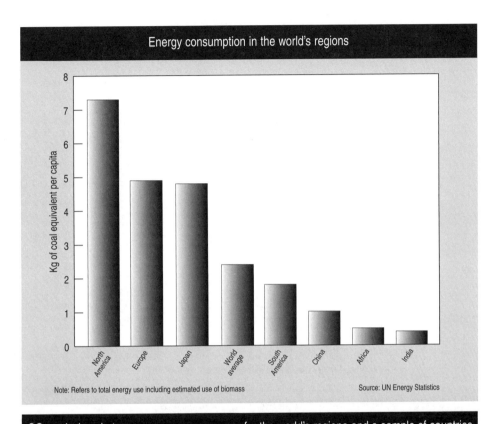

Energy consumption in the world's regions

Note: Refers to total energy use including estimated use of biomass   Source: UN Energy Statistics

Table 3.3

CO$_2$ emissions in tonnes per person per year for the world's regions and a sample of countries	
World	4.21
Regions	
North America	17.37
Former USSR	12.31
Aust./Oceania	11.24
Europe	8.20
Asia	2.11
South America	2.00
Africa	1.03
Countries	
United States	19.53
Canada	15.21
Australia	15.10
Germany	12.13
United Kingdom	10.00
Japan	8.79
Spain	5.64
Mexico	3.92
China	2.20
Brazil	1.43
India	0.81
Kenya	0.18

Emissions from industrial processes for the year 1991   Source: World Resources, 1994–95

Figure 3.8

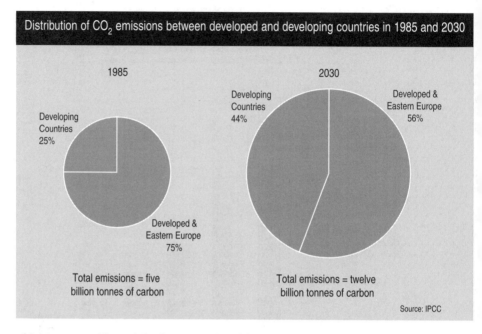

Distribution of CO_2 emissions between developed and developing countries in 1985 and 2030

1985

Developing Countries 25%

Developed & Eastern Europe 75%

Total emissions = five billion tonnes of carbon

2030

Developing Countries 44%

Developed & Eastern Europe 56%

Total emissions = twelve billion tonnes of carbon

Source: IPCC

of Asia now extend beyond the tiger economies of South Korea, Taiwan, Hong Kong and Singapore to include India, China, Thailand, Malaysia, Indonesia and the Philippines. They have a share of world trade equal to that of the European Union, bigger than that of the USA and twice that of Japan. The average economic growth rates in the region are around 7 per cent per annum, more than twice that of the OECD countries. Other emerging NICs include Pakistan, Egypt, Turkey, Columbia, Chile and Peru.

During the next ten years, for the first time, the prosperity of these Southern economies will not depend on what happens in the North. Of the world's 5.8 billion people, 3.5 billion live in Asia alone. The population of China is 1.2 billion and that of India has climbed from 0.8 billion to one billion. Chinese and Indian domestic markets are already of sufficient size that they need not depend on overseas markets for economic growth. The regional distribution of world population by 2025 suggests the potential strength of emerging Asian markets (see Figure 3.9). For instance, Asia is now the world's largest producing region of crude steel (see Table 3.4).

The top 20 NICs also include Brazil, Indonesia and Thailand. These countries, with India and China, are projected – in a recent report by the UK Treasury – to move into the international economic league table of top ten economies by 2015, by sheer size if not by income per head.[43] They will displace France, the UK and Italy from the top country Group of Seven. For overall size of economies, the Treasury suggests the line-up in 2015 (in descending order) will be China, the USA, Japan, India, Germany, Brazil, Indonesia, France, Thailand and the UK. This ranking can be compared with current GDP, calculated according to purchasing power rather than exchange rates, which puts China and India at second and fifth respectively (Table 3.5). If the countries of East Asia sustain recent growth rates, the whole region will, in the span of one generation, have about the same per capita GDP as the OECD does today, but twice the population of the OECD plus the former Eastern Bloc. Yet, as recently as 20 years ago, countries such as China, India, Malaysia and Indonesia were viewed as having underdeveloped, mainly agricultural, peasant economies.

43 H M Treasury *Strategic Considerations for the Treasury 2000 to 2005* London: HMSO, 1996

Figure 3.9

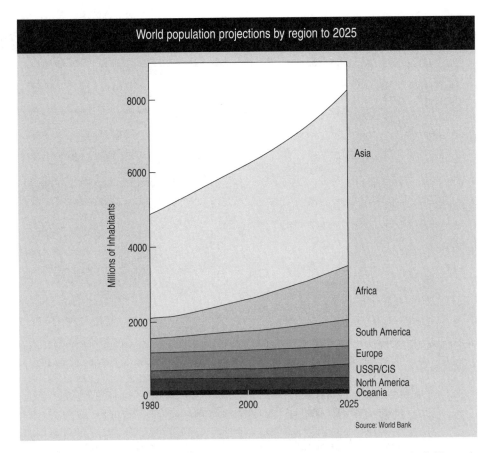

World population projections by region to 2025

Asia

Africa

South America

Europe

USSR/CIS

North America
Oceania

Millions of Inhabitants

8000

6000

4000

2000

0

1980   2000   2025

Source: World Bank

The development opportunities in NICs are enormous, as can be seen from the growth of cities such as Hong Kong, Kuala Lumpur and Jakarta. But the environmental risks are also huge – depending on the development path. For example, in China only one-fifth of the people need achieve USA-style mid-level incomes to generate volumes of consumption and pollution equal to that of the USA. When per capita CO_2 emissions in China eventually hit five tonnes per year, less than one third of the American rate, China's contribution to global emissions will be around 20 per cent of the global total. South Korea, with just 44 million people, already ranks eleventh in the world for total energy consumption and fifteenth for GNP. Per capita consumption is still only 60 per cent of the OECD average.

Even with a stable world population, the ecological implications of rapid economic growth in NICs on the current industrial model is worrying. However, global population may continue to grow for some time. Both the USA and China have current growth rates of around 1 per cent, for example. At this rate, around 500 million Chinese will be added to the country's population by around 2030. This corresponds to the fact that the bulk of the world's population growth will be in Asia in the first half of the next century.

The overall global growth rate has declined from its peak of around 2 per cent in 1970 to a current 1.6 per cent, with 90 million additional people on earth per year.[44] However, given that only 14 per cent of humanity lives in countries with stable populations, considerable additional growth is likely. UN projections suggest that the world's 1997 population of 5.9 billion will reach 6.2 billion by the year 2000 and 7.2 billion by 2010. Current estimates suggest a steady state in the 22nd century but a levelling off at

44 Brown, L
op cit p12

Table 3.4

World crude steel production			
Regions/Countries	Total Production (million tonnes) 1995	1996	% Change 1995/96
Africa	10.55	9.95	–5.7
Middle East	10.36	11.10	7.1
Asia	282.14	291.97	3.5
China	94.00	100.35	6.8
Japan	101.64	98.77	–2.8
North America	107.88	108.63	0.7
Other America	47.82	49.87	4.3
Oceania	9.34	9.16	–1.9
Europe	283.89	270.16	–4.8
World	751.98	750.83	–0.2

Source: UN Economic Commission for Europe

somewhere between 9.4 and 11 billion by around the year 2050.[45] Nevertheless, it is important to remember that it is not the number of humans, but the impact of human activity and consumption which is most influential in terms of environmental impact. In the next chapter we argue that a more balanced distribution of global resources, North–South, on the equity principle will foster a decline in the rates of population growth, and thus environmental pressure, by encouraging the spread of sustainable prosperity.

The real challenges to global sustainable development, therefore, are, in order of priority, existing and growing overconsumption in the North, the threat of overconsumption in NICs, and the mutually reinforcing nature of the two parallel trends. For example, on a business-as-usual scenario, Chapter 2 noted that we will need to find room on our planet for an additional 1000 million motor vehicles, and room in our atmosphere for their pollutants. But the North has already overloaded the sink capacity of the atmosphere to absorb carbon dioxide, and no amount of improvement in vehicle technology during that short period of time is likely to overcome the fact that three times as many vehicles are polluting. If the 20 threshold NICs adopt the existing scenario for automobility and industrialisation, within a few decades they will be discharging just less than half of global climate-changing gas emissions into a dangerously polluted atmosphere. Beyond this, there should also be concern for the amounts of energy and materials required to produce the vehicles.

Clear thinking on the problem, however, is difficult because domestic vehicle production is seen as a key factor in NIC industrialisation programmes, as it has been in the North, and is therefore an element of national pride. It is not surprising that Asian cities such as New Delhi, Jakarta and Shanghai are banning bicycles as old-fashioned in favour of the motor car when the car is touted in international marketing efforts, and over new satellite television links, as the *sine qua non* symbol of modernity. Indeed, car ownership confers many short-term benefits, so it is hard to argue that the benefits may not be as great as they first appear. In any event, automobility has virtually become the foundation of social

Table 3.5

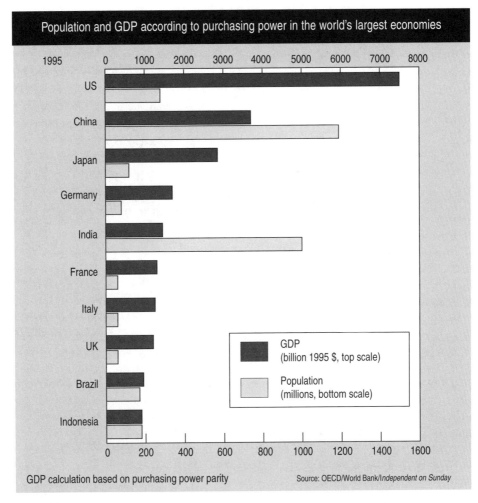

Population and GDP according to purchasing power in the world's largest economies

GDP (billion 1995 $, top scale)

Population (millions, bottom scale)

GDP calculation based on purchasing power parity

Source: OECD/World Bank/*Independent on Sunday*

life and land use in the North, and we have reorganised our cities and societies around the car. Efforts to contain traffic growth and its contribution to global warming in most Northern countries are either weak or almost non-existent. Given this situation, it is morally impossible to fault the South either for its lack of political will to reduce automobility and urban sprawl, or for valuing the car-based lifestyle as the highest form of modern living.

46 In United Nations Development Programme *Human Development Report 1996* New York and Oxford: Oxford University Press, 1996

We have for over a century been dragged behind the chariot of the prosperous West, choked by the dust, deafened by the noise, humbled by our own helplessness and overwhelmed by the speed. We agreed to acknowledge that this chariot drive was progress, and progress was civilisation. If we ever ventured to ask, 'progress towards what, or progress for whom?' it was considered ridiculously oriental to entertain such ideas about the absoluteness of progress. Of late, a voice has come to us to take count not only of the scientific perfection of the chariot but of the depth of the ditches lying in its path.

Rabindranath Tagore[46]

Can We Manage It? – Environmental Policy: Too Little, Too Late

If the North's record of environmental management was better, there would be far less need to be concerned about development patterns in NICs – they could adapt Northern environmental policy and practice to their needs. But the past record of managing pollution and land degradation shows clearly that our understanding of the need to reduce damaging effects is almost always too little, too late. Problems are usually not recognised as worthy of study until they already harm human health or the biosphere or both. Even then, politicians find it expedient to wait for firm scientific evidence before making the necessary, but difficult, political decisions. Interest groups representing polluting industries work hard to confuse the scientific consensus. People who sound the ecological alarm are labelled doomsayers. But firm scientific evidence of serious problems is seldom available, by definition, until the problems are critical and therefore damaging. Once they are critical and often endemic, such as with organochlorine pollution, managing the problem becomes much more difficult. The legacy of the 60 or so chemicals now identified as 'gender benders' may be with us for a century or more, even assuming political will arises to tackle the problem.

Failure to address the long-term, cumulative impacts of industrial processes in sufficient time, when they are still manageable, is therefore a basic weakness of current approaches to environmental management. Ozone depletion, greenhouse gas emissions and nitrate pollution of freshwater aquifers are other examples. For example, a study of organochlorine pollutants in fish for the UK's Department of the Environment (DoE) notes that:

> *Most of the regulatory information required for the licensing of new materials has been based on short-term, acute toxicity tests and formal measurements of properties such as solubility coefficients, leaving the most dangerous properties of long-term accumulation and biological impact largely untested.*[47]

Overall, there are too many sources of biophysical stress and pollution, such as urban sprawl, factories, autos and energy-inefficient houses, and too many interactions between them, to imagine that we can exert the necessary degree of rational control over polluting outputs, even in the most highly organised of countries with good environmental track records.

Environmental space analysis is intended to address both of these challenges: consumption patterns in industrialised countries, North and South, and the chronic failure of end-of-pipe pollution control. It starts from the recognition that tackling these end-of-pipe outputs of industrial processes, such as air or chemical pollutants, in a full world economy is not enough. We know it is not enough because the kinds of thresholds charted in the Chapter 2 are being exceeded with increasing regularity. These kinds of problems will grow in magnitude and complexity as more countries industrialise, as more people in the world join the consumer society, and as world population increases.

47 Department of the Environment *Chlorinated Organic Pollutants in Fish from the North East Irish Sea* London, 1991, cited in McLaren, D, Bullock, S and Yousuf, N *Tomorrow's World* London: Earthscan, 1997

Environmental Space – Development Path for the 21st Century

What is to be done? One possibility is to continue the present pattern of production and consumption, with mild environmental control policies, which we have called business as usual. This development path could, for a short time, sustain current levels of consumption among the world's consumer class, but at the growing expense of the middle income group and the poor in terms of their current and future access to resources and the planet's sink capacity. This would widen the development gap between North and South, which is increasingly highlighted in the South by the persistent messages of global television and film.

Business as usual also reinforces persistent and accelerating environmental degradation: too many social and economic trends presage dire consequences when their cumulative impacts are assessed against global carrying capacity, at least in the absence of positive action. Business as usual, at best well-meaning but ultimately disdainful of the future, is not a sufficient approach to organising a modern global economy. The scale of the problem is such that even without any further growth in the pollution of industrialised countries, the environmental impact of each unit of consumption must decrease by more than 75 per cent by 2050 to maintain the current unhealthy situation.[48] In other words, we have to run to stand still.

The viable alternative is to focus on the inputs of production processes and to tackle problems at source. The Sustainable Europe Campaign began by recognising that to achieve a sustainable economy in Europe it is necessary to act on the precautionary principle and to shift our focus away from end-of-pipe pollution control; the emphasis should be on a more proactive management of the economy and the environment based on sustainability principles. The environmental space concept is intended to help do that, with gradual, targeted alterations to production and consumption, as determined by consensus-building around national sustainable development strategies.

The result is a challenge to business-as-usual industrialism, but without suggesting any loss of the obvious quality of life it has brought to many millions of people. Environmental space builds on the strengths and energies of market economies – it is a revolution 'with the grain' rather than against it. The approach considers simultaneously global and regional carrying capacities, appropriate national resource consumption patterns and national rights to global resources to generate quantifiable, global, long-term sustainability targets. The campaign envisions a steady transition in national economies to sustainable patterns of production and consumption, and sets out a philosophy and methodology to achieve:

- a necessarily high level of reduced resource use of the world's consumer class, but little or no reduction in quality of life in those countries; and
- a managed increase in living standards among the middle and lower income groups, within the bounds of sustainable levels of resource extraction and pollution.

These objectives, taken together, highlight the need for a new relationship between North and South in the next century. The North can no longer afford to take an excessive amount of the Earth's resources, if only because it is starkly apparent that the ecological and human health cost is too high. The South is entitled to a greater share of the Earth's resources and, as we have suggested, the growing number of NICs will increasingly demand and take it. However, this is not without cost unless new paths to national development are found.

48 Ekins, P *The Gaia Atlas of Green Economics* New York: Anchor Books, 1992

Box 3.2 Environmental space is like money in the bank

Compare the planet's resources to a large sum of money which pays interest. If you live on the interest alone, the capital stays intact, and you can live well indefinitely. This interest is our available environmental space. On the other hand, if you use even a small part of the capital each year as well as the interest, the end will come surprisingly fast. After all, because of a decrease in the capital, the annual interest will also decrease at an increasing rate. One will therefore eat faster and faster into the capital. This is the foolish way we are living now.

Source: adapted from *Action Plan Sustainable Netherlands*

Policies directed towards sustainable production and consumption therefore offer a big advantage: while business as usual can only offer high consumption to a limited number of people for a limited time, the sustainable option can offer a reasonable level of consumption to a much larger group of people for a much longer time. The best guarantee for achieving these objectives and for increasing global prosperity is to recognise that while the Earth has ecological limits, there are no limits to the creative powers of human beings who wish to achieve quality of life within the limits of environmental space. The mobilisation of that creativity is of profound social, ecological and economic significance.

Using Resources Effectively to Enhance Quality of Life

Environmental space involves accepting quantitative ceilings, or upper limits, on resource consumption, and a minimum use of resources to meet basic needs. We will demonstrate in subsequent chapters that the ceiling will involve a reduction of global material flows by around half. This can be achieved by the combined application of efficiency measures – that is, in terms of the amounts of products or services produced per unit of natural resources – and a redefinition of quality of life to encompass sufficiency as a way of life – that is, the degree of well-being gained from a product or a service. Efficiency is discussed in detail in Chapter 6 and sufficiency in Chapter 7.

By reducing resource inputs to production processes, a significant decrease in environmental problems can be anticipated. A particular innovation of the environmental space approach is to recognise that the sum of the problems associated with materials consumption, including pollution and waste disposal problems, resource depletion and biogeological disruption, are approximately related to the total amounts of materials moved during the entire life-cycle of the economic activity. These are called the ecological backpacks or rucksacks. The world's mining industry, for example, moves 28 billion tons of soil and rock every year, with enormous energy, erosion and siltation costs.[49] Subsequent smelting releases large quantities of arsenic, cadmium, lead, sulphur dioxide and other toxic substances into the air, land and water. Mining, smelting and metal processing use around 9 per cent of energy consumption in the OECD each year, which rises to 13 per cent if non-metal minerals such as cement are included. If these kinds of total amounts can be lowered, by reducing consumption of the minerals themselves, it will almost always be the most efficient and effective means of minimising the impacts of production. Ecological backpacks are discussed in more detail in Chapter 6.

49 Young and Sachs op cit p13

It is also the contention of the environmental space approach that the resources which societies use inefficiently to fight environmental problems at the end-of-pipe level, and the resources which are currently squandered by inefficient production processes, can be allocated in future to important aspects of economic and social development, such as life-long education, training or employment creation. The potential national benefits are very great – but can only be achieved if there is the political will and courage to shift to a proactive stance. Here we join other voices in arguing that quality of life in a sophisticated society is about more than company profits – conventional economics may suggest it is efficient to eliminate jobs, but this is a very blinkered and ultimately self-defeating kind of efficiency.[50] So, while efficient markets may be necessary for a high quality of life, they are never sufficient. This also suggests that creative interaction between business, government and the civil sectors of society are essential for a high quality of life. These issues are discussed in Chapters 7 and 8.

A second challenge, therefore, is to reduce the material intensity of production, or dematerialisation, without loss of welfare or quality of life. It is important to stress that environmental space is not the same as end-use. For example, radically increased efficiency in the use of resources – for instance, the continuing reuse of materials such as aluminium, the development of sustainable technologies, such as solar energy, as well as the alteration of lifestyles, such as reducing the need to spend frustrating hours commuting to work – means that reducing end-use benefits, such as consumption of soft drinks, a warm house in winter, or the opportunity to meet friends, is not necessary to live comfortably within available environmental space. The environmental space concept challenges all countries to use their knowledge base and new technology to achieve a high-quality standard of living within ecologically sustainable boundaries. This is the sufficiency dimension of the concept.

No Presumption against Economic Growth

It is important to note that the environmental space concept implies no judgements about the possibility for continued growth of GDP, either in developed or developing countries. Assuming that graduated but stringent targets for reducing wasteful land use and materials and energy consumption are met, economic growth in GDP terms is compatible with the concept and may be considered sustainable. It is already the case that industry's energy efficiency increases substantially as economies grow. Unfortunately, on our current development paths, the volumes of energy consumption more than outweigh gains in production efficiency, just as the volumes of car traffic always seem to outstrip improvements in vehicle technology. This simply reinforces the need to consider production efficiency and consumption sufficiency at the same time. It is likely, therefore, that in the growing number of advanced economies, technologically sophisticated and dematerialised sectors, such as information and knowledge applications, will offer the greatest potential for efficient economic growth if appropriate human skills are available. The market for efficiency gains in industry could also be huge. The *Financial Times* estimates that the market for energy efficient goods and services could be US$1800 billion over the next 40 years.

This is not to minimise the enormous challenge of achieving sustainability in the first half of the next century. Rather, it reinforces the point that intense creativity and ingenuity on the part of all countries and peoples will be required if we are to realise production and consumption patterns within the limited environmental space available to us and still live comfortably. Given this creativity, there is no reason for sustainability and economic competitiveness to be seen in opposition. The following chart, from the

50 Rowe, J 'Honey, We Shrunk the Economy!' Yes – *A Journal of Positive Futures* Spring/Summer, 1996

Table 3.6

Reconciling sustainable development with economic growth		
	Internationally Competitive	**Internationally Uncompetitive**
Ecologically Sustainable	Scenario 1: Sustainable development	Scenario 2: Utopian approaches – economic and/or social crisis
Ecologically Unsustainable	Scenario 3: Business as usual – ecological crisis	Scenario 4: Development crisis

Sustainable Germany report, shows how there is only one broad option for sustainable development which is also competitive and compatible with economic development. It is the fundamental nature of that development which we seek to change and not the high-quality goods and services it delivers. Of course, some parts of the economy will contract, others will grow, as is always the case in a dynamic economy. Economic structures, policy options, technology and individual preferences can all adapt in a sustainable direction. There will be a reorientation of national economies to favour resource-efficiency, reduced volumes of unnecessary transport, product durability and enhanced use of renewable raw materials.

Nor does the implementation of strategies for living within our environmental space imply any sort of central planning of resource allocation. Rather, the targets, derived by discussion, debate and consensus-building in each country, are beacons for policy steering towards sustainability. The policy mechanisms for moving towards sustainability are a matter for national concern. They could be achieved, for example, by promoting more sophisticated and satisfying forms of consumption, and by appropriate market reform, together with bans on dangerous products such as CFCs. Environmental tax reform, such as carbon taxes, is one such policy option, currently favoured in Europe; tradeable permits and extraction quotas, preferred by the US Government, might be another option for achieving the necessary reductions in a socially responsible and economically feasible way, if equity considerations are factored into the calculations. These are discussed again in Chapter 8. Whatever the policy mechanisms chosen, there is ample evidence that government and business can work together to achieve the necessary advances from a matrix of options. Political will is the essential ingredient.

In particular, the environmental space concept challenges us to think about sustainable pathways to national development. While adopting the principles of environmental space can be seen as a global project, environmental space analysis itself is a project for each nation, best undertaken within a national sustainable-development strategy process, and by making use of each country's unique blend of cultural orientation, political policy, scientific technology and the ability to adjust values. What needs to be accomplished to generate sustainable development is indicated by the analysis, but how best to achieve this is down to national and local ingenuity and creativity. Later we will make use of the benefit of Sustainable Europe's and the North–South Project's experience of environmental space analysis in 38 countries.

This process of positive change – of heading in the right direction – is the true meaning of the term sustainable development, which we see as a process of living and managing wisely rather than some eventual utopia. But to achieve this, Europeans and citizens of other regions and nations must take full responsibility for their use of environmental space, must stimulate creativity and broad participation in developing alternatives, and must generate widespread commitment to redirecting current economic activities in a sustainable direction.

First Steps for the North

Agenda 21 stated that 'the major cause of the continued deterioration of the global environment is the unsustainable pattern of consumption and production, particularly in industrialised countries'. All parties at the Rio Earth Summit challenged developed countries, in particular, to take the lead in promoting and achieving more sustainable production and consumption patterns.

The environmental space approach recognises that global renewal must begin in the North. There are four reasons.[51] Firstly, the two previous centuries of industrialisation have left a legacy of environmental degradation for which the North is largely responsible. This is both in terms of transnational pollutants which enter the atmosphere and the seas and in terms of resource exploitation, such as zinc or bauxite mining, in Southern countries; this has generated localised pollution as it develops the industrial infrastructure and feeds consumption in the North. Secondly, Northern countries command far more technological and financial resources for the necessary shift to sustainable production and consumption than do countries in the South. Thirdly, the lifestyles of the North, for better or worse, have become the model for many people in the South, to our potentially and seriously mutual disadvantage. Finally, the North can make no demands on the newly industrialising countries unless it changes first. If the North wishes to enter into global negotiations to avert the emerging environmental crisis and to achieve genuinely sustainable development, it must improve its bargaining position by putting its own house in order. This does not mean just decreasing emissions of polluting substances within national borders. It also means a decrease of environmental pressures on countries that produce and export resources to the North.

And a Leapfrog for the South

51 Loske, R 'Sustainable Germany: Contribution to Global Sustainable Development' in Report on International Conference on Sustainable Economy for the North – Implications for the South, Berlin: Carl Duisberg Gesellschaft, 1995

Of course, sustainable development cannot be achieved by the North on its own, certainly not in an integrated, global economy with the Asian 'tigers' industrialising rapidly. Nor is it a case of the North reducing consumption of raw materials unilaterally, causing prices to sink and driving poor Southern countries into greater poverty with less ability to develop sustainable national policies. It is in the obvious interest of the South to achieve sustainability within the context of its countries' development goals and within the context of an overall global strategy; this will achieve sustainable production and consumption in a manner which enhances the development opportunities of individual countries and regions. The combined principles of boundaries for environmental space and equity of resource consumption provide an intellectual and information framework for both organising an international effort, and for marshalling the necessary information about every country in the world.

This is certainly true of advanced NICs and former Eastern Bloc countries who need to diversify from labour-intensive production, heavy industry and reliance on imported technology to more sophisticated, hi-tech manufacturing and services. NICs such as Singapore, Taiwan and South Korea are well on the way; larger NICs such as China, India and Brazil are making progress in the development of scientific and

GUEST ESSAY 3.1

Josefa Rizalina M Bautista

Global Cooperation for Sustainable Development: the View from the Philippines

As one travels worldwide, basic disparities in language, colour and the physical build of people are readily apparent. But the differences are diminishing. Technology and its applications, especially through trade and media, are harmonising tastebuds, preferences and even lifestyles across the globe, generating a distinct and pervasive global culture. Capital cities almost all have their McDonalds, Toyotas and Benzes, Ninna Riccis and Florshiems available in one-stop-shop malls, surrounded by skyscrapers and air conditioned houses with state-of-the-art gadgets. This is the growing culture of materialism and consumption. The extension of this culture's reach has, unfortunately, led to the felling of forests, aggressive harvesting of marine life, and massive production of consumables contributing to the deterioration of air and water quality.

On the other hand, poverty, hunger and turmoil continue to plague some places. Rwanda, Bosnia and Afghanistan exemplify this other culture – the culture of deprivation. The culture of consumption and the continuing crises of deprivation, with their inherent disparities, are the real-life battlegrounds of sustainable development and environmental space. In any jurisdiction – whether country, region, province or local area – corresponding disparities exist. Global cooperation necessitates managing the social, technological, economic and political changes that need to take place in both cultures.

Developing countries such as the Philippines must satisfy basic and higher needs in ways that do not invite unsustainable materialism. We have to decide as a nation what are truly sustainable growth standards and then work to realise them. We have to leapfrog foreign development modes characterised by high use of non-renewable energy and resources. We have to look back to our ancestors' culture and reinculcate its treasures of sustainable living – organic farming, herbal healing, waste minimisation, community spirit and many others. We have to deal seriously with the impacts of cable TV, Coca/Pepsi Cola culture, rock bands, the World Trade Organisation (WTO), etc so these support rather than deflect us from sustainability. We have to practice what we preach in terms of defending our remaining forests and rivers. We have to sustain our gains in dealing with poverty as well as in forging peace.

From the North we can use relevant technological and financial support – but less dictation of lifestyles and measures of progress. Ultimately, global solidarity in sustainable development necessitates equitable sharing of the world's wealth across political jurisdictions – big words and yet translatable into concrete actions so long as leaders and peoples truly have the desire to do so.

Josefa Rizalina M Bautista is Vice President of the Development Academy of the Philippines and Managing Director of its Center for Sustainable Local Development.

52 ibid

technological capability. That Asian NICs may already be on their own unique development paths compared to old industrialised countries is indicated by the fact that their rapid economic growth is taking place against a background of higher national levels of income equity.[52] Similarly, China has adopted policies since the 'four modernisations' of 1980 to change the structure of production and investment in favour of labour-intensive industries, together with open trade.

In the long term, it may be vital for the less industrialised countries, many rich in natural and human resources, such as the 52 states and 640 million people of Africa, to bypass 20th-century patterns of industrialisation. These foster an overdependence on the environmentally damaging export of unprocessed raw materials, whose prices will be subject to periodic and destablising declines due to reductions in the material intensity of goods. These countries need to create the option to move directly into a 21st-century, knowledge- and information-based mode of development, consistent with environmental space. At the same time, many of these countries are fortunate to have indigenous and rural populations who are often rich in ecological knowledge that has been tried and tested over generations, even if they are not rich in material goods. In all countries and regions, wherever the political will and the general support of the people exists, a window of opportunity exists to fashion new pathways to sustainable development.

4

Fair Shares in Environmental Space – Basic Principles

Introduction

Living within the environmental space made available to us by the planet avoids the need to anticipate the dangerous effects of industrial processes. It does this by reducing the volume of material inputs to those processes, and hence their polluting outputs, but without lessening quality of life. This is the only way to stay within the earth's biophysical boundaries in a world of rapid economic expansion.

In the first chapter, environmental space was defined as the total amount of energy, non-renewable resources, land, water, wood and other resources which can be used globally without lasting environmental damage and without impinging on the rights of future generations, within the context of equal rights to resource consumption and concern for quality of life for all peoples of the world. A more specific definition of a fair share in environmental space is the maximum average resource use per person for each world citizen in a specific target year to achieve a good life. Using this rule-of-thumb the amount available can be compared to current consumption to give an indication of distance-to-sustainability for consumption of various key resources. In Chapter 5 some examples will be given of how a fair share in environmental space can be assessed. This chapter focuses on the general ideas behind the three main principles of the environmental space concept.

Of course, achieving environmental space and global equity is not possible solely by individual, household or local action. Rather, it demands linking of top-down political commitment at a national and international level with bottom-up initiative to tackle structural opportunities and constraints in production, and to encourage adjustment in human values towards sustainable consumption patterns. The latter is brought about by a combination of individual initiatives and national programmes which build on cultural diversity and national creativity. Environmental space is therefore calculated at the level of the

---

Box 4.1 Basic principles of environmental space

Three basic principles:

- commitment to living within the Earth's biophysical limits by the middle of the 21st century;
- global equity of access to the Earth's resources by all nations and all peoples;
- production and consumption should enhance total quality of life within a framework of national and cultural diversity.

nation – by aggregating environmental space per capita. Each country's entitlement is termed a fair share of environmental space.

First Principle: Commitment to Living within the Earth's Biophysical Limits

In the long run, our economies and our quality of life are dependent on the environment – not the other way around. The global environment provides:

- a *home* for the human race;
- *sources* of energy and materials;
- *services* to human, animals and plant life, such as carbon absorption and climate regulation; and
- *sinks* for waste energy and waste materials.

These flows are shown in Figure 4.1 – which indicates points of action available to people to influence the system which is, after all, our only home. It is folly, therefore, to degrade or destroy the environment, equivalent to fouling one's nest or destroying one's home. The alternative is to live comfortably within the boundaries of the system, so that it continues to provide the vital services for sustaining human life. This requires that we pay attention to a few simple but crucial criteria for a healthy planet:

- renewable resources, such as soils, forests and fish, should not be depleted or harvested in such a manner as to cause environmental damage or diminishment of stocks past their replacement threshold.
- Non-renewable resources should be increasingly used in closed systems to minimise waste and the damaging environmental impacts of their extraction.
- The amount of pollution and CO_2 emissions may not exceed thresholds that can be coped with by the biosphere.

These may be simple rules-of-thumb, but we are nowhere near realising them. As we saw in Chapter 2, we are moving too often in the wrong direction.

Figure 4.1

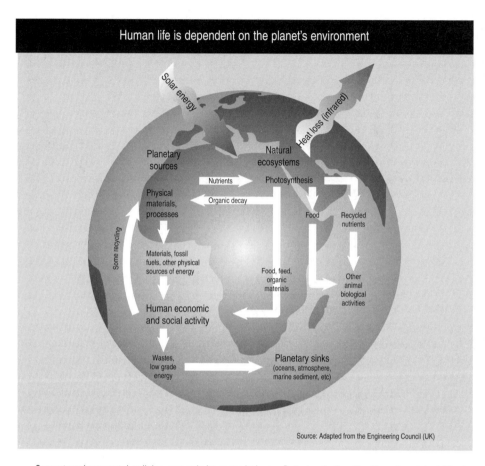

Current environmental policies can only be regarded as a first step in the direction of sustainability; in many cases a complete analysis reveals that environmental improvements are outstripped by increases in pollution caused by rising resource consumption. Sometimes it appears that the domestic environment is improving – instead, the environmental degradation has been exported to other, often poor, countries. Dutch environmental policies, for example, are highly esteemed by world experts. Indeed, positive results are being achieved. The emission of various polluting substances has decreased during the past few years although economic growth has continuously increased. The most important exceptions, however, are CO_2 emissions, mainly from growing transport intensity, and waste. These failures of policy are obvious.

What is hidden and therefore not discussed within Dutch society is that during the ten years between 1985 and 1995, the use of primary (newly produced) metals increased very substantially with a range of environmental impacts in the Netherlands and abroad, particularly in developing countries. The report *Sustainable Netherlands Revised* charts these increases including zinc (+89 per cent), lead (+25 per cent), copper (+33 per cent) and aluminum (+25 per cent). The 'consumption' of agricultural land from outside Europe to grow fodder for the intensive Dutch animal husbandry industry has doubled as well. These are the 'ecological backpacks' mentioned in the last chapter. So, within The Netherlands the environment may be cleaner, with some important exceptions, but the total Dutch environmental burden on the planet is increasing. Gains in pollution control are being overtaken by volume growth, mainly associated with resource and land consumption. The effects of Dutch production and consumption patterns increasingly lie outside their borders, although few Dutch people are aware of that. Few are also aware that the material- and energy-intensive lifestyles of the Dutch, and other wealthy countries, cannot be followed by developing countries without causing a tremendous increase in global environmental damage.

If we are to move to a constructive, proactive approach, with a truly global perspective, sustainable development must be underpinned by a systematic understanding of the measurable limits to the earth's resources and its sink capacity – at least by approximation. With this knowledge in hand, we can:

- change the technology of industrial transformation to improve efficiency, reduce consumption of resources and generate equal utility for less polluting inputs;
- adjust our population numbers by promoting economic prosperity and by spreading knowledge about options for family planning;
- alter our value systems so that we need less material goods and value family and community life more.

These are all reasonable options, and we can mix and match approaches to suit national and cultural frameworks.

Assessing Sustainable Resource Use

Within environmental space, which preserves the biophysical basis of life, human beings can exploit the natural environment in a sustainable manner. To assess whether this is happening, we need to do three things:

- firstly, establish some principles and norms which express the notion of sustainability in a way which could achieve widespread consensus.
- Secondly, measure resource consumption or develop proxy values.
- Thirdly, develop targets – so that we are confident we are moving in the direction of sustainable development rather than away from it.

Each of these steps are discussed. Firstly, principles and norms must be established which express the notion of sustainability both in terms of sustainable limits to resource use as well as in terms of quality of life, determined by factors such as measures of social cohesion, employment, and health. The principle of fair share in environmental space gives targets for a maximum allowable use of several natural resources in terms of their primary consumption; that is, the use of newly produced material from virgin resources. The concern is to limit the primary use of resources, as well as to give equal access to resources. As far as recycled, or secondary, materials are concerned, the main concern is with the amount of energy and material use it takes to get them recycled. Both primary and secondary resource use have to stay within the earth's biophysical limits regarding its capacity to produce renewable resources and to cope with polluting substances without (serious) changes in ecological systems.

Box 4.2 Club of Rome revisited?

On the whole, environmental space calculations are input-oriented – that is, they do not measure the pollution of natural systems per se but rather focus, wherever possible, on reducing inputs that guarantee sustainable use of non-renewable resources with minimum waste and pollution. Calculations are based not on resource availability, but on the environmental impact of resource use in which the impacts of extraction loom large.

The environmental space approach is not, therefore, concerned with whether amounts of non-renewable resources are static or not, since technology can increase the exploitable potential of resources. Rather, it is concerned with the fact that, even if resources are not limited, the environmental impacts of resource exploitation set limits to the sustainable extent of that exploitation. These are the real limits to growth, not the resources themselves.

In principle, consumption of non-renewables is unsustainable in the long term because reserves, however large, will run out. But that is seldom the issue; as minerals become more scarce, their prices rise and more effort (in terms of capital, labour, energy, water, landscape destruction) will be put into finding and developing new reserves or substitute materials. With prices rising, the environmental impacts of extraction and processing may well grow as more overburden is removed, more energy used in processing, and more wastes, some toxic, are generated in the production process.

Human societies could go to the Antarctic and extract yet more resources. The bottom of the ocean is also relatively virgin territory. And there are still (a decreasing) number of areas of natural beauty that could be exploited for oil, gas, metals and other resources. But continuing this pattern of resource exploitation in the 21st century could be construed as a dramatic mistake in human history. It would threaten an already diminished biodiversity and generate yet more energy use and pollution. The problem, therefore, is not resource scarcity but ecological scarcity: the capacity of the planet to absorb the pollution which is associated with excessive resource exploitation. The environmental space approach involves a self-determined decision to abstain or reduce our use of those resources which result in ecological scarcity.

Secondly, it is necessary to measure, by approximation, the net resource consumption at a national level. Adding and subtracting product and goods imports to national production, and correcting for changes in stock, gives the net resource consumption in a given year. Obviously more work is required to achieve standardised reliable data. But, in principle, these calculations can already be made for the high-consuming OECD countries. Examples are given in the next chapter. Thirdly, comparisons should be made between current net resource consumption and the fair share in environmental space, which is calculated globally in most cases, but regionally for freshwater. For example, the fair share in environmental space for energy in terms of CO_2 emissions is around 1.7 tonnes per capita per year (discussed in the next chapter), compared to 29 tonnes in the USA, German emissions in the order of 12 tonnes and a European average of 7.3 tonnes. Plotting CO_2 emissions on a year-by-year basis and plotting the sustainability target in a target year will clearly indicate whether the distance-to-sustainability target is decreasing. For emissions, this is already common practice, though not yet for net resource use.

Key Areas of Resource Consumption and Indicators of Fair Shares in Environmental Space

The following resources are generally identified as key areas of sustainable production and consumption.

- *Energy*: it is fundamental to modern economies and ways of living, facilitating most production and consumption; the use of fossil fuels underlies many pressing environmental concerns including global climate change and acidification of forests and lakes.
- *Key non-renewable resources*: including pig iron for steel, which still accounts for around 90 per cent of metal input in a modern economy; aluminium, whose use is growing and which is highly energy-dependent, consuming 1 per cent of world energy use; cement, a major construction material whose manufacture accounts for 2.5 per cent of world CO_2 emissions; and chlorine which, as part of a compound, is usually the largest chemical input to a modern economy and which is implicated in ozone depletion, organochlorine pollution and dioxin production.
- *Freshwater*: without it there would be no life, no food, no drink and virtually no production and consumption; clean water is essential to health and development but is increasingly in short supply, and therefore a source of conflict.
- *Wood*: it is used not only in paper production and construction materials, but, more importantly, as carbon sinks in the carbon cycle, regulators of the water cycle, woodland habitats for species and sites for landscape protection and recreation. Deforestation accounts for almost one fifth of global carbon dioxide emissions through burning and decay. Wood is a specific aspect of land use.
- *Land use*: land provides living space and is a source for renewable resources, supporting 98 per cent of global food production and natural ecosystems. Economic growth is urbanising vast amounts of land which is now alienated from rural functions.

Within these categories, a very broad range of industrial processes and types of resource consumption are represented, covering about 90 per cent of all material flows. For these categories, indicators have been selected (see Table 4.1). These indicators are at the apex of a chain of industrial processes and their reduction generates positive ramifications throughout production systems. In part, this occurs because of the often large expenditures of energy and movement of secondary, waste materials which are involved in securing the benefits of the primary resource – the ecological backpacks or rucksacks, discussed below. They are the hidden environmental costs of production and consumption which we can no longer ignore. Where precise and complete measurements are not available as indicators, the precautionary principle is applied.

It would, of course, be possible to analyse the environmental space for pollutants and other forms of degradation, rather than resource use per se. However, on the whole, there is an important and practical reason for focusing on resource consumption: while the number of pollutants and sources is very large, the major inputs to production which are associated with many environmental problems can be subsumed under a few headings. In spite of this, CO_2 emissions are used as a proxy for the atmosphere's sink capacity because of the critical nature of global warming and its influence on all ecological systems, and because it is currently the best environmental indicator for fossil-fuel consumption.

For each of the indicators shown in Table 4.1 there is a measurement of actual per capita consump-

Overview for the European Union of actual per capita consumption of the various categories of environmental space			
Resource	Present use per capita per year	Optimum reductions	Interim targets
CO_2 emissions [1]	7.3 t		
Primary energy use	123 GJ		
Fossil fuels [2]	100 GJ		
Nuclear	16 GJ		
Renewables	7 GJ		
Non-renewable raw materials			
Cement	536 kg		
Primary steel	273 kg		
Aluminium	12 kg		
Chlorine	23 kg		
Land use EU-12 [3]	0.726 ha		
Arable area	0.237 ha		
Pasture land	0.167 ha		
Add. area	0.037 ha		
Unpr. wooded area	0.164 ha		
Protected area	0.003 ha		
Built-up land	0.053 ha		
Unused area [4]	0.000 ha		
Wood [5]	0.66 m^3		
Water	768 m^3		

1   1995 emissions and energy sources for continental Europe
2   Coal, lignite, oil, gas.
3   Use for 12-member countries of the European Union in 1995
4   This is a category which will be useful in future environmental space analysis
5   European Union countries plus the European Free Trade Area countries plus Central and Eastern European countries

Table 4.1   tion of the various environmental space categories in appropriate measures, such as tonnes of CO_2, gigajoules of energy (GJ), kilogrammes of non-renewable raw materials, hectares of land consumed at home and abroad by import of foodstuffs and non-food agricultural products (ha), and cubic metres of wood and water (m^3). These have been estimated for the 12 countries which belonged to the European Union at the time of calculation in 1994. The remaining columns will be filled in later to demonstrate environmental space calculations and distance-to-sustainability measures. The assumptions which underpin these calculations are discussed in the next chapter.

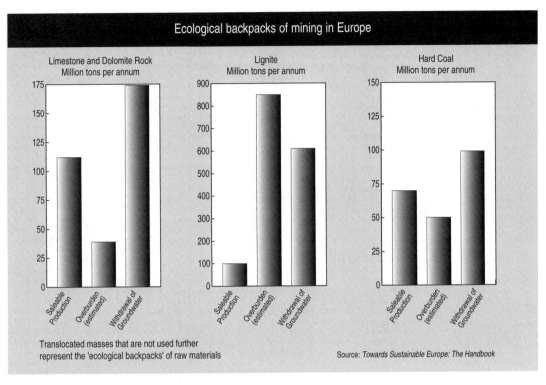

Figure 4.2

The Ecological Backpack

Every year, to secure the resources which flow into production processes, billions of tons of materials are displaced by human activity. Twice as much material is shifted by machine as is moved by geological forces on the earth's surface.[1] These include rocks, sand, gravel, water and fossil fuels. This suggests that environmental and materials analysis must acknowledge that for every resource extracted and used, there is a concomitant expenditure of energy and substances. These include, for example, materials moved to access the resource; overburden intentionally removed to extract ores; toxic wastes released onto the earth's land surface and into water; or soil unintentionally eroded by timber harvesting. On a global basis, for instance, mining today moves a total of 28 billion tons per year, only a tiny percentage of which ends up in usable form. Mining and smelting also consume 5 to 10 per cent of world energy each year.[2]

Similarly, every product and every service is linked throughout its entire life-cycle with energy and material throughputs. Large proportions of these are not economically utilised but are dumped back into the natural environment, often in a way which makes absorption difficult. These translocated masses of materials consumed at the beginning, or during, a product's life-cycle can be thought of as 'forgotten megatons'.[3] Their reduction could make an enormous contribution to sustainable development and environmental protection. For example, Figure 4.2 shows the translocated masses for some mining operations in Europe.

The ecological backpack concept can also be applied to finished goods. For example, the backpack of a car includes the weight of its constituent primary, process and recycled materials (metal, glass and plastic), as well as the weight of soil, rock and wastes moved during the extraction and processing of

1 Factor 10 Club, *Carnoules Declaration* Wuppertal, 1995

2 Young, J and Sachs, A *The Next Efficiency Revolution: Creating a Sustainable Materials Economy* Washington: Worldwatch, 1994

3 Spangenberg, J (ed) *Towards Sustainable Europe: The Study* Brussels: Sustainable Europe Campaign, 1995

Figure 4.3

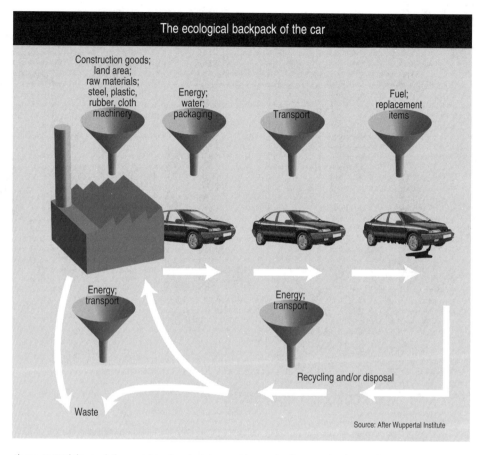

The ecological backpack of the car

Construction goods; land area; raw materials; steel, plastic, rubber, cloth machinery

Energy; water; packaging

Transport

Fuel; replacement items

Energy; transport

Energy; transport

Recycling and/or disposal

Waste

Source: After Wuppertal Institute

4 OECD Workshop on Sustainable Production and Consumption: Clarifying the Concepts; Final Report, Paris: OECD, 1995

5 Hinterberger, F, Luks, F and Schmidt-Bleek, F 'Material flows vs. "natural capital": What makes an economy sustainable?' in Ecological Economies, 1997, forthcoming

those materials, and the weight of materials used in production, packaging and transportation (see Figure 4.3).[4] As noted earlier, the vast bulk of materials associated with production are often derived from locations outside of the country where production takes place. We argue that they must be considered in terms of the environmental space of the car-producing country. Since the South is largely a supplier of raw materials, it bears the greater burden of ecological consequences. And since the ecological backpacks of Northern imports are greater than those of Northern exports, foreign trade mechanisms encourage the shift of environmental burdens from North to South.

These calculations can be part of an industrial ecology which examines material and energy flows, attempts to achieve closed-loop systems in the reuse of materials and wastes as well as integrated life-cycle management of products and processes to minimise environmental impacts at every stage of the product from cradle to grave. These are discussed in Chapter 6. In summary, according to the first law of thermodynamics, neither matter nor energy can be destroyed. Every waste flow is the result of material inputs into the economic system. Hence, reducing material inputs means waste reduction.[5] Environmental space measurements are intended to provide a quantitative basis for input reduction to production processes. By reducing the amounts of inputs, called material flows, a significant decrease in environmental problems can be anticipated.

Box 4.3 Organised debate in the Sustainable Europe Campaign

The Sustainable Europe Campaign links 30 countries in action and research around production and consumption issues. The main goal of the first phase, completed in 1994, was to develop a more thorough understanding of the requirements for sustainable production and consumption in continental Europe for a interim target date of 2010. During this phase, the German Wuppertal Institute for Climate, Environment and Energy was responsible for scientific input and the development of a common methodology for assessing environmental space at both European and national levels, building on an approach pioneered in *Action Plan Sustainable Netherlands*.

This first phase of analysis resulted in the published study *Towards Sustainable Europe* and a methodological handbook providing national groups with guidelines to analyse current and sustainable uses of environmental space in their country. The report was produced as a discussion document for the campaign. This report has been translated into most European languages and several summaries of varying lengths have been compiled.

During the second phase, from 1995, studies were made at national levels using a common methodology, set out in the handbook, which ensured methodological consistency among the 30 national reports. In each country parallel discussions were initiated to allow national groups to hold debates with key figures from relevant target groups. During this phase, these key stakeholders considered the problems and possibilities of closing the sustainability gap in different economic sectors – the sustainability gap being the difference between present usage and sustainable usage of resources in each country. For example, in Germany, Friends of the Earth (BUND) teamed up with a Christian human-aid organisation (Misereor) to undertake the environmental space analysis, hold debates with various target groups (such as political parties, trade unions, religious organisations and business groups) and to present the finding as a basis for discussion at more than 600 meetings around the country. More than 95,000 copies of the long or short version of the report have been sold, and 350 articles have appeared in the print media discussing environmental space. The German Federal Environment Minister said the report, *Sustainable Germany*, is 'endowed with the breath of what is manageable'. The most important German news magazine, *Der Spiegel*, called the study 'the green bible of the millennium transition'.

The third phase of Sustainable Europe, covering 1996–97, consisted of integrating national findings at a European level, further widening the debates in all countries and the EC, and preparation for follow-up campaigning activities by national groups and Friends of the Earth, Europe and International to promote consensus around the way forward to sustainable development.

Fair Shares in Environmental Space is about Debate

Of course, environmental space is really only partially quantifiable. This is for three reasons.

■ Firstly, the science at each level of analysis is always challenged by the complexity of biophysical systems, and by the intensely dynamic nature of human–environment interactions.

- Secondly, human values and cultural preferences play an important role in any points of action which might give rise to sustainable development. The view that the needs of future generations is of equal value to that of our own generation is a value judgement in itself, but one fairly easy to defend.
- Thirdly, the natural restorative powers of nature and good husbandry enter into the equation. Land which is allowed to lay fallow can recover its fertility, polluted water can gradually recover its quality if pollution levels fall to reasonable amounts, and so on. In other words, good management is a tactic for restoring environmental space, which can then be used for sustainable consumption. The Earth's restorative powers means that we can potentially regain resources we have squandered in the past for sustainable use.

This means that the concept of environmental space has a subjective element. As a result, there is lively debate over which are the most appropriate measurements or indicators of sustainable development, such as within the Sustainable Europe Campaign.[6] The measurements of environmental space, and the methods which give rise to them, are definitely intended to encourage discussion and debate, rather than be the last word in indicators. The debate is a positive process because it contributes to, and helps refine, our ability at a national and continental level to assess the sustainability of production and consumption patterns.

Second Principle: Global Equity of Access to Resources Among All Nations and Peoples

The second principle of environmental space is a commitment to global equity. The equity principle states that each person in the world has the same right (but not obligation) to use an equal amount of global resources, now and in the future. In advocating the equity principle, the environmental space approach parts company with much thinking on sustainable development, which either ignores the issue of distribution or, like the Brundtland Commission, overtly assumes that Northern consumption would remain far in excess of Southern consumption for the foreseeable future.

There are a number of reasons why equitable in access to resources is important. Chapter 2 discussed a few of the many serious environmental problems which are threatening the common inheritance of the planet and its resources, which we, of this generation, are bequeathing in stewardship to our children and subsequent generations. The magnitude of these problems, such as global warming, means that the resource base of existing production and consumption systems for all people on earth is at stake. As long as rich countries continue to consume a high amount of renewable and non-renewable resources per capita, developing countries can also morally command the right to do so, if they too ignore the biophysical limits to natural resource use. As a result, the planet will be locked in a vicious and downward cycle of environmental, and ultimately socio-economic, degradation. As developing countries such as China choose to increase resource use per capita in the near future to the level of existing advanced industrial countries, and these advanced economies continue to overconsume resources, then world production and consumption will exceed the environmental and ecological limits of the planet even further, by a factor of up to ten. The destructive cycle of overconsumption and environmental degradation will steadily erode our quality of life, for all peoples of the world.

6 See, for example, Hille, J *The Environmental Space Concept: Implications for environmental reporting, policies and assessments* Copenhagen: European Environmental Agency, 1996

GUEST ESSAY 4.1

Alan Durning

Ecological Backpacking in Seattle – the Ghost of Coffee's Past

My name is Alan and I'm a compulsive drinker. Coffee is my brew. I used to drink it daily, sometimes hourly. I drank it by the pot... cappuccinos, frappacinos, even Folger's drip. Now I'm on the wagon, drinking locally grown herbal tea. You see, this terrible thing happened. A dream straight out of Scrooge. I saw where my coffee comes from.

It started one morning in the kitchen. As I poured the beans into the grinder, I suddenly found myself in a clouded forest on a mountain above the Cauca River in Colombia. The lush vegetation was disappearing all around me as a coffee plantation grew. Farm workers were spraying the trees with pesticides made in the valley of the River Rhine in Europe. I began to choke on the poisonous fumes when I was transported... to New Orleans. Burlap sacks of coffee beans were being unloaded from a freighter burning oil from the Orinoco River Valley of Venezuela. It was like a spin on the house that Jack built: the freighter was made in Japan out of steel forged in Korea from iron mined in the lands of Australian aborigines. Workers were pouring the beans into a roaster, which was fuelled with natural gas piped in from Oklahoma. Out the other end, my beans poured into bags of nylon, polyester, and polyethylene – plastics from New Jersey – and aluminum foil from a smelter in Oregon. That smelter was powered by electricity from dams that have nearly wiped out wild salmon in the Columbia River.

Suddenly, I was in my kitchen again, but hovering by the ceiling, looking down. My beans, now disintegrating in the grinder, had come to my home inside a brown paper bag made from pines in the northern Rockies. On the trip from the supermarket, my car had burned a sixth of a gallon of gasoline, spewing carbon monoxide, carbon dioxide, nitrogen oxides, and volatile organics into the air. The gas had come from Alaska's North Slope by way of Prince William Sound and a refinery in northern Washington.

Hovering above myself in the kitchen, I watched as I took that first sip of the day. But from the cup came pesticides, oil, molten steel. My ecological wake. And it wasn't just the coffee. My T-shirt. My newspaper. My radio. The wake of it all washed over me. I buckled under its weight. Then, my bathroom scale appeared, flashing 115 pounds. My daily consumption of natural resources. I fell to the floor, crushed and bloated. I can't shake this dream. I've gotta get off this consumption kick. And I'm starting with java. I don't know how to do it but I gotta find a way of using less. Can we make things better? Figure out better ways of getting around? Get stuff from closer to home? I don't know, but I do know this, my name is Alan, I'm a compulsive coffee drinker, and there's a world in my cup.

Alan Durning is Executive Director of Northwest Environment Watch in Seattle. This commentary was first heard on the radio show 'Living on Earth' on KPLU, adapted from Alan's *This Place on Earth* (Sasquatch Books).

> We will either come together across socio-economic circumstances and cultures in the common task of local and global sustainability or we will all go to hell together.
>
> Dato Mahathir Mohamad, Prime Minister of Malaysia

Nevertheless, it is also important to recognise that grappling with the problem of over-consumption is generally a post-materialist task insofar as the concern tends to arise after most wants and needs are met, or where consumption is already at an excessive level. The problem for the world's environment is that only a small minority of the world's population is in any position to adopt a post-materialistic perspective, and only a minority of these choose to do so.

Conversely the 75 per cent of the world's population not yet anywhere near the materialistic standards of the overconsuming North feel, with ample justification, that they have every right to fulfil their material needs and desires through industrialism, just as the rich world has done. A steadily increasing number of people will demand this right, whether we like it or not. They have an ethical right to do so in terms of fair shares of resources for all, up to the upper limit of sustainable consumption of resources. If we are to live within those limits, environmental space calculations may prove essential starting points for worldwide political negotiations on sustainable production and consumption patterns. Equity is both a moral and political necessity.

Among these high consumers of the future, 70 per cent will be concentrated in just eight countries: China, India, Indonesia, Brazil, Pakistan, Bangladesh, Nigeria and Mexico. The Chinese and Indians alone comprise 2.2 billion people, or 38 per cent of the world's population: 1.2 billion Chinese and 1 billion Indians. Their approach to sustainable development, along with the other six countries, will be a major factor in terms of planetary quality of life in the next century. But the developed world can hardly have expectations that these countries might act sustainably – unless the developed world itself is prepared to make radical changes in their unsustainable lifestyles.

The equity principle accounts for this situation. The principle is straightforward: on a per capita basis, by a designated year sometime in the first half of the next century, each country will be entitled to consume the same amount of natural resources relative to its population size, and to contribute the same reasonable amount of pollution to the environment. Each individual in the world will, accordingly, be entitled to a theoretically equal amount of environmental space and therefore development potential. The equity principle argues that we are all equal in terms of access to planetary resources and pollution. What could be more logical as the starting point of international discussions on our common but differentiated responsibilities for the planet? What is more in accord with the principles of natural justice, or more in keeping with a liberalised world economy committed to equal opportunity for all, but to recognise the biophysical limitations of the planet? The equity principle is fundamental to a modern, humane capitalism, and its proponents should support free and fair access to resources as the crux to providing quality of life for all.

Overall, environmental space analysis suggests that an approximate 50 per cent reduction in the current levels of materials input into the global economy is necessary to reduce pollution and waste from non-renewables consumption to sustainable levels, as shown in Figure 4.4. However, given current consumption patterns, the focus of this reduction would fall on few countries. For example, as of 1991,

Box 4.4 Target years

Environmental space means more than targets; it is only meaningful when connected to challenging but realistic target years. Within the period of one generation, industrialised countries should be well on the way to a sustainable society. In the year 2010 we should have started to redistribute most categories of environmental space. The year 2010 is also near enough to foresee, and capitalise on, potentially beneficial developments in technology and to influence socio-economic patterns in society. We need to remember that changing habits by changing values takes years, but changing values by changing habits can take only weeks. New habits engender new values.

Beyond that, 2050 could be chosen as the year when it is possible to achieve full sustainability of resource use on a global basis – if we begin now. The years are, of course, arbitrary – any date could be chosen for the purposes of the analysis. But the important thing is that the magnitude of the challenges we face, and the rapid growth of negative environmental effects, means we need to quickly start a purposeful process of achieving sustainable resource consumption. Otherwise the problems get worse, and the task more difficult, day by day.

seven countries, with 11.6 per cent of the world's population – the USA, UK, France, Germany, Italy, Japan and South Korea – consumed 59 per cent of the world's aluminium and 43 per cent of overall crude steel.[7]

One obvious consequence of accepting the equity principle is that primary resource use in rich countries must be cut back significantly. For example, we noted that the environmental space available for fossil-fuel energy consumption is 1.7 tonnes of CO_2 emission per capita per year compared to Europe's 7.3 tonnes and North America's 19 tonnes. These figures indicate the critical importance of early reductions to the health of the planet. For non-renewable raw materials, wood, land use and water similar calculations can be made by using the environmental space methodology.

The Population Basis of the Calculation

Although global population growth is an issue requiring serious attention, the effect of population growth in the South on resource consumption is relatively minor compared to the effect of high per capita resource consumption in the North. This is shown by Figure 4.5

It is important to note that, in Europe and generally in the North, the degree of current, wasteful overconsumption, and the reduction of materials consumption required to allow equitable access to resources, means that environmental space calculations are relatively robust even where populations will continue to grow after 2010, or other cut-off dates, in the underconsuming developing world. However, the issue also points to the challenge the world faces if populations continue to grow in countries such as China and India in tandem with growth in materials consumption. The historical precedent is that population growth levels off as material prosperity reaches more households, and there is no particular reason to suppose this will not be the case for NICs. In countries such as Indonesia and Malaysia, for

7 Friends of the Earth *Tomorrow's World: Britain's Share in a Sustainable Future* London: Earthscan, 1997

Figure 4.4

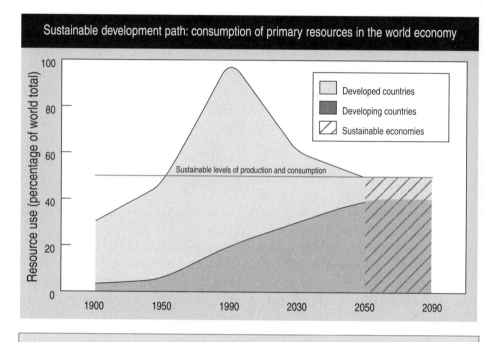

Sustainable development path: consumption of primary resources in the world economy

Legend:
- Developed countries
- Developing countries
- Sustainable economies

Sustainable levels of production and consumption

y-axis: Resource use (percentage of world total) — 0, 20, 40, 60, 80, 100

x-axis: 1900, 1950, 1990, 2030, 2050, 2090

Box 4.5 Is environmental space the same as the ecological footprint?

There is some confusion over the difference between the concepts of environmental space and the ecological footprint. An ecological footprint is the total area a person occupies in terms of land used for agricultural purposes, wood consumption and to absorb polluting emissions. In the analysis, these are aggregated at the city or the country level to show the relative impact on the planet of land consumed, compared to population levels.[8] Both environmental space and the footprint approach arise from the same concern for excessive production and consumption in the North and for development prospects in the South.

Footprints reduce all forms of production and consumption to a hypothetical measurement of hectares required to generate production and consumption patterns (the footprint) compared to the actual physical space occupied by the city region or country under analysis. This calculation is not, however, to be confused with analysis of real land use.

Environmental space is the more complex approach because it analyses various key resource sectors at the national level. It is also probably more difficult to understand and communicate because its calculations are grounded at the policy level of the nation state, and because it encompasses energy and non-renewable resource consumption. Footprints are simpler and easier to communicate because resources are aggregated to one indicator. Both concepts foster discussion and debate on sustainable production and consumption within sound biophysical limits. In terms of policy formulation, environmental space moves beyond the impact of unsustainable lifestyles to suggest sustainable levels of production and consumption and the targets needed to achieve them. It also links North and South in a common framework of responsibility and action.

8 Wackernagel, M and Rees, W *Our Ecological Footprint – Reducing Human Impact on Earth* Gabriola Island: New Society Publishers, 1995

Figure 4.5

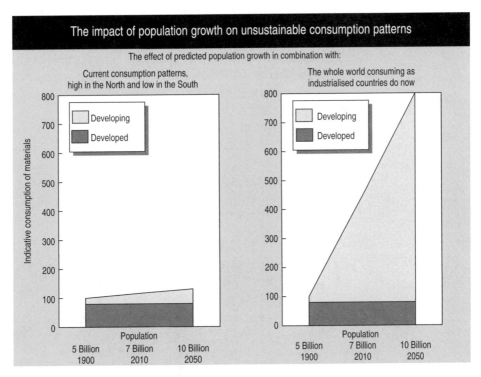

The impact of population growth on unsustainable consumption patterns

The effect of predicted population growth in combination with:

Current consumption patterns, high in the North and low in the South

The whole world consuming as industrialised countries do now

Indicative consumption of materials

Developing
Developed

Developing
Developed

Population
5 Billion   7 Billion   10 Billion
1900   2010   2050

Population
5 Billion   7 Billion   10 Billion
1900   2010   2050

example, a clear indicator of tiger economy status is a decline in birth rates. This also underlines the fact that if sustainability is to be achieved and environmental crisis averted, the North must cut back on consumption to allow the South to achieve development levels which will help lower birth rates. Since the North is overconsuming in many areas, and since overconsumption is increasingly perceived as a negative factor in the quality of life, this is a logical development path.

Implications of Equity

A long-range implication is that countries around the world will share common environmental space targets, common responsibility or common stewardship for all the earth's resources and have an equal opportunity for development. The other side of the equity coin is that global resources are made available, or kept in reserve, for development purposes for those newly industrialising or less-developed countries, up to the common limit of environmental space indicated in the analysis.

Europe, for example, has mostly exhausted its own supplies of raw material resources, which are easily exploitable and of which the minerals have a high ore content. Europe, therefore, imports its requirements mainly from Africa, showing the influence of former colonial relations. But in so doing, Europe may be foreclosing the development prospects of African countries in two ways. Firstly, it narrows the options for countries which may later require easily exploitable minerals of high ore content. These may have to be produced or imported at considerable economic and environmental cost. Secondly, Europe's unsustainable rates of production and consumption are using up the planet's sinks for waste, which will no longer be available in future.

Following on from this, the impacts of any national economy on sustainability in other countries must be assessed. It was argued earlier that analysis of ecological backpacks demonstrates how trade allows the ecological burden to be shifted from country to country – mainly from North to South. For example, although most European countries have both environmental monitoring systems and pollution control, these say nothing about the environmental pressures created by exploiting resources abroad or the European import of goods from other continents, which do not show up in any European statistics. The environmental space approach argues that it is necessary to have indicators of real consumption of energy and materials at national and European Community levels, which account for imports and exports. This is important since there may be a tendency for production to be shifted on a global basis to countries with weak or non-existent pollution control systems. There is not the space in this book to describe the intricacies of import and export of environmental space, but the reader is referred to the technical litera- ture of the Sustainable Europe Campaign.[9]

Box 4.6 German recognition of the import and export of environmental space

Regarding the impacts of the German economy on the countries of the South, it is quite possi- ble for a country to pursue ecologically sustainable development within its boundaries while consuming the resources of other countries to an extent that it robs the latter of the possibility to develop sustainably and, from a global perspective, endangers sustainable development. Broad examples of the effects of the German form of economy on the countries of the South are: the exploitation of the global commons in the form of the atmosphere and oceans, and the exploitation of land, raw materials and biological resources in the South.[10]

Third Principle: Commitment to Total Quality of Life within National Cultures

Living within the boundaries of environmental space, and commiting to global equity in resource consump- tion, requires changed attitudes in order to initiate a bold restructuring of production and consumption processes. This restructuring should not be seen as a sackcloth and ashes project, but as an exciting opportunity to increase quality of life in our communities, for our benefit and that of our children and grandchildren. One way to initiate change is to build on the growing recognition that economic prosperity is necessary, but hardly sufficient, for total quality of life. In many developed countries, for example, there is substantial evidence that, although GNP and GDP continue to grow, quality of life has been declining for 20 years or more. Chapter 7 takes up these issues.

Of course, any vision of total quality of life will vary enormously from continent to continent and from country to country. Within the environmental space approach, there is no prescription beyond the general commitments outlined in the first two principles. Indeed, it is assumed that ingenuity at the national and local levels is essential to achieving a framework for sustainable production and consumption which is

9 Spangenberg, J (ed) *Sustainable Europe: The Handbook* Brussels: Sustainable Europe Campaign, CEAT, 1994

10 Loske, J 'Sustainable Germany: Contribution to global sustainable development' in *International Conference on Sustainable Economy for the North – Implications for the South* Berlin: Carl Duisberg Gesellschaft, 1995. See also BUND and MISEREOR *Sustainable Germany* English résumé, Berlin: Carl Duisberg Gesellschaft, 1996

sensitive to local values and needs. A first step in developing this more sophisticated vision is to be more realistic in our understanding of the ecological basis of the overconsuming Northern lifestyle and in our expectations of the meaning of quality of life. Unfortunately, global television, purveying fantasy shows such as 'Dynasty', 'Dallas' and even 'Lifestyles of the Rich and Famous' only show one, unrealistic side of the Northern lifestyle on the growing number of television screens around the world. Similarly, advertising and even packaging can mislead and distort our views of what is important in life.

Box 4.7 Automobility moves from North to South

A fundamental change is taking place in the world, in the perceptions of successful people and what they think should be part of the new automobile. These models offer authentic quality of life and a totally new concept of design, space, technology, safety and mobility. They are a response to the individual's freedom of choice and a declaration of efficiency in harmony with the environment.

Car advertisement in the *Ghanaian Times*, Accra

The side-effects of the Western model of consumption are never made clear to potential consumers. Take the effects of automobility, for example, now sweeping the world. In Britain traffic danger has reached such a deplorable condition that the number of children (aged seven and eight) allowed to walk to school without parental supervision has declined from 90 per cent to just 9 per cent in the 20 years between 1970 and 1990. Many children are driven to school by their parents – these trips are in the order of 50 million journeys per week, adding to the vicious cycle of congestion and pollution. The cost to parents in lost time is valued at around US$26 billion. In terms of child development, research has shown a dramatic decline in the freedom and independence of British children because their opportunities for unsupervised travel and play have become so restricted.[11] Children are described as prisoners in their own homes.

At the same time, in Britain there has been a sharp rise in the incidence of childhood asthma, which can be triggered by air pollution, caused principally by motor vehicle emissions. Does this situation really reflect quality of life and a sophisticated lifestyle in harmony with the environment? It is important for societies to start asking these questions across a broad range of issues. Unfortunately, many politicians in all parts of the world are convinced by the fairy tale that a continuing increase of consumption leads to a steadily increased quality of life. They forget, however, that the GDP measures welfare without taking into account future losses and environmental costs. Traffic accidents generate GDP, especially if many people are badly injured. Polluted soils and water increase welfare too, according to current methods of national economic analysis.

For some time it has been obvious that if external costs such as ozone depletion, atmospheric pollution, car accidents, noise, water pollution and loss of wetlands are subtracted from, instead of added to, GNP, overall quality of life in many developed countries might well be decreasing. The existence of poverty, and an underclass of unemployed persons and working poor, also tarnishes the image of prosperous societies. Social and economic inequality generate a range of dysfunctions. Therefore, besides monitoring the net primary use of resources within the environmental space analysis, it is important to

11 Hillman, M, Adams, J and Whitelegg, J *One False Move: A Study of Children's Independent Mobility* London: Policy Studies Institute, 1990

Box 4.8 The folly of using GNP to measure quality of life

The gross national product includes air pollution and advertizing for cigarettes, and ambulances to clear our highways of carnage. It counts special locks for our doors, and jails for people who break them. The gross national product includes the destruction of the redwoods and the death of Lake Superior. It grows with the production of napalm and missiles with nuclear warheads.

And if the gross national product includes all this, there is much that it does not comprehend. It does not allow for the health of our families, the quality of their education, or the joy of their play. It is indifferent to the decency of our factories and the safety of streets alike. It does not include the beauty of our poetry, the intelligence of our public debate or the integrity of our public officials.

The gross national product measures neither our wit nor our courage, neither our wisdom nor our learning, neither our compassion nor our devotion to country. It measures everything, in short, except that which makes life worthwhile.

Robert F Kennedy, 1967

consider social and cultural aspects of well-being, and the quality of public or community life as well as private consumption. Correcting GDP for negative environmental and social effects is the first step towards a more a realistic understanding of total quality of life.

Conclusion

Given the importance of using global resources wisely, the difficulty of doing so is no excuse for business-as-usual, or for compromising environmental needs to secure short-term economic benefits. The kinds of environmental problems documented in Chapter 2 already indicate that weak sustainability is not sufficient. A more sophisticated approach is required, which monitors whether we are moving towards or away from sustainability. In this context, environmental space analysis provides indicative policy guidance – that is, it can cut through the rhetoric of sustainable development and help us to consider, as a society, whether we are moving towards sustainability or away from it.

The challenge of living within our available environmental space, and of reducing resource use and pollution, can be met in two ways. Firstly, it can be achieved through managerial and technical creativity, for which the environmental space concept and measurements provide guidance on goals and objectives. Secondly, and more importantly, it can be realised through a growing political consensus around the world on the paramount importance of sustainable primary resource use to quality of life for present, and especially future, generations and societies. This consensus needs to develop locally and nationally in each country and on a continental and global level, involving government, business and citizens' groups in partnership. Friends of the Earth organisations and their affiliates have made a modest start in advocating environmental space by promoting discussion and debate among relevant organisations.

The next chapter looks more closely at how environmental space can be assessed. Subsequent chapters consider the contributions of ecoefficiency and sufficiency to sustainable production and consumption.

CHAPTER 5

Assessing a Fair Share in Environmental Space

Introduction

In a full world, we must come to terms with the fact that environmental space is limited, and that we are already exceeding many of those limits. This means that we must reorganise production and consumption in a coherent and targeted manner if the planet, our home, is not to be further despoiled. The limits are determined by the carrying capacity and recuperative power of ecosystems, the availability and renewability of resources, and the limited ability of the planet to absorb pollution.

Environmental space analysis helps us to understand the magnitude of those limits. There is, for example, a limited amount of acceptable CO_2 emissions because of the greenhouse effect; there is only so much good agricultural land that can be used sustainably; non-renewable resources are limited by their ecological backpacks and the environmental impacts of their use, and so on. Later we discuss key resources which stand at the apex of production and consumption systems.

Assessment of these limits requires that we:

- estimate approximately the maximum level of sustainable resource use on a global scale, including a value-based assessment of acceptable risks.
- Calculate the sustainable level per person based on realistic projections of the global population.
- Compare the estimated sustainable level per person with the current per person net consumption of resources – to generate distance-from-sustainability measures.

A basic assumption of the analysis is that end users should be responsible for the full damaging effect of the ecological backpack and not the residents of the exporting country – for instance, in the case of

GUEST ESSAY 5.1

Jacqueline Aloisi de Larderel

Sustainable Production and Consumption: Two Sides of a Coin

The report *Global Environmental Outlook*, published by UNEP in association with 20 of the world's most important research institutes, shows we are not yet on the path to sustainable development. Here you will find the critical trends: climate change, freshwater scarcity, pollution, land degradation, deforestation, loss of biodiversity and dispersion of toxic materials.

But it is more important to look at the causes. These worsening environmental problems are due to the wasteful extraction and use of energy, water and other natural resources. Of course, the earth's reserves of fossil fuels and mineral resources are immense. New extraction techniques are available. That is not the issue. In the long run, environmental problems can only be resolved by limiting extraction of mineral resources.

It is therefore clear that we need not only reduce unwanted outputs – pollution – but must increase substantially the productivity of raw material use, from cradle to grave. In short, we need to dematerialise our economies. If we are to make real progress, a reasonable target is to improve resource productivity by a factor of five to ten by the year 2030. But this target will not be attained by just improving current production processes and products. Ecoefficiency also requires drastic innovations in all industry sectors, and changes in consumption patterns, to move from concern for quantity – or more consumption, to quality, that is, different consumption.

Production, or supply, and consumption, or demand, are two sides of the same coin. Up to now, focus has been on the supply side of eco-innovation. A demand side strategy also has to be developed, leading to a delinking of peoples' needs and satisfaction from the consumption of natural resources. This means not only using less raw material in production, but focusing more on quality of life and less on quantity of consumption. Here, UNEP continues to push forward the frontiers of industrial environmental management; to disseminate information and practical tools; and to help in the implementation of a preventative approach through cleaner and safer industrial production and consumption.

Jacqueline Aloisi de Larderel is Director, Industry and Environment, the United Nations Environment Programme (UNEP).

agricultural products, or bauxite for making aluminum, or copper. In other words, fair shares in environmental space places the responsibility for the impacts of resource consumption on the final consumers of products and services, at least wherever it is possible to assess those 'embodied' exports and imports. This is an extension of life-cycle analysis, which assesses the impacts of production and consumption throughout product or service life, from the cradle to grave. Life-cycle analysis is taken up in the next chapter.

Since the equity principle argues that all countries should have access to the same amount of environmental space per capita, they can all, in principle, develop a similar standard of living during the 21st century. However, producing and consuming within a limited environmental space, and living comfortably at the same time, can only be realised by a highly efficient use of a limited amount of resources; this contradicts the steadily increasing and often inefficient use of resources and energy which characterise the current pattern. To make the general concept of environmental space relevant at a political level it needs to be continually refined to incorporate policy measures based on specific goals and targets. This process has been initiated for Europe. The overriding purpose of the Sustainable Europe Campaign has been to encourage informed discussion and debate on production and consumption issues as a key to moving towards European-level and national consensus. An important advantage of the environmental space approach over well-meaning but vague commitments to sustainable development is that debate is underpinned by realistic, quantitative resource analysis. This chapter describes the assumptions and methods upon which the general measurement approach is based.

In the European analysis, values for the environmental space available per capita in 2010 and 2050 have been calculated. The national environmental space available is defined as the environmental space per capita multiplied by the expected number of a country's inhabitants. Comparing the current, actual use and the sustainable use of environmental space gives the input reductions that must be achieved in order to bridge the sustainability gap in any resource sector. Output reductions – for example, waste – should be achieved by reducing the corresponding inputs. Where the outputs are a critical limiting factor to sustainability, such as for CO_2 emissions, they have been taken into account in setting the environmental space for the relevant input, such as energy supply.

It is important to note that all environmental space calculations are approximate; nevertheless, they give a clear indication of the order of magnitude of change needed in the resource use of industrialised countries. They are robust and therefore good indicators of the trends in production and consumption and the degree of movement towards sustainability. The rest of this chapter looks at the methods and assumptions for calculating indicators as set out in the previous chapter.

Energy

The environmental space for energy is assessed by looking at outputs of greenhouse gases that are emitted when using fossil energy. In terms of potential levels of substitutable renewable energy which could be tapped from solar, wind, water, biomass and geothermal sources, it is necessary to assess the limits imposed by the use of other resources (for instance, materials, land and water) in production. There are two categories of energy sources:

- non-renewable energy sources, with limited reserves and various environmentally damaging emissions; and
- renewable energy sources, which also have impacts in terms of materials and land consumption.

Non-renewable Energy and Planet Sink Capacity

Current patterns of energy consumption are connected with a wide range of ecological and social problems. Fossil fuels are the dominant source and cause landscape destruction through their extraction, pollution from transportation, health risks and atmospheric pollution from inefficient combustion and, dramatically, climatic change. A major portion of the energy supply of most national economies comes from burning coal and oil products. This results, among other things, in the production of carbon dioxide and other greenhouse gases. The major man-made contribution to the greenhouse effect is produced by the burning of 23 billion tons of fossil fuels annually, contributing about 7 gigatonnes (thousand billion) of carbon annually to the 1.2 gigatonnes absorbed by vegetation. The result is that the atmospheric concentration of CO_2 is rising steadily, from 315 parts per million (ppm) in 1950 to more than 360 ppm in the mid 1990s.[1]

On a business-as-usual scenario, the International Energy Agency predicts that fossil fuels will be the mainstay of world power generation well into the next century, and will go on developing faster than either nuclear or hydroelectric power. In OECD countries, for example, an increase of 2.1 per cent per year compares with 1.2 per cent for other power sources. Fossil fuels, in particular coal and gas, will account for 65.5 per cent of total electrical energy supply in OECD countries in 2010, compared to 61.2 per cent in 1990.[2] Carbon dioxide emissions in the OECD area will rise over the same period from 10.3 billion tonnes to 13.3 billion tonnes. Rising use of fossil fuels is likely to be even more marked in countries outside the OECD. These countries lack the finance required to invest in major renewable sources. Many of them, such as China, also have large reserves of exploitable coal.

A related concern is air pollution in the form of photochemical smog – a growing threat to life and health in the difficult-to-manage, emerging megacities housing ten to 30 million people, in which the majority of the earth's inhabitants will live in the next century. There will be 24 megacities in Asia alone with populations in excess of ten million persons. Air pollution also has been shown to spread to rural areas and to damage health and crop and forest production.

Using IPCC Information to Calculate Overall CO_2 Reductions

The Intergovernmental Panel on Climate Change (IPCC) assesses the impact of climate change and responses to it as a basis for international cooperation. This is a good example of global consensus-building around environmental space. Considerable progress has been made since 1990 in the understanding of the science of climate change, and new data and analyses have become available. The *1995 Second Assessment Report* recognised that, for the first time: 'The balance of evidence suggests a discernible human influence on global climate.' IPCC scientific studies indicate that there has been a 30 per cent increase in CO_2 concentration since the start of the industrial revolution; and the observed warming trend is unlikely to be entirely natural in origin. The report says that given the current increases in emissions of most greenhouse gases, their atmospheric concentrations will grow through the next century and beyond. This may lead to a total warming of the globe by 2°C by 2100, 'representing an average rate of warming greater than at any time in the last 10,000 years'. Interference with the climate system is expected to increase, with a greater likelihood of adverse effects. Computer modelling suggests that sea levels will rise by up to 50 centimetres, with more severe floods or droughts in some areas and more extreme rainfall, such as tropical cyclones. The geographical distribution of these effects remains uncertain.

According to the IPCC, a business-as-usual scenario will see total world energy consumption nearly double by the year 2025 as a result of yearly growth of 1.3 per cent in North America, 0.7 per cent in Europe and 3.6 per cent in developing countries. Despite the high growth rate in developing countries,

1 Pearce, F
'Chill winds at
the summit'
New Scientist
1 March 1997

2 Union of
International
Associations
*Encyclopedia of
World Problems
and Human
Potential*
Brussels: Folio
Infobase, First
CD-ROM Edition
1996

the per capita use of fossil fuels in rich countries by 2025 will still be six times greater. The IPCC predicts that current energy policies will result in an average global rise in temperature of 0.3°C per decade. A rise of 0.1°C per decade is regarded by the IPCC as the maximum level that will enable ecosystems to adapt or to migrate. To stabilise the concentration of greenhouse gases at a little higher than today's levels a halving of current global CO_2 emissions is needed in the coming decades. The environmental space for energy is therefore calculated according to the IPCC's recommendation to avoid a global temperature rise of more than 0.1° per decade or a cumulative increase of more than 2°C. This means that the emission of CO_2 has to decrease by 50 to 60 per cent within the coming decades. Current emissions are around 25 billion tonnes per year globally but the sustainable level in 2050 lies in the range of 10 to 12 billion tonnes of CO_2 per year globally. However, it is important to note that the emission of other greenhouse gases such as methane and nitrogenous oxides need to decrease as well. If not, CO_2 emissions would need to decrease even more to compensate.

On a per capita basis, and depending on the rate of population growth, the environmental space for fossil fuels in 2050 is:

- 1 to 1.2 tonnes of CO_2 per capita if population increases to ten billion persons;
- 1.4 to 1.7 tonnes of CO_2 per capita if population growth remains limited to seven billion persons;
- approximately two tonnes of CO_2 per capita if global population remains at approximately 5.9 billion persons.

In addition to setting targets, this calculation also demonstrates rather vividly that population growth makes little difference to the overall magnitude of reductions required in developed countries, where the range of current emissions is between seven and 20 tonnes of CO_2 per capita per year. For European countries, for example, the long-term required reduction for high emission countries to stay within environmental space is between 80 per cent and 90 per cent.

Differentiated Responsibilities to the Year 2020

So far, we have an indication of overall reduction targets, calculated for Europe, for the year 2050. But a more exact and refined scenario is needed for practical, phased reductions. A scenario developed by the Energy Working Group of Friends of the Earth Denmark (Figure 5.1) shows that in the intermediate phase to the year 2020 developing countries can still increase their use of this environmental space. After 2050, however, they too will have to decrease their per capita levels of fossil-fuel use to long-term,

Box 5.1 The environmental space for fossil fuel use in the year 2050

An estimated 10 to 12 billion tonnes of CO_2 per year is a sustainable level of emissions compared with a current level of 25 billion tonnes.

Figure 5.1

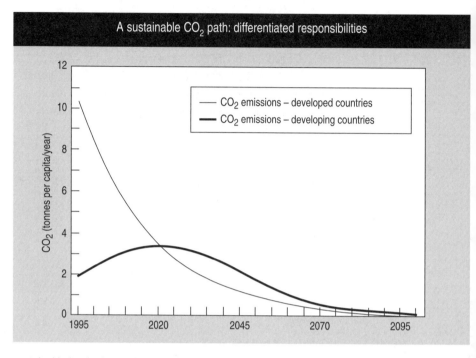

A sustainable CO_2 path: differentiated responsibilities

— CO_2 emissions – developed countries
— CO_2 emissions – developing countries

CO_2 (tonnes per capita/year)

3 The target of 450 ppmv is higher than the lowest proposed option of 350 ppmv but not as high as IPCC scenarios which range upwards from 550 ppmv. As the allowable ppmv ranges upwards, the very long-range impacts escalate and the point where accumulated CO_2 begins its necessary decrease moves further into the future, even into the 22nd century. A figure of 450 ppmv, therefore, represents a practical and sustainable option, although not the most rigorous possibility. For a more full discussion, see Global Climate Institute, 'Contraction and Convergence': a Global Solution to a Global Problem London, 1997

sustainable levels. It seems reasonable that developing countries can take advantage of the initial increase when building up their modern infrastructure – as industrialised countries have done. Such a scenario could help compensate developing countries in climate change negotiations where claims are made that developed countries should be held responsible for historical greenhouse gas emissions.

To stabilise the climate at a level of 450 ppmv (parts per million volume; pre-industrial concentration: 280 ppmv), global man-made CO_2 emissions between 1995 and the end of the next century (2100) have to be around 1600 billion tonnes of CO_2.[3] This calculation assumes a stabilisation of current levels of methane and nitrogenous dioxide emissions. These 1600 billion tonnes can be emitted in a variety of different patterns: everything could be emitted in earlier years or emissions could be spread evenly over the period. Figure 5.1 (starting in 1995) uses the United Nations' middle population projection. It shows a curve for industrialised countries with the following targets:

- 1995 – 10.3 tonnes of CO_2 per capita (maximum emissions);
- 2010 – 5.3 tonnes of CO_2 per capita;
- 2020 – 4.1 tonnes of CO_2 per capita;
- 2050 – 0.9 tonnes of CO_2 per capita.

After 2050 this scenario suggests an almost total phasing out of fossil-fuel use, comparable with a scenario developed by the Stockholm Environment Institute, discussed below. Compared to the current average European emissions, this gives a reduction of over 50 per cent between 1995 and 2010 and of 90 per cent between now and 2050. For developing countries, the curve is rather different:

- 1995 – 1.8 tonnes of CO_2 per capita;
- 2010 – 3.1 tonnes of CO_2 per capita;
- 2020 – 3.4 tonnes of CO_2 per capita (maximum emissions);
- 2050 – 1.7 tonnes of CO_2 per capita.

After 2050 a phasing-out follows as well. Compared to current average emissions of a little less than two tonnes of CO_2 per capita, this scenario gives an increase of 70 per cent between 1990 and 2010 and of almost 90 per cent between 1995 and 2020.

Overall to 2050, the intended outcome of scenarios based on the environmental space approach is a substantial reduction in the use of fossil fuels. A recently published scenario by the Danish Energy Agency suggests a target emission of 1.2 tons of CO_2 per capita in the year 2100 for industrialised countries. This is in the range of the European target derived by environmental space analysis.

Nuclear Energy Is Not Appropriate

Due to the unacceptable and very long-term risks of nuclear energy and disposal problems for nuclear waste, a gradual phase-out of the 437 or so nuclear reactors in operation throughout the world is proposed as a corollary of the environmental space approach. This is based on risk assessment of the technology, and a clear-headed view of decommissioning and clean-up costs. Whatever our faith, or lack of it, in the safety record of the nuclear industry, it cannot be sustainable to create wastes which remain highly vulnerable to ecological dislocation, social disruption and technological breakdown for unimaginably long periods of time. For example, the zirconium used in cladding-reactor fuel rods has a half life of 1.5 million years – the time it will take for the radioactivity of the material to fall to half its original level. Uranium 235 has a half-life of 710 million years; if uranium had been buried long before the first dinosaurs showed up, it would still harbour half its radioactivity and be highly dangerous.[4] Due to these very long-term risks, the environmental space for nuclear energy is therefore set at zero in the long term. However, given that a 1000 megawatt (MW) gas-fired plant can be built for US$600 million in two years and a similar nuclear plant would cost US$4000 million and take six to eight years, it is likely the market for nuclear generation without state subsidy will disappear.

This may coincide with an emerging trend. The Swedish Government, for example, has announced a programme to phase out all of its nuclear power stations, currently providing half of its electricity.[5] The intention is that the closure programme will trigger intensive research and development on reasonable cost-alternative sources. The Worldwatch Institute reports that in the year 1997, for the first time in 40 years, work did not begin on a single nuclear power station anywhere in the world, while wind power is now growing more rapidly than any other source of energy.[6] In terms of the future of the nuclear industry, construction is yet to start on two new (Canadian-funded) reactors in China, but these are seen by Worldwatch as the 'emptying of the pipeline of new orders'. When realistic decommissioning costs are factored into the cost-benefit equation, nuclear power is not economical. This accounts for the fact that in the recent privatisation of energy suppliers in Britain, nuclear power plants had no market value. However, a number of Asian countries, including Indonesia, are still considering construction of nuclear plants.

Nuclear energy is an extreme example of short-term decision making. It is not a sustainable policy option to saddle innumerable future generations with the costs of harbouring dangerous wastes.

4 Hall, J *Real Lives, Half Lives* London: Penguin 1996

5 *Financial Times* 6 December 1996

6 Worldwatch Institute *Vital Signs 1996–97*, Washington, 1996

Renewable Energy

When one considers the environmental space for energy from the perspective of climate change, the result is substantial limits on the use of fossil energy sources. Conversely, there is enormous potential in renewables. For example, the earth receives 1.5×10^{18} kilowatts per hour (kWh) of energy from the sun every year. The current energy demand of the world's population is 1.5×10^{14}. Calculating the environmental space for energy from this solar perspective means that, in theory, the environmental space for this source is limited only by the materials and land consumed in its production. However, based on current technology, only a limited area of the land surface can be made available to convert solar power to usable energy. Another constraint is the amount of non-renewable materials used in production.

> It is not clear, apart from inertia, ignorance and institutional complacency, what the obstacles are to energy efficiency.
>
> Michael Jefferson, World Energy Council

The amount of solar energy, wind energy and water energy that can be used acceptably in a sustainable manner also depends not only on ecological but social values. Societies will need to define, for example, the maximum levels of energy taken from wild rivers and the acceptability of windfarms in the landscape. Dams are contentious in many countries; in Britain windfarms are seen by some as the industrialisation of the rural countryside. For the use of crops as sources of bio-energy, land-use conflicts also have to be taken into account to determine the maximum contribution of this source to the environmental space offered by renewable energy.

A more precise calculation for renewable energy's environmental space is derived by the Stockholm Environment Institute (SEI).[7] In their *Fossil Free Energy Scenario*, the SEI takes as an hypothesis that global energy demand will continue to increase but that fossil fuels and nuclear sources will be phased out. The scenario then examines the potential of renewable sources, given the assumption that fossil-fuel use within the interim period to 2050 stays within the boundaries proposed by the IPCC for limiting global climate change. SEI calculations for Europe give an environmental space for renewable energy sources of 60 exajoules (EJ) in 2100.* In 1988, renewable energy consumption in Europe stood at 6.9 EJ while total energy consumption in that year amounted to 72.8 EJ. The SEI scenario suggests that by 2030 renewable sources could contribute 53 GJ per capita. A modest decrease in energy consumption, therefore, is part of the scenario. Not every research institute involved in Sustainable Europe agrees with this. Estimates by the Wuppertal Institute argue that the proposed levels of renewable production, especially from biomass sources, might be too high since the scenario does not account for other claims to the limited land area in Europe. The Wuppertal Institute estimates that in 2030 renewables could contribute 36 GJ per person. In this latter scenario, the reduction in primary energy use would need to be higher to remain within interim targets.

Whatever the differences in medium-term scenarios, these fruitful debates give a flavour of the use of environmental space analysis to inform public policy. Both studies agree that renewable potential is

7 For a discussion see Spangenberg, J (ed) *Towards Sustainable Europe: The Study* Brussels: 1995

* An exajoule, or 1×10^{18} joules: a joule is a unit of energy equivalent to the heat generated by a current of one ampere flowing for one second against a resistance of one ohm. A gigajoule is 1×10^9 joules.

Figure 5.2

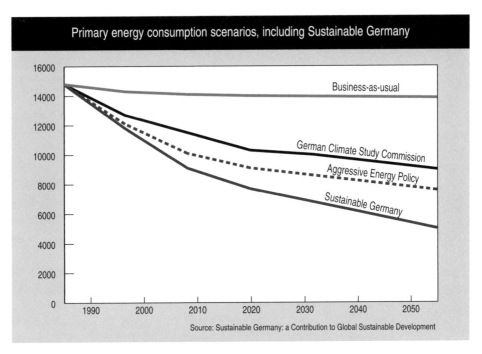

Primary energy consumption scenarios, including Sustainable Germany

Business-as-usual

German Climate Study Commission

Aggressive Energy Policy

Sustainable Germany

Source: Sustainable Germany: a Contribution to Global Sustainable Development

considerable, but also that a reduction in overall energy consumption is essential. This suggests the direction in which public policy must move to stay within available environmental space.

It also suggests that the use of energy is never environmentally neutral, even from renewable sources, and that energy use as a whole in industrialised countries must be reduced to lower levels. To achieve this, consumption patterns should be reduced and the development of energy-conserving technologies intensified. In Germany, for example, the study Sustainable Germany proposes the following policy direction: that energy production from renewables increase by 3 to 5 per cent per year, combined with energy productivity increases of 3 to 5 per cent per year, for example, by reducing loss during transmission, against a background of halving primary energy consumption by the year 2050. Figure 5.2 shows primary energy consumption scenarios for Germany, including that of Sustainable Germany.[8]

The overall conclusion of the assessment is that national energy policy should emphasise:

- energy conservation through resource-efficient lifestyles;
- efficiency enhancement, that is, reduction of energy input per service unit of output;
- substitution of high-carbon by low-carbon fuels;
- renewable sources of energy (sustainable production) on a least-environmental and social-impact basis; and
- a gradual phase-out of nuclear and fossil fuel sources.

Conservation should be the primary option, particularly because technological advances make it entirely feasible to deliver equivalent units of utility or life satisfaction with greatly reduced fossil-fuel energy consumption. Goals can be achieved by energy price regulation, consistent enforcement of energy-

8 See also Loske, J 'Sustainable Germany: Contribution to global sustainable development' in International Conference on Sustainable Economy for the North – Implications for the South, Berlin: Carl Duisberg Gesellschaft, 1995

Box 5.2 First option – saving energy

There are innumerable practical ways to reduce energy demand. They range from energy-saving light bulbs to high-efficiency house insulation to passive solar water heating. In Denmark, for example, a test group of households had their major electrical appliances replaced with the most energy-efficient models on the market. Overall a 47 per cent reduction in electricity consumption was achieved. For space heating, there was a 78 per cent reduction. The World Energy Council estimates that such energy efficiency measures alone could deliver cuts in carbon dioxide emissions of between 20 and 30 per cent. Other practical options include high-efficiency vehicles combined with land-use planning which minimises the need to travel by locating home, work, shopping and recreation all within a safe walk or bicycle of one another.

efficiency standards in final products, and through a policy of implementing energy-efficient technologies.

It is also important to be aware of the trade impacts on import consumption of environmental space from other countries. A growth in imports of energy-intensive manufactured products can indicate a trend towards shifting negative environmental impacts to other countries. This is a form of inequitable energy consumption, and runs counter to the equity principle. Conversely, however, energy from renewable sources could be exported. The Sustainable Norway analysis, for example, suggests that a final national consumption level of around 60 GJ per capita is considerably lower than the country's renewable energy production potential of 158 GJ per capita per year. Norway could, therefore, export energy from renewable sources.

Finally, it is important to note that energy inefficiency is a squandering of scarce resources which could be used for other investment purposes, such as business or public investment. For example, scientists have estimated that, with some political will, the USA could cut its CO_2 emissions per unit of GDP in half – to the current Japanese level.[9] This could be achieved by a combination of energy-efficiency measures and expanded use of renewables. The savings to the US economy would be in the order of US$2.3 trillion per year, not to mention the benefits to the world environment and future generations.

Key Non-Renewable Resources

9 Union of Concerned Scientists et al *America's Energy Choices: Investing in a Strong Economy and a Clean Environment* Washington, 1991

The Earth is like a container full of elements. Some of these elements are extracted as a raw material for production processes from the earth's crust, others from the sea, the air or as biomass. As raw materials, they find their way into the economy to satisfy people's needs and wants at an ever increasing rate. When people have finished using them, they are discarded and end up back in the environment. They do not disappear, they just move from one ecosystem to another, usually changing form *en route*. The industrial age has seen enormous increases in global production of metals (see Figure 5.3).

This movement is the origin of many environmental problems. As stressed in the previous chapter, the environmental and social impacts of non-renewable resource consumption constitute the primary constraint on environmental space, and not the levels of reserves themselves. In many cases, discussion

Figure 5.3

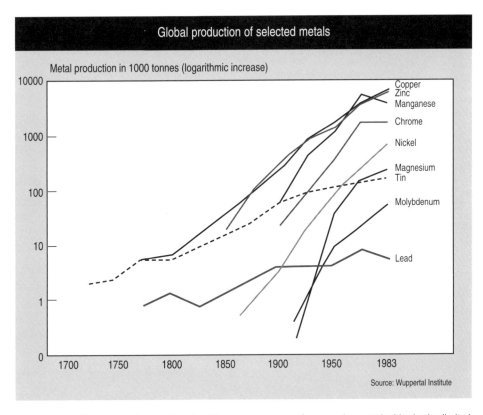

Global production of selected metals

Metal production in 1000 tonnes (logarithmic increase)

Source: Wuppertal Institute

of non-renewable reserves is a red herring. The reserves may, of course, be sustainable, in the limited sense that they will last a long time at current rates of consumption, but that is simply not the issue.

Environmental space for non-renewables, therefore, is a function, not of reserves, but of a number of factors: environmental impact and resource-use in exploration; the environmental costs of production and consumption, such as land disruption and soil erosion, toxicity, energy use, including CO_2 emissions, and leakage; the potential for recycling of non-renewables; the substitution of renewables for non-renewables; and the overall amounts of consumption and resultant toxicity released. For minerals, the environmental damage done in extracting a mineral is determined by such factors as the ecology of the mining site, the quantity of material moved, the depth of the deposit, the chemical composition of the ore and the surrounding rocks and soils, and the nature of the processes used to extract purified minerals from the ore.[10]

After centuries of mining to fuel the industrial requirements of the North, many sites containing the richest ores both North and South have been exhausted and the average ore content is declining. Opening up mines with lower ore concentrations results in higher energy costs and environmental impacts per extracted tonne. It is very clear that the costs of the historic development path followed by the developed countries will have to be borne mainly by the developing countries. For example, the European Union's recent State of the Environment Report (the Dobris Assessment) states that mineral resources with a high ore content in Europe are already depleted. Today, Europe mainly imports mineral resources from Africa. As a result, Europe is now depleting the easily exploitable African resources. This forecloses a development

10 Young, J E 'Mining the Earth' State of the World 1992 Washington: Worldwatch Institute, 1992

Box 5.3 Mining as a source of non-renewable resources

As far as mining companies are concerned, the most economic means of extracting raw materials is opencast mining. This allows a larger proportion of the raw materials to be extracted and is cheaper than deep mining. The amount of soil moved and hence potential environmental damage is also much greater. Opencast mining activities, particularly in developing countries, often result in the original inhabitants either being driven away from the areas where they have traditionally lived, or being forced to live with poisoned water in a degraded landscape.

The mining of metals is almost always a highly polluting process with considerable quantities of toxic and non-hazardous waste contributing to pollution of land and aquatic resources. Up to 90 per cent of materials moved to access metal ore ends up as tailings dumped in huge piles near the mining site. This overburden is nutrient poor and seldom supports vegetation.

The trend is towards mining lower ore concentrations. The lower the raw material's ore concentration, the greater the consumption of energy for extraction and the greater the quantity of mining tailings to be disposed of in the surrounding environment. Dangerous chemicals are also needed to process the raw materials, often on-site; these end up in the water, soil and air. Such chemicals commonly include acids, mercury, cyanide and arsenic. The amount of energy needed for both mining and primary production is so vast that giant hydroelectric dams or coal-fired power stations may also need to be constructed to power mining activities.

option for African countries based on domestic exploitation of resources with a high ore content.

In terms of the current balance of overall consumption between renewables and non-renewables, the Wuppertal Institute has found that around six times more abiotic (non-renewable) mass is withdrawn each year to feed German industry than biotic (renewable) mass, when the rucksacks are included. Industrial sectors particularly dependent on material-intensive intermediate inputs are: mining, iron and steel and associated semi-finished products, and building and finished metal products. These sectors correspond to the proxy indicators of environmental space listed below.

As noted, the Sustainable Europe analysis indicates that to reduce the environmental impacts of mineral extraction, the flows of raw materials in the global economy must be reduced by half. This, is of course, a first approximation as a rule-of-thumb; more detailed analysis is currently considering the environmental impacts of extraction and toxicity of a range of non-renewable resources.[11] However, to be clear, if current global metal extraction is decreased by half, this would not necessarily mean a cut of metal consumption by half. The available consumption, and hence environmental space, also depends on the effort of countries to increase the durability of products, and the reuse and recycling of metals when products are discarded.

Recycling often means substantial advantages in terms of backpack reduction and reduced energy consumption (see Table 5.1). For example, each ton of recycled steel saves 2500 pounds (1135 kilogrammes) of iron ore, 1000 pounds (454 kilogrammes) of coal and 40 pounds (9 kilogrammes) of limestone.[12] The Sustainable Scotland study showed that Scottish households throw away enough quantities of metals and other materials each year to make all the new cars that Scotland imports every

11
Spangenberg, J
(ed) op cit

12 *State of the World 1996* Washington: Worldwatch Institute 1996, p157

Box 5.4 The impacts of mining in Papua

Since the opening of the Ok Tedi Copper Mine in Papua New Guinea in the mid 1980s, the Australian mining company BHP has simply been dumping wastes from the mine into the nearby Ok Tedi and Fly rivers. Copper concentrates are also regularly spilled during transport downriver, and transport vessels are cleaned using river water. The rivers are permanently yellow or grey, and the vegetation along the banks has died.

The mining spoil is accumulating on the beds of the rivers, which are becoming shallower and will lead to frequent flooding. In the summer of 1995, downriver landowners started legal proceedings against the company. They are demanding compensation and a dam to prevent the mining spoil flowing into the river. This example is not unusual. Similar cases could be cited in Guyana, India, Indonesia, Brazil, Canada or in the Rocky Mountains of the USA.

year. Similarly, Sustainable France found that if France were to double the quantities of non-renewables reused and recycled each year, it would be possible to consume 60 per cent less primary raw materials.

In calculating environmental space, it is also important to assess final consumption. The Sustainable Czech Republic analysis, for example, found that although pig iron production in the republic amounts to some 451 kilogrammes per capita per year, the country is an important exporter of steel. Its net annual export is almost three million tons of steel to countries such as Slovakia, Russia, Norway, Germany and other EU countries. Net consumption is therefore some 183 kilogrammes per capita per year, compared to the EU average of 273 kilogrammes per capita per year. Similarly, the Sustainable Republic of Georgia study noted that the country carries the burden of the copper production which it exports to Russia and the rest of Europe. Copper production is almost 200 times the European per capita average. In the environmental space calculations, the responsibility for this consumption is included with that of the final consuming country.

In terms of overall consumption, the example below of environmental space calculations for European aluminum consumption demonstrates that recycling, although helpful, cannot usually substitute entirely for longer-term reductions in consumption of primary materials.

The Proxy Indicators of Non-renewable Resource Use

Environmental space analysis makes use of proxy indicators of non-renewable resource consumption which, as noted, account for about 90 per cent of global primary resource consumption when backpacks are included.[13] These indicator materials are:

13 Friends of the Earth Scotland *Towards a Sustainable Scotland* Edinburgh 1996

- *aluminium*: whose extraction produces substantial amounts of waste and whose production is extremely energy intensive, but which can be readily reused and recycled.
- *Pig iron*: when combined with carbon, this is the main material in steel production and is used extensively for construction; it also can be made from recycled material.

Table 5.1

Energy requirements using virgin and recycled materials		
Material	Virgin Production GJ/ton	Recycled Material GJ/ton
Plastics	80–220	50–160
Steel	24–45	9–15
Aluminium	150–220	10–15

Gigajoule: Unit of energy, factor of 10^9 Source: Worldwatch Institute, Friends of the Earth Scotland

- *Cement*: this is mainly made from primary materials extraction with large backpacks and substantial environmental impacts.
- *Chlorine*: used in many products whose wastes are highly toxic or carcinogenic and which last an extremely long time – for instance, organochlorines.

Because of the serious negative environmental impacts of chlorine production, the Sustainable Europe analysis argues for a complete phase-out by the target date of 2050. Not all participants in the various debates agreed. As might be expected, representatives of chemical industries argued that this was overly stringent. There is not the space here to discuss the issue except to note that major reductions are possible almost immediately. For example, the Sustainable Finland study reports that since 1990 chlorine use in Finland's forest industries has decreased from 110 million kilogrammes per year to 15 million kilogrammes per year. This is due to the active campaigning of environmental organisations against the use of chlorine in bleaching pulp and paper. A first step is to switch from elemental chlorine to chlorine dioxide, which reduces organochlorines dramatically. There are many similar switches in industrial processes which can be made almost immediately to bring interim environmental space targets within reach.

Besides this, the methods of analysis for proxy indicators involve a similar series of calculations, and the remainder of this section uses one area of environmental space – aluminium consumption – as an example. A similar approach can be used to assess the environmental space for other non-renewables as required.

Environmental Space for the Use of Non-Renewable Metals such as Aluminium

The use of metals is increasing worldwide, with consumption of primary aluminium rising fast, especially in developed countries. Britain, for example, with just 1 per cent of the world population, consumes 5 per cent of the world's environmental space for aluminium. Analysis of the results of the Sustainable Europe national studies suggests a strong correlation between GDP and aluminium consumption. Aluminium consumption in countries such as Norway and Switzerland is significantly higher than in Eastern European

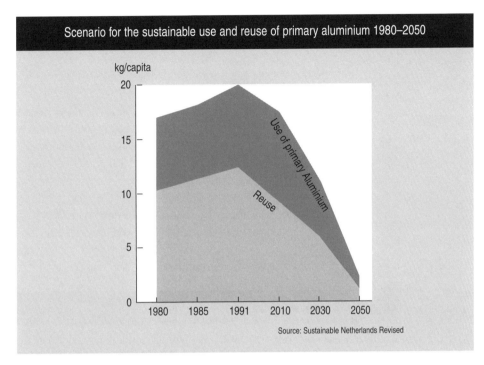

Figure 5.4

Scenario for the sustainable use and reuse of primary aluminium 1980–2050

kg/capita

Use of primary Aluminium

Reuse

Source: Sustainable Netherlands Revised

countries, even when corrected for exports via products. Within the category of non-renewable resources, aluminium is a good indicator of consumption of environmental space. If this can be reduced, it triggers a chain of pollution reductions across space and time in a vertical industrial process.

Calculation of the primary and secondary use of aluminium for the years 1980 to 2050 is shown in Figure 5.4. Reuse in both 2010 and 2050 has been set at 90 per cent of primary aluminium use. In 1991 reuse amounted to 60 per cent of primary use, so this a reasonable target. The graph clearly illustrates the change necessary in order to achieve a sustainable closed-loop system in this industrial sector: primary aluminium use must be reduced sharply, while reuse will increase, relatively speaking, but will still have to be reduced in absolute terms. In other words, recycling is necessary but not sufficient for Europeans to live within the available environmental space.

The implications can be worked back to give national targets. By the year 2010 for The Netherlands, for example, this means that 9.2 kilogrammes of primary aluminium per capita could be used in the Dutch economy. Reuse of 90 per cent of this 9.2 kilogrammes produces 8.3 kilogrammes of secondary aluminium, which results in a total of 17.5 kilogrammes per capita. This represents a reduction of 12 per cent in relation to the total use in 1990.

The calculations, considering equity criteria, allow comment on the global situation. The current consumption of primary aluminium amounts to 18 billion kilogrammes globally per year. A 50 per cent cut gives an environmental space for aluminium of 9 billion kilogrammes. Divided by ten billion people, this gives an environmental space of 0.9 kilogrammes per person and when divided by seven billion people yields 1.2 kilogrammes per person.

Current aluminium consumption in the USA amounts to over 20 kilogrammes per person and in the European Union an average of around 12 kilogrammes per person. Thus the reduction requirement for

Europe is –90 per cent while Americans need to reduce their primary consumption by 94 per cent. In line with its general approach, Sustainable Europe set the final reduction target date of 2050. This means that by 2010 a 25 per cent is necessary. For other metals, similar calculations can be made to create sustainability targets. These distance-to-sustainability targets are essential to assess and focus economic and environmental policy.

Because of a tendency to substitute one material for another, environmental space analysis ultimately would need to extend to a range of metals. To do this, distinctions would need to be made between various metals on the differential rates of energy and material intensiveness and toxicity of materials and byproducts. Judgements will be required on the relative costs and benefits of different mixes of production and consumption. This process should combine the best scientific evidence with a measure of political consensus over the best way forward in terms of different scenarios, considering not only product mix but North–South relations. To tackle this vexed issue, the Sustainable Finland team proposed the establishment of an Intergovernmental Panel on Non-Renewable Resource Use, the equivalent of the IPCC. Such a panel would need to develop alternative scenarios of global non-renewable production and consumption to foster discussion and debate. The next section considers what this might look like.

Table 5.2

Scenarios for non-renewable resource use to 2050					
	Doubling of global resource use and equal sharing		Current global resource use and equal sharing		Halving of current global resource use and equal sharing
Population assumption	No growth	Doubling	No growth	Doubling	No growth	Doubling
Figures below are compared to the current situation					
Per capita resource use for developed countries	–50%	–75%	–75%	–88%	–88%	–94%
Per capita resource use for developing countries	+400%	+800%	+200%	+400%	+100%	+200%
Total global resource use	Twice the current level		At the current level		Half the current level	

A Scenario-Based Approach to Non-Renewable Consumption

It is possible to postulate a variety of scenarios for non-renewable consumption, all of which embody the equity principle. Here we make an assessment for:

14 Friends of
the Earth, EWNI,
*Tomorrow's
World: Britain's
Share in a
Sustainable
Future* London:
Earthscan, 1997

Box 5.5 A cool drink and aluminium consumption: a British case study

The drink, in a beer or soft drink can, is the end of a long and complex process which might take bauxite mined in Ghana in West Africa across to Jamaica to be processed into aluminium before it is fashioned into soft drink cans to be sold, after considerably more transport, in Europe. Here the aluminium, if not recycled, becomes part of a massive not-in-my-backyard waste disposal problem.

Aluminium-can consumption is not inevitable but is determined in part by consumer preference and by government policies on deposit containers and recycling. Britain, for example, has the largest aluminium can market in Europe, with an annual consumption of 6.79 billion cans – accounting for 13 per cent of total British aluminium consumption.[14] The British predilection for aluminium cans is demonstrated by the fact that the average British citizen gets through 117 aluminium cans every year, of which only 33 are recycled. The French, on the other hand, consume only ten cans per person per year.

Although the rate of aluminium recycling in Britain is increasing, the consumption of aluminium cans is growing at a faster rate. Therefore, in spite of increasing the recycling rate from 2 per cent to 28 per cent over six years, the British are throwing away more cans every year. The situation is unsustainable – given that making aluminium from bauxite consumes 20 times as much energy as recycling, not to mention the ecological backpack. The potential for recycling is exemplified in Sweden where 91 per cent of all aluminium cans (and 60 per cent of all aluminium) are recycled. Other impressive examples include Canada, where every bottle and can carries a deposit. In Denmark, metal containers for beer and soft drinks are banned, and 99.5 per cent of soft drink and beer bottles are returned for reuse, due to the stringent deposit system.

- doubling the extraction of global non-renewable resources and an equal sharing of the outputs;
- stabilisating at current levels of extraction all global non-renewable resources and an equal sharing of the outputs;
- halving the current extraction of global non-renewable resources and an equal sharing (the Sustainable Europe scenario).

The implications of these different scenarios are set out in Table 5.2. If the Sustainable Europe scenario of halving global metal consumption is adhered to, developing countries are entitled to a growth in consumption of 100 to 200 per cent, depending on anticipated population growth. Developed countries need to reduce, on average, consumption by 88 to 94 per cent. These calculations prove to be robust. They demonstrate that global population growth does not affect the distance-to-sustainability targets for developed countries very much.

Given these scenarios, the required policy direction for any developed country committed to sustainable development is quite clear. Even in the short term, the only sustainable path is substantial cuts in consumption of non-renewable resources. If the environmental space target of Sustainable Europe – that

15 Friends of
the Earth, EWNI,
op cit

Box 5.6 The environmental space for land

Land resources should be shared fairly between the people of the world, just as energy and material resources should be. The products of land use are already globally traded. In a sustainable world this could continue.

However, calculating a fair share of land's environmental space is not as simple as dividing the total area of productive land between the world's people. The quality of land varies widely, and any nation will naturally first make claim on land within its national territory. One approach is to compare the average productivity of land with the global average (adjusted for potential changes under sustainable agricultural techniques) to estimate a 'quality factor'. If, as in Britain, the land is above average quality, then, in areal terms, the country has a smaller claim on the world's productive land. If, as in many developing nations, it is of poorer quality, then the area that country can claim increases in size. For example, Britain currently lays economic claim to around 21 million hectares, including 'import of land', although its agricultural land area is only around 17 million hectares. A fair share of global average quality land would be almost 30 million hectares, but the land of Britain is around twice as productive as the global average. So Britain's claim on land is reduced to 15 million hectares. Britain needs to become a net exporter of land, rather than a net importer. This does not mean that British people cannot enjoy tropical produce such as coffee, bananas and chocolate. Trading of agricultural goods can continue. It is merely the net balance which must change.

Friends of the Earth for England, Wales and Northern Ireland[15]

global levels of resource use need to be halved – proves overly precautionary, the scenarios show that this should not affect the short-term goals of developed countries. It also has little impact on the long-term goals they should adopt. Curtailment of non-renewable resource use is therefore a key policy of sustainable development.

Land Use

The wise use of land is one of the most important and challenging aspects of sustainable development. In the full world economy, we are beginning to realise that land is a finite resource. But pressures to use land in a less than sustainable fashion are enormous, and once land is alienated from its best use, say prime farmland by low-density suburbanisation, it is difficult, if not impossible, to undo the damage. For example, the land-take for building in developing countries alone is half a million hectares per year. Of course, cities and townships need to expand and not all farmland or forests can be retained. But land use is too seldom in sync with the emerging requirements for reduced transport emissions of CO_2, conservation and biodiversity, and so on. Most countries share the pressure to relinquished protected or rural areas to expanding tourism, resource extraction and quasi-industrial uses, including plantation forestry, and to alienate rural land in favour of urban functions. These problems are exacerbated because

Figure 5.5

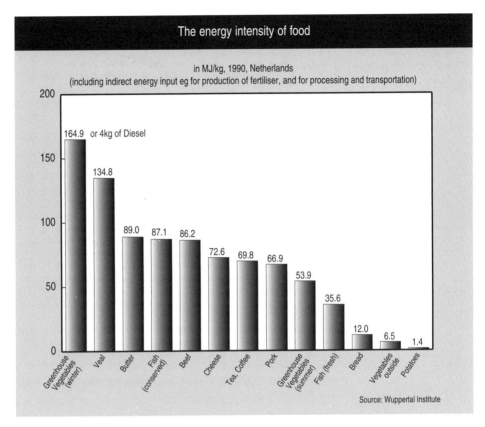

The energy intensity of food

in MJ/kg, 1990, Netherlands
(including indirect energy input eg for production of fertiliser, and for processing and transportation)

164.9 or 4kg of Diesel

134.8

89.0 87.1 86.2

72.6 69.8 66.9

53.9

35.6

12.0 6.5 1.4

Greenhouse Vegetables (winter) · Veal · Butter · Fish (conserved) · Beef · Cheese · Tea, Coffee · Pork · Greenhouse Vegetables (summer) · Fish (fresh) · Bread · Vegetables outside · Potatoes

Source: Wuppertal Institute

the legal and value systems of many countries still treat land as an infinite resource. There is also a widespread tendency to elevate individual property rights over land above any land-use planning controls, or land redistribution requirements, which might be exerted for the common good of present and future generations.

Perhaps more than any other sector of analysis, sustainable use indicators of land require considerably more sophistication, beginning with the basic databases on existing land uses. In Europe, these databases are of limited value, and there are as yet no common, agreed categories for land classification. The Sustainable Europe methodology has made a start in this regard, but we would not pretend that the methodology is as sophisticated as need be. Four indicators are being used so far:

- proportion of organically farmed land to indicate the rate of transition towards less intensive, sustainable agriculture (national level statistic only);
- net import, or appropriation, of land from other continents;
- extent of protected land – noting IUCN (the International Union for the Conservation of Nature) guidelines which suggest a national minimum of 10 per cent; and
- extent of built-up land – to warn of overconsumption by urbanisation and urban-type functions, such as tourist hotels and golf courses.

The statistics and targets for European indicators are given later in Figure 5.11.

Rural and Agricultural Land

Worldwide, there are 0.27 hectares of arable land for each human being. Current, unsustainable production methods are decreasing the amount of high-quality arable land by about 16 million hectares per year, mainly due to soil erosion and salinisation of irrigated land. At this rate of decrease, in 2010 there will be only 0.22 hectares of arable land per person in the world – a decline of 25 per cent. If this trend continues to 2025, the area of land available will drop to 0.17 hectares per person, assuming a world population of 8.4 billion. Sustainable means of agricultural production, with no land degradation, is therefore of vital importance.

In terms of rural land use, the environmental space methodology suggests, firstly, that agriculturally productive land is preserved to guarantee global food supplies and to provide necessary renewable materials such as fibres, biomass for energy and wood. This is especially important as citizens of new industrialising countries increase their protein and meat intake, which increases land-take, and energy consumption per unit of food produced. Figure 5.5, for example, gives us an idea of the varying energy intensity of different foodstuffs, which is part of their ecological backpack.

Secondly, the environmental space approach recommends that each country, especially in the industrialised world, conform to the IUCN recommendation that a minimum of 10 per cent of the land base is devoted to undisturbed natural areas. These need to be interconnected by conservation corridors, and the same proportion of land devoted to forest cover. This is the minimum necessary to preserve or reestablish diverse natural ecosystems, especially those threatened by global warming and to foster CO_2 reduction by carbon absorption. Vegetation currently absorbs between one and two gigatonnes (thousand billion tonnes) of carbon which can be compared with the fossil fuel output of about seven gigatonnes. Protected corridors between protected areas are important to allow the migration of species, especially during the outset of climate change.

In part, both these indicators also suggest conservation of biodiversity, although there is no broadly accepted direct measure. But both sustainable farming practices – for example, retaining wild vegetation at field boundaries – and protected land will contribute to, or maintain, biodiversity levels. Beyond this, criteria for biodiversity and sustainable land use will tend to be qualitative rather than quantitative.[16] An exception is the Sustainable Switzerland study which identified natural forest borders to agricultural and other land uses as critical to biodiversity. A doubling of this land use has been set as a quantitative target. Beyond this, agriculture and forestry are the main uses of the countryside, which are potentially compatible with the ecological use of the soil base. The environmental space approach assumes sustainable forestry practices based on endemic species, and a gradual but steady shift from intensive chemically based farming towards sustainable agriculture, of which organic agriculture is at present closest to a sustainable approach.

Sustainable agriculture is important in order to avoid the endemic pollution of agricultural products, rivers, streams, lakes and groundwater by fertilisers, biocides and the erosion of nutrient-rich soils. In Europe, and many other areas, the nitrate content in extracted groundwater continues to rise, with safe tolerance limits exceeded in many areas. The consumption of organic agricultural products also reduces

16 For a discussion see Lehmann, H and Reetz, T *Sustainable Land Use* Wuppertal Institute: paper 26, 1994

17 Carley, M
Policy
Management
Systems and
Methods of
Analysis for
Sustainable
Agriculture and
Rural
Development
Rome: FAO and
IIED, 1994

18 For a full
discussion see
Hille, J The
Environmental
Space Concept:
Implications for
environmental
reporting,
policies and
assessments
Copenhagen:
European
Environmental
Agency, 1996

19 UK
Departments of
the Environment
and Transport
Reducing the
Need to Travel
through Land
Use and
Transport
Planning
London: HMSO,
1995; Carley, M
'Settlement
Patterns and the
Crisis of
Automobility'
Futures
September
1992; Figure
5.6 is from May,
T 'Transport
Policy and
Management' in
Banister, D and
Button, K
Transport, the
Environment
and Sustainable
Development
London: E and
FN Spon, 1993

20 Worldwatch
Institute, op cit
p81

Soil erosion and degradation – for example, from excess irrigation – is also a serious problem related to intensive agriculture. Currently, the UN Food and Agriculture Organisation (FAO) reports that 12.7 million tonnes or 1 per cent of world grain output is lost each year because of land degradation and damage to crops from pollution.[17] The accumulated effect of this soil degradation is a major threat to global food security.

the health risks of organochlorine consumption. That it is possible to make a substantial shift to organic agriculture is indicated by the fact that there are 23,000 organic farms in Austria, accounting for 12 per cent of all farmland. Sweden, Denmark and some German states are committed to putting 10 per cent of land into organic production by the year 2000. On the other side of the coin, the Sustainable Poland study warns that the current changeover from traditional smallholdings to big farms threatens a major loss of biological diversity in that country.

The equity principle also comes into play where developed countries use their economic muscle to import land from developing countries through food consumption preferences; this curtails food production that meets basic needs. For example, the use of fodder that is imported from developing countries should be reduced where developing countries need that land to feed their own population, instead of feeding Northern-based cattle. Although an export-oriented specialisation can be an appropriate strategy in the first stages of economic development, a balanced import–export relation between developed and developing countries is a long-term prerequisite for sustainable land use.

The argument is not always straightforward. For example, in the case of land use, the Sustainable Europe approach has defined environmental space on the basis of continental resources. The premise is not that Europe should be absolutely self-sufficient and self-contained but that Europe should be sufficient in the sense that the amount of land used to grow export crops in Europe balances that used in other continents to grow crops, including timber, that are imported to Europe. This means Europe will no longer exploit the land resources of other continents, nor export its agricultural pollution; however, it leaves open the possibility of beneficial trade while recognising the finite nature of the land base. However, Hille takes a different view, arguing that timber and agricultural products should be considered global resources because of the differing resource endowments of continents.[18]

Urbanisation and Transport

In terms of urban land use and its integration with transport, sustainable management presents a complex problem. There is substantial evidence that the typical modern urban sprawl of housing, shopping and employment, triggered by economic development, needs to be contained (see Figure 5.6).[19] This is in order to reduce the take-up of increasingly scarce rural land for lower-density urbanisation – for example, 2.4 million acres (one million hectares) of prime farmland converted in the USA in the past decade, and 20,000 hectares lost in Java annually[20] – to reduce the emissions associated with unsustainable automobile transport; and to reduce the proportion of land paved over by settlements and transport infrastructure, which carry an ecological backpack inversely related to settlement density. Figure 5.7 shows a typical expanding metropolis.

Figure 5.6

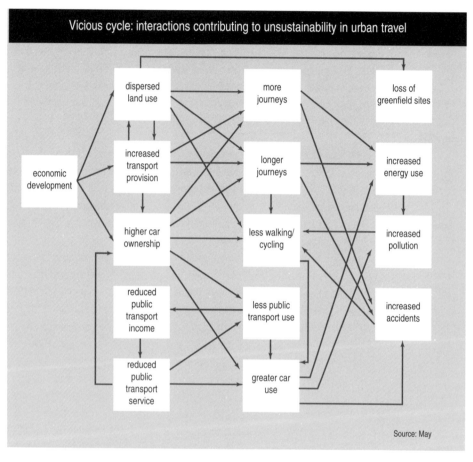

Vicious cycle: interactions contributing to unsustainability in urban travel

Source: May

Once a suburbanised land-use pattern is established, it is almost impossible to revert to a more sustainable pattern of concentrated, nodal density, and even rail-based transport is no solution as destinations spread over the landscape. As urbanisation penetrates into the countryside, political pressure grows for yet more road-building. A related problem is the cost of congestion, which wastes billions of dollars annually – money which could be devoted to social or economic investment for development. For example, the annual cost of congestion in Bangkok is US$272 million, accounting for 2.1 per cent of regional GDP.[21]

21 Euisoon, S et al 'Valuing the economic impacts of environmental problems: Asian cities' World Bank, Urban Management Programme, Discussion Paper, 1992

Higher, urban densities are more likely to generate sustainable development than are lower, suburban densities. The energy and pollution reduction advantages of higher densities are suggested by Figure 5.8. Higher densities also reduce the pressure on the diminishing rural land base and reduce the need to use private vehicles to access shopping and workplaces, thus reducing CO_2 emissions and air pollution; they also make it easier to run public transport on an economic basis. However, higher density living runs counter to suburban values, and to a propensity in many cultures for households to desire large detached houses with sprawling private yards or gardens. Control of automobility and suburbanisation is thus politically sensitive, and options for managing the situation must be socially feasible.

Figure 5.7

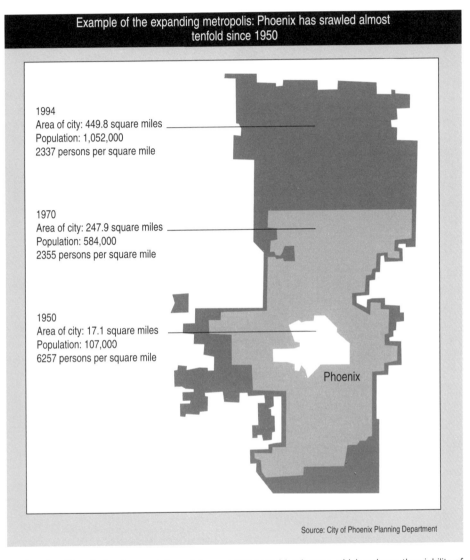

Example of the expanding metropolis: Phoenix has srawled almost tenfold since 1950

1994
Area of city: 449.8 square miles
Population: 1,052,000
2337 persons per square mile

1970
Area of city: 247.9 square miles
Population: 584,000
2355 persons per square mile

1950
Area of city: 17.1 square miles
Population: 107,000
6257 persons per square mile

Phoenix

Source: City of Phoenix Planning Department

22 Council for the Protection of Rural England and Countryside Commission *Special Report: Tranquil Areas: A New Way of Seeing the Countryside* by Ash Consulting Group, November 1995

A related problem is the fragmentation of the remaining rural landscape, which reduces the viability of ecosystems, and the subtle but relentless destruction of what has been defined as rural tranquillity by the Council for the Protection of Rural England (CPRE).[22] Rural tranquillity can be dissipated by mining operations, traffic, aircraft noise, power stations, touristic developments, such as large hotels, and intensive recreational uses, such as golfcourses. The process described is the suburbanisation of the countryside and it is occurring all over the world. For example, the Sustainable Greece team, Nea Ecologia, warns that intensive tourist developments, exceeding biophysical and social carrying capacities, is a main challenge of sustainable land management in the country. Many local, island people are aware of the dangers of misusing their limited land resources. But the current framework for land-use planning is weak and too easily manipulated to generate short-term economic gain at the expense of long-term needs.

Figure 5.8

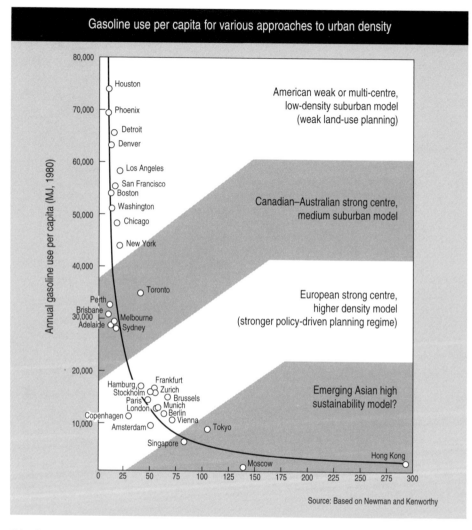

Urbanisation as a result of growing prosperity at the expense of agricultural production usually means that an increasing proportion of foodstuffs are imported. This contributes to transport emissions to global warming as well as to the occupation of foreign land by developed countries.

Wood

The earth's forests currently cover about a quarter of the land surface: around 3604 million hectares. Tropical forests account for a little over half of this but are diminishing rapidly. Growing forests absorb carbon dioxide and store carbon, thus reducing the build-up of greenhouse gases. Forests provide society with wood for paper production, construction and energy generation. Other functions include the preservation of biodiversity, the balance of water supply, the protection of the landscape and the use as recreational and leisure areas.

23 Walker, H
quoted in The
Scotsman 30
September
1996

Box 5.7 Transport intensity and land use

The world, and Europe, is engaged in an epidemic of motorisation. In the EU the number of truck kilometres travelled has increased by 700 million in the past five years. Goods, such as a pair of trousers, travel 3000 kilometres across Europe to be stitched because wages are cheaper in Eastern Europe, and the cost of road transport, highly subsidised by governments and the European Union, is cheap. The cost of health and other damages is around US$150 billion per year.

The energy intensity of motorised transport is very high and hugely inefficient. Fussler notes that less than 2 per cent of the energy content of gasoline is converted to moving the driver or passenger, with most displaced by heat and friction. Britain provides a good example: its 22 million cars travel 350 billion kilometres per year and consume 30 billion litres of fuel or 1000 litres per second.[23] Railways are three to six times more energy efficient, depending on load factors, which is shown in Figure 5.9.

Even if high vehicle fuel-efficiency is achieved using, say, solar cells or advanced engines, CO_2 emissions could be reduced, but the take-up of land for urbanisation would still increase – generating social nuisance, automobile accidents and disruption of natural areas. For this reason, the distance travelled by automobile may be a useful indicator of unsustainability. If the index goes up, it is unavoidable that there will be pressure for yet more roads to be built to avoid congestion. A related factor is the materials costs and ecological rucksacks of infrastructure. Finally, even if the index is low, but roads are built through natural sites, this cannot be construed as sustainable transport.

A three-month experiment in Vienna, in the course of which 40 car owners did without their cars on a trial basis and instead became members of the car sharing association, shows a reduction of automobility by more than 80 per cent (two-thirds of which was substituted by public transport, one third by bicycles). This encapsulates what needs to happen on a global scale. Energy efficiency in travel may also need to be complemented by 'demobilisation' – that is, a reduced need to travel. Growing interest in compact cities and urban villages recognises the need to contain mobility without diminishing (or often enhancing) quality of life.

Achieving sustainable management of the world's forests means reversing deeply ingrained patterns of both production and consumption. The determining factor in how to use forests should not be the demand for timber but the ecological capacity of the forests. However, the result of current rates of deforestation is a dramatic reduction in biodiversity; by 2020, up to 10 per cent of the world's 13 million species may disappear on a business-as-usual scenario. Wood consumption is therefore a proxy not only for carbon dioxide absorption but is also related to the maintenance of biodiversity.

Industrial timber cutting is a major cause of primary forest destruction in both temperate and tropical forests. The world's annual trade in forest products is in the order of US$90 billion annually, having expanded by 50 per cent since 1965. The most rapid current rates of deforestation are in Africa, where 72 per cent of rainforests have been decimated, cut almost entirely for timber exports. Average rates of deforestation suggest that most of the tropical forest will have disappeared by 2100. However, tropical

Figure 5.9

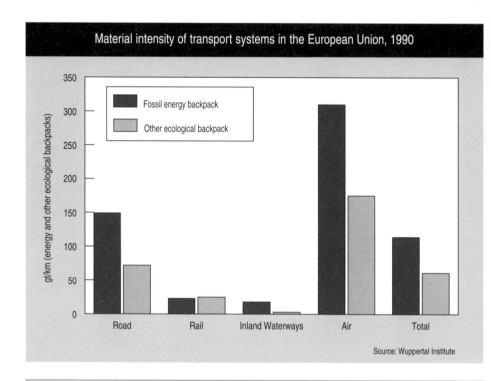

Material intensity of transport systems in the European Union, 1990

Source: Wuppertal Institute

> Wood is removed from Swedish forests at less than the annual growth rate. This does not mean, however, that the forestry sector is ecologically sustainable. Forests are managed with the explicit purpose of maximising production of wood, in particular for pulp. This limited approach has negative effects from an environmental perspective. For example, the number of tree species is kept low, and the natural mix of ages of trees in the forest is altered. These reduce biodiversity.
>
> From *Targets and Calculations for a Sustainable Sweden*

deforestation merely emulates the disappearance of primary forests in the Northern countries. Virtually all of Europe's virgin forests have disappeared, replaced by a few species in intensive plantations. In the continental United States, less than 6 per cent of primary forest is intact. In Canada, at current rates of harvesting, the last swaths of old-growth temperate rainforest will disappear by 2010, with the exception of a few isolated stands. In Ontario, only 3 per cent of old-growth forest remains and that is under threat.

Forests are essential for a continuation of life on earth. They are life support systems which regulate climate and atmosphere and maintain watersheds. Already deforestation is causing dangerous soil erosion in mountain areas, resulting in loss of life from landslides in countries as diverse as Spain, Greece, Brazil and the Philippines.

The environmental space approach argues that concern for biodiversity and natural heritage implies that there must be no more logging of the remaining 2173 million hectares of primary forest. These virgin forests, and other forests of special value, should be set aside for nature protection purposes, above and beyond the 10 per cent IUCN figure, and without any commercial exploitation such as logging. The

> Noteworthy is the extent of protected woodland in Cyprus, which means we are well within our environmental space. This is partly due to the efficient and well-planned forestry policies of the country's Forestry Commission.
>
> From *Towards a Sustainable Cyprus, National Data and Inventory*

remaining 1431 million hectares of secondary forest should be used on a sustainable basis, without threatening biological diversity, regeneration capacity or the economic and social needs of local and indigenous people.

The environmental space for wood is then based on this sustainable exploitation of forests, which will allow production of some two billion cubic metres annually on a global basis. Calculations of the sustainable yield on a global basis are difficult to deduce since the total area of the various forest types and sustainable yield per hectare are not yet scientifically determined. A fair share in environmental space between 0.4 and 0.5 cubic metres of wood per person can be used sustainably, forever. This can be compared to far higher, current consumption rates of 1.1 cubic metres per person per year in the rich countries, and a much lower 0.1 cubic metres per person per year in the developing countries.

Wood is a truly renewable resource and, when harvested and used with care, maximum use can be made of it. In order to remain within environmental space boundaries, primary wood consumption can be cut back by:

- reducing wastage during logging, transport and processing;
- switching from chemical to a thermo-mechanical processes in paper production, which reduces the amounts of woodpulp needed;
- reducing the unnecessary use of wood, especially in short-life applications, and reusing according to the cascade principle of extracting maximum lifespan from every piece of wood; and
- improving paper reuse and recycling.

Finally, it is worth noting that sustainable forest practices tend to be more labour intensive, and this can contribute to employment creation and rural development.

Water

Although some regions will have plentiful water for the next millennium, other areas will start running critically short of water in the next 30 years. The situation could become worse as global climate change begins to take effect. Total water consumption worldwide has been growing at 2.5 per cent per year, and has risen sixfold this century, roughly twice the rate of population growth. By 2025, 27 countries in Asia, Africa and the Middle East will fall within the UN's high water stress category. Figure 5.10 shows global water use by region and by sector, indicating another area of explosive growth in resource consumption.

Of course, the water balance sheet varies enormously from region to region, as does the rate of withdrawal. There are three key issues:

Figure 5.10

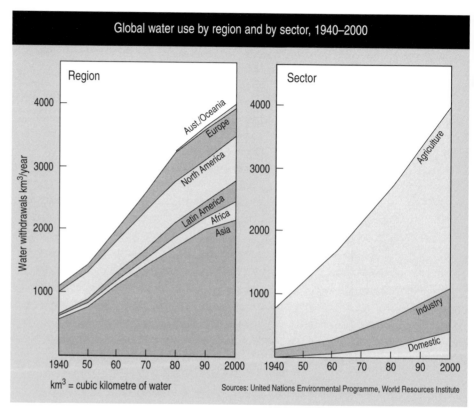

Global water use by region and by sector, 1940–2000

Region

Water withdrawals km³/year

Aust./Oceania
Europe
North America
Latin America
Africa
Asia

Sector

Agriculture
Industry
Domestic

km³ = cubic kilometre of water

Sources: United Nations Environmental Programme, World Resources Institute

- water scarcity through withdrawal from riverine transboundary sources, which could engender regional conflict, such as in the Middle East or the Nile Basin; and which is causing many rivers to dry up far from their outlets to the sea;
- overexploitation of groundwater resources which is usually a function of population growth or prosperity – watertables are falling because underground aquifers are being drawn down at unsustainable rates in the American Great Plains, China, India, Mexico and the southern ex-USSR republics;
- pollution of basic drinking water supplies, which means that around 20 per cent of the world's population has only limited access to clean water supplies, but also that supplies in developed countries are increasingly degraded by agriculture, mining and industry.

Conflict also arises when there are opposing demands for water, such as agricultural purposes versus the extraction or production of non-renewable resources. Industrialisation and intensification of agriculture has resulted in an enormous upsurge of freshwater consumption and numerous problems of overconsumption, pollution, ground subsidence from depletion of aquifers, disappearance of lakes, rivers and wetlands, and soil siltation from excess irrigation. In some countries, per capita consumption currently exceeds national supply.

Measuring the consumption of water to establish sustainability targets presents methodological challenges. For example, national statistical systems often ignore agriculture and energy generation when

Water consumption in Spain is far beyond the boundaries of environmental space. Water consumption per capita is the third highest in the world and the highest in Europe, although most of the territory is dry. The main contributor is agriculture, which accounts for 80 per cent of total abstraction. Also important is water loss in distribution, estimated to be 40 per cent. Spain is the European Union country with most natural areas in a good state of conservation. Fifteen per cent of Spain's territory could be declared a protected area, which represents 50 per cent more than the sustainable target for 2010 set in the Sustainable Europe Study.

From *Sustainable Europe, Sustainable Spain*

reporting consumption by sector.[24] Ground or surface water, furthermore, is often consumed but then returned to local watercourses in a more polluted state. Given the current recording situation, gross abstraction is probably the best feasible indicator.

The environmental space for provision of freshwater is best calculated regionally, by aquifer, for example. Regional targets will depend on factors such as rates of runoff and aquifer recharge. The calculation is complex: it is also influenced by climatic surplus precipitation, the hydrogeology of the water system, vegetation cover and the manageability of over and underground water flows.

Water consumption depends on population density, standards of living, habits of consumption and patterns of agricultural and industrial production. The differences are enormous: Americans consume on average $2150m^3$ (cubic metres) per year, Canadians $1500m^3$ per year, and Nigerians $45m^3$. But these rates still do not tell us the whole story because of the nature of supply. The Dutch and the people of Jordan consume less than the Americans at around 1000 and $175m^3$ of consumption respectively but, given the regional available supply, could still be said to overconsume available freshwater supplies. Comparing local or national availability with local or national consumption gives a first indication of whether current water abstractions are sustainable. Strategies for water management, identified in *Towards a Sustainable Scotland* include:

- direct water reuse involving using treated sewage effluent or non-potable 'grey' water for purposes that do not require potable supply;
- dual-supply systems in new developments – for example, for flushing toilets;
- leakage control and pressure reduction;
- domestic conservation, including water efficient technologies which can reduce domestic consumption by 30 per cent;
- industrial conservation;
- licensed abstraction control and permitting;
- domestic metering; and
- integrated catchment management to promote conservation in an ecologically sound and holistic manner.[25]

24 Hille, op cit

25 Friends of the Earth Scotland, op cit pp67-68

European Calculation for Environmental Space

In this final section, by way of example, current use of key resources in Europe, fair shares in environmental space to 2050 and intermediate targets for 2010 are presented for energy, some non-renewable resources, wood and land use (see Table 5.3). For wood and land use, calculations have been made at the continental level instead of the global level. Water, because it is considered a regional resource, is not included at this European level of analysis. In the third and fourth columns, the distance-to-sustainability is presented as the difference between current consumption and the fair share, for the final target year of 2050 and the interim target year of 2010.

It is important to note that these figures are approximate but that they give a clear indication of the magnitude of change needed in the resource use of industrialised countries. Here the assumption is that global population stabilises at seven billion in 2010. However, the table can easily be recalculated at the UN mid-range population projection of around ten billion people by 2050, in which case the per capita environmental space for global resources will be reduced by around one third. This will lead to a relatively small increase in the environmental space challenge to the industrialised countries. These conclusions are summarised in Figure 5.11 and Table 5.3.

Dialogue and Debate Complement Calculations of Environmental Space

The relevance of the environment space methodology is demonstrated by its recently tested applicability that spans the length and breadth of Europe: from Scotland to the Ukraine and from Finland to Malta.

Box 5.8 Environmental space calculations

The environmental space for CO_2 is based on recommendations of the IPCC. Divided by the world population in 2010, this gives a fair share of environmental energy space of 1.7 tons per capita. For non-renewables, the impact of non-renewables on a global scale needs to be about halved. This leads to reduction percentages for Europe of 80 to 90 per cent. For land use it is calculated on how much land is needed to feed the European population with sustainable agriculture. The overimport of agricultural products, especially fodder, that claim land needed for food production in developing countries should be stopped. The intention is to promote a balanced import–export relationship between continents.

The natural area of Europe should be expanded to 10 per cent of the territory. Wood consumption should be slightly reduced to allow forestry management regimes based on mixed, natural forests, of which the harvest matches the annual growth rate. The environmental space for water should be calculated on the national and local level. It is important to stress that the figures here are rough and approximate, but they give us a good directional policy guidance.

Source: *Towards a Sustainable Europe: The Handbook*

Figure 5.11

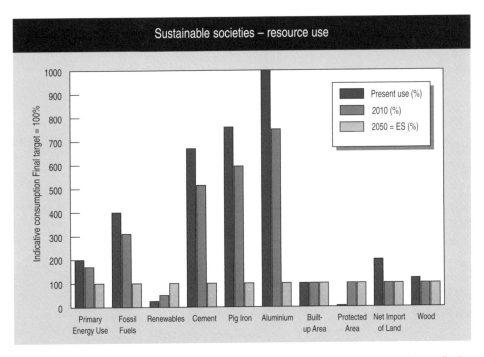

But it is also important to note that quantitative calculations are of little use without the qualitative process of dialogue and debate which the measures are intended to kindle. This final section touches on this key aspect of the approach.

All the Sustainable Europe teams organised a participative process in which, literally, thousands of representatives of governments, businesses and NGOs across Europe discussed, in an open-minded manner, the sustainability targets and distance-to-sustainability measures for their countries. Debate was carried on in face-to-face seminars, and in the media. In the Republic of Macedonia, for example, Sustainable Macedonia researchers debated, in a constructive manner, with the Minister for the Environment on prime time television. This is important in a country which is already living, in many areas, within the bounds of environmental space but is under pressure to modernise the economy.

Often contact led to further constructive outcomes. In Italy, the Sustainable Italy team has been asked to assess the national environmental policy from an environmental space point of view. Similarly, the Sustainable Slovakia report has become a supplement in the government's strategic environmental assessment manual. In Estonia, the study was influential in the Estonian Parliament during the passing an act on sustainable development which sets out a legal basis for the sustainable use of natural resources and establishes guidelines for environmental protection. Although there was surprisingly widespread agreement in most countries on the appropriate nature of the environmental space approach, and the underlying assumptions, as would be expected, not everyone agreed wholeheartedly with the calculations or the assumptions. Some people found the calculations too absolute and not sufficiently reflective of scientific uncertainties. The national action–research groups did not always agree with the common methodology which guided them in calculating distance-to-sustainability figures for the various resources, suggesting, in some cases, that the common methodology did not always reflect particular local requirements.

Current European consumption of environmental space with interim reductions for the year 2010 and fully sustainable consumption levels for 2050				
Resource	Present use per capita per year	Optimum reductions for final target year 2050		Interim targets target 2010
Energy CO_2 emissions	7.3 tonnes	1.7 tonnes	–77%	–26%
Non-renewable raw materials				
Cement	536 kg	80 kg	–85%	–21%
Pig iron	273 kg	36 kg	–87%	–22%
Aluminium	12 kg	1.2 kg	–90%	–23%
Chlorine	23 kg	0 kg	–100%	–25%
Land use EU-12				
Protected area [1]	0.003 ha	0.061 ha		+2000%
Built-up land [2]	0.053 ha	0.051 ha	–3.2%	–3.2%
Net import of land[3]	0.037 ha	0.0185	–50%	–50%
Wood	0.66 m[3]	0.56 m[3]		–15%
Water [4]				

1   The assumption is that 10% of national land area should be fully protected conservation areas.
2   Assumes that urban densities will increase slightly and low density settlement will be controlled.
3   The use of land in other countries to generate foodstuffs and other items for European consumption. Does not preclude imports but assumes a better balance towards self-sufficiency.
4   Because of the large variation in water regimes from country to country and area to area, environmental space for water is calculated on a national, bioregional or local basis.

Table 5.3

On the other hand, there was very little contention about the absolute need for major reductions in excessive consumption. It was almost unanimously agreed by stakeholders that, whatever disagreement might exist over long-term targets, the directional guidance provided by environmental space analysis was clear and correct and present trends towards more and more unsustainable production and consumption must be altered. During debates it was indicated that setting an objective of a 50 per cent reduction in the use of primary raw materials and energy, for example, is seen as highly feasible as far as the design and development of new products is concerned. It became apparent that such an objective could be helpful in starting a process of developing and producing radically different products and services, which could offer equal levels of utility with greatly reduced environmental impacts.

Despite various reservations, the majority of the participants in the Sustainable Europe campaign were convinced of the importance of quantifying environmental space, and of the validity of the measurement approach. In particular, gaining an insight into long-term independent policy objectives appealed to many who participated in national forums. Furthermore, the need was expressed for long-term sustainability objectives to be converted into short-term financial and economic reforms. These can be based, in part, on a drive to innovation in ecoefficiency, which is the subject of the next chapter.

CHAPTER

6

Eco-Innovation: More from Less

Introduction

Environmental space provides a sustainable context for human action while preserving the natural basis for life, with each generation bequeathing to the next an Earth full of possibility. Within this framework of stewardship there are many options for positive action. The previous two chapters explained why and how to assess our world's available environmental space as a means of progressing towards sustainable societies. In this and the next chapter we argue that living well within fair shares of environmental space comes about through a combination of:

■ *efficiency* in materials and energy management, combined with technological advancement, called eco-innovation; and
■ changing values which recognise that, beyond meeting basic needs, quality of life derives from a *sufficiency*, rather than an excess, of consumption.

In a nutshell, we must either increase resource efficiency or reduce consumption, and probably both. This chapter considers the ecoefficiency side of the equation, the next, sufficiency.

Towards a Revolution in Production Efficiency

1 von
Weiszäcker, E,
Lovins, A and
Lovins, H *Faktor
Vier* München:
Droemer Knaur,
1995

There is no doubt that some sort of revolution in production efficiency is needed to achieve a high quality of human life by the middle of the next century – with the inflow of materials and energy to production systems reduced by a factor of eight to ten. This will allow everyone on earth to live within the earth's capacity for renewal and with fair shares of consumption for all.[1] However radical this 'factor ten' reduction may seem from current vantage points, change can be brought about by an evolution of materials' management and the application of technology – in a way which is already within our reach and which will bring significant benefits in terms of both reduced costs and reduced pollution. But we need to force the pace of change if we are to get ahead of rising patterns of consumption.

For example, in Western Europe over the past 25 years, material and energy efficiency has improved greatly. This suggests that the technological capacity exists to make major efficiency gains. Typically, however, these gains have been more than outstripped by absolute increases in consumption. For instance, the efficiency of building services (lighting, heating, cooling, equipment) is increasing by about 1 per cent per year, but the quantity of energy consumed for these purposes is increasing by 2 per cent per year.[2] The technical efficiency of the car improves by 1 to 1.5 per cent per year, but this is outstripped by growth in travel (2 to 2.5 per cent per year) and the upgrading of vehicle power (0.5 per cent per year). As a result of these types of trends, European energy consumption has increased by 40 per cent since 1970. The extent of built-up land has doubled, and so on. These absolute increases in consumption reinforce the need for innovation in ecoefficiency if sustainability is to be achieved, but also highlight the need for sufficiency.

In this chapter we argue that the pace of change in ecoefficiency should be dramatically increased by technological and managerial innovation, and by a better understanding of the processes of innovation to foster a reduction in materialism, concepts elaborated below. They are important because they are overall societal objectives for achieving environmental space, and they frame ecoefficiency at the level of the firm or the sector.

2 Bleijenberg, A and Swigchem, J van 'Efficiency and Sufficiency: Towards sustainable energy and transport' Delft: report by Energy Conservation and Environmental Technology for Sustainable Europe Campaign, 1997

3 Schmidt-Bleek, F 'MIPS A Universal Environmental Measure' *Fresenius Environmental Bulletin* vol 2, 1993; see also Adriaanse, A et al *Resource Flows: The Material Basis of Industrial Economics* Washington: World Resources Institute, 1997

Development and Growth within Environmental Space

The environmental space approach argues for a shift away from traditional, material-intensive growth (called here business-as-usual) to global and national strategies for delinking economic growth from resource consumption. Material intensity is the total material and energy input (measured in weight) per unit of a good, assessed during the entire life-cycle of the good, from cradle to grave.[3] Given the enormous range of negative outputs from production processes, and our chronic inability to get ahead of these problems, the emphasis on reducing inputs is the only practical way to tackle the problems of waste, pollution and the depletion of natural resources, such as topsoil.

Delinking needs to be followed by a more stringent and fully sustainable stage of 'dematerialisation' of industrial production processes, which can be defined as an absolute reduction in the use of energy and materials (and possibly a stabilisation of land use), whatever the levels of production. A minimum factor ten reduction of material and energy inputs per unit of service output is probably necessary to meet environmental space targets.

Material-intensive growth is an increase in GDP associated with higher material inputs, usually at the rate of GDP growth or greater, and subsequent outputs of waste materials. The obvious implications of business-as-usual is suggested in Figure 6.1, which shows the near linear relationship between GNP and domestic waste production in the recent past. However, we argue that this kind of linear relationship need not be the case – the pattern can and must be changed dramatically towards dematerialisation.

Figure 6.1

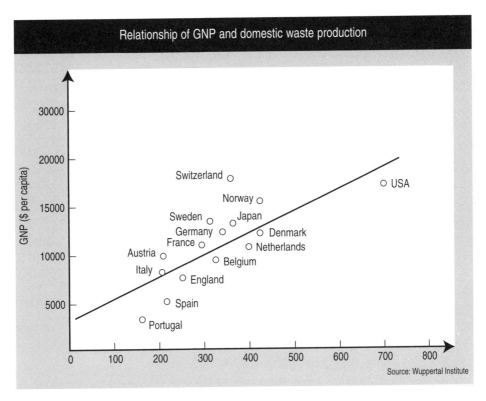

Relationship of GNP and domestic waste production

Source: Wuppertal Institute

Delinked Growth

An interim stage is the application of increasingly stringent ecoefficiency standards to delink economic growth from materials, land and energy use, where any increase in the growth rate of these factors is less than the growth rate of GDP. Delinking begins by considering the most efficient means of providing a service to the consumer, rather than simply goods per se. Aspects of a delinking strategy include: detailed analysis of material flows at the national, industrial and firm levels; closing industrial process cycles; improved quality of products; cradle-to-grave product responsibility; and production processes located close to the consumer according to the proximity principle. Also relevant are economic instruments and ecological tax reforms intended to discourage environmentally unsound practices and to reward sustainable behaviour, without damaging market competitiveness.

Delinking is already possible: this is indicated by the substantially different rates of energy consumption per unit of GNP in Japan, Germany and the USA, shown in Figure 6.2. These differences are not necessarily reflected in the quality of life of the citizens, nor in the economic prosperity of the nations. This suggests that energy consumption patterns could be made more efficient, or delinked, from GDP growth.

The result of delinking is a more efficient use of resources. Some industries are currently delinking their company's growth pattern from materials consumption. This is obviously good business, especially where materials use or waste disposal is moving towards covering true costs. However, at the national level, there is a problem where growing levels of consumption outstrip ecoefficiency gains.

Figure 6.2

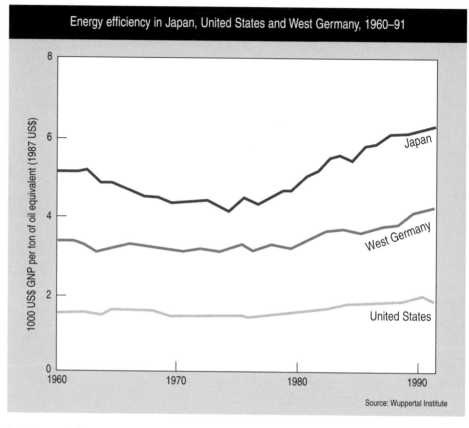

Energy efficiency in Japan, United States and West Germany, 1960–91

Source: Wuppertal Institute

In this case, delinking is no more than relative to GDP and real, absolute levels of waste and pollution will continue to rise.

The implications of this situation is shown in Figure 6.3 where traditional business-as-usual GDP growth is compared with increasing stringency in the application of delinking. Relative delinking is shown by (1) – while some ecoefficiency is in place, it cannot offset the environmental impacts of growth in production and consumption. This is the current situation in industrial sectors in many countries, even those with relatively strict end-of-pipe pollution control. Even more of a problem arises in terms of land consumption, because very few countries have sufficiently stringent land-use planning regimes, or the political will to mediate between private development rights and the greater good, to prevent growing consumption of the land resource in terms of suburban sprawl.

Because delinking is only a step towards genuine sustainability, the more stringent variation of dematerialisation is necessary, shown by (2) and (3); here, absolute reductions are given in the use of energy and materials whatever the levels of production and consumption. This is genuinely sustainable, since resource use is declining. At (3) a sustainable level of development is achieved within the boundaries of environmental space.[4]

The implication of dematerialised growth is that it is within long-range (say the year 2050) environmental space targets and therefore comprises sustainable growth. Other terms for this state of affairs include extensive growth and low MIPS growth (material intensity per product or service unit).

4 Schmidt-
Bleek,
F,'Revolution in
Resource
Productivity for a
Sustainable
Economy: a new
research
agenda'
*Fresenius
Environmental
Bulletin* vol 2
pp485–490
1993

Figure 6.3

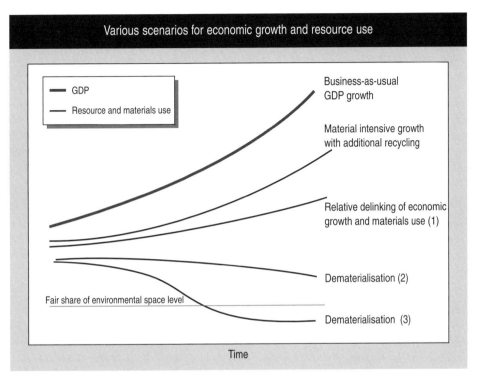

Various scenarios for economic growth and resource use

- GDP
— Resource and materials use

Business-as-usual
GDP growth

Material intensive growth
with additional recycling

Relative delinking of economic
growth and materials use (1)

Dematerialisation (2)

Fair share of environmental space level

Dematerialisation (3)

Time

Dematerialisation is an important positive threshold; depending on global population, the achievement of dematerialised growth is sustainable in the sense that all people on earth could enjoy the benefits brought by current Western standards of living. The Sustainable Europe methodology makes clear that the general principle is a reduction in raw materials, but that some processes and products would need to be phased out altogether (such as nuclear energy or CFCs).

Box 6.1 A simple test of dematerialisation

Can this product or service be acquired and used by seven to ten billion people without causing environmental damage to the planet or social damage to its people?

Dematerialised Growth

In terms of dematerialised growth, it is important to note that the term growth refers not to levels of production or consumption, but only to growth in monetary flows. This reinforces an underlying premise of environmental space: if materials consumption can be brought within sustainable limits, this imposes no particular limitation to economic growth per se. In this tightly defined, ecologically sound concept, economic growth can be sustainable.

Ernst Ulrich von Weizsäcker

Dematerialisation of Production and Consumption

In terms of material flows into production and consumption, including their ecological rucksacks and their impacts on the planet, the environmental space concept demonstrates a fact that is both surprising and embarrassing for the North. China and India don't look overpopulated on current figures, while countries such as the USA, Germany and The Netherlands are.

If we aim for global equity, we ought to reduce drastically the ecological rucksacks. Two mutually supportive strategies exist in this regard: efficiency and sufficiency. Macroeconomic efficiency increases as large as factor four are available to us already. Resource productivity can be quadrupled for houses, cars, appliances, food, textiles, office equipment and industrial processes. But this efficiency revolution will not materialise by itself. Conditions conducive for the new technologies should be established. Least-cost planning, especially in the energy sector, and ecological tax reform are highly desirable. Both can be designed in a way that strengthen, rather than weaken, the economy and help combat unemployment.

Ernst Ulrich von Weizsäcker is President of the Wuppertal Institute for Climate, Environment and Energy in Germany and coauthor, with Amory and Hunter Lovins, of *Factor Four*.

Box 6.2 Dematerialising a television

Industrialised countries will need to reduce overall resource use by a factor of ten (or 90 per cent) in the coming 30 to 50 years to meet a 50 per cent global reduction target. This might sound outlandish at first, but research shows there are ways to achieve this while maintaining equivalent end-use satisfaction. If one takes the example of the service 'television watching per hour', we can dematerialise this by 80 per cent if we double the lifespan of the TV set, reduce its weight by 30 per cent and use 50 per cent recycled parts in its construction.

From *Sustainable Germany*.[5]

However, there is a further important step which is to distinguish growth, a quantitative process, from development, which implies a positive change in the quality of life. Growth is not necessarily better than no growth or limited growth, and in no way guarantees the achievement of development. For example, the founder of ecological economics, Herman Daly, argues that there is a fundamental misunderstanding about growth, which is generally taken to be synonymous with an increase in wealth. Thus, it is commonly argued that we must have growth because only if we become wealthier will we be able to afford the cost of environmental protection. But it does not take much imagination to question whether economic growth, at the current margin, is really making us wealthier, given the kinds of problems discussed in Chapter 2. Rather, economic growth can push our societies beyond optimal scales relative to the biosphere and can make us poorer as a result. The next chapter considers the possibility of what might

5 BUND and
MISEREOR
*Sustainable
Germany* English
Summary 1996

Box 6.3 Sustainable dematerialised growth

Sustainable dematerialised growth
exists when:

*annual economic growth = the annual increase
in resource productivity,*

given that the economy is within environmental space limits
at the start of the period.

be called a post-consumer society and aspects of quality of life, such as the quality of family, work and community life on the one hand, and the pressures of stress on the other.

There is a last important point with regard to growth and development. In the long run, under demate-rialised growth, annual economic growth will have to be limited to the annual increase in resource productivity, which is approaching an objective definition of sustainable development, at least from an input–output perspective of materials consumption. Resource productivity could be expressed per unit of service or per unit of GNP.

The remainder of this chapter discusses the potential for technological advancement and eco-innovation to contribute to sustainable development, including the potential for what might be called quantum leap technologies to accelerate technological development for sustainability purposes. In all cases, these are intended to decrease resource use without decreasing the quality of life.

Eco-Innovation and Technology

Eco-innovation can be defined as a deliberate process of entrepreneurship, design and product life-cycle management that contributes to the ecological modernisation of industrial societies by integrating environmental concerns into product and process development. Eco-innovation promotes integrated solutions to reduce resource and energy inputs while increasing the quality of a product or service. Technological innovation is one route to eco-innovation.

Technology is, of course, a two-edged sword. Toffler calls it the 'prime motor of capitalism' and Freedman 'the fundamental force in shaping the patterns of transformation of the economy'.[6] Technology is, without doubt, a key contributory factor in the globalisation of economic activity. Before Hiroshima, technological development could be perceived as the equivalent of progress, at least by its beneficiaries. Since then, many people have an ambivalence or outright suspicion of technology, not least because of the role of technology in environmental degradation, such as ozone depletion, and in militarism and war. As we approach the 21st century, however, it is possible to be cautiously optimistic; we have a better understanding of the strengths and limitations of technology and a more reasoned view of its potential contribution to human development – as well as an acceptance of inherent dangers and the critical need

6 Toffler, A *Future Shock* London: Pan, 1981; Freeman, C 'Introduction' in Dosi et al (eds) *Technical Change and Economic Theory* London: Pinter, 1988

to apply the precautionary principle to new technology. However, given the enormity of the task of planetary management, and the role of technology as one of the driving forces of capitalism, governments, industrialists and many environmentalists expect technology to make a positive contribution to sustainable development.

It is important to stress that technology is neither value-neutral, culture-free nor independent or autonomous.[7] Technology is in a constant interplay with both economic structures and cultural values. The economy, through price mechanisms, plays an important role in determining the types of technology developed and marketed, but the choices are entirely human and therefore social and political: the technology of mass destruction? atmosphere-destroying technology? environmental technology? intermediate technology? technology for the good of the human race? The choice is not preordained, and it is vitally important to influence technological development so that it contributes to, rather than dominates, socio-cultural development. This is especially true because not only do we influence technology, but it profoundly influences us. Chapter 2 documented how, for better or worse, much of human society reorganised itself in the 20th century around the motor car. The next chapter discusses the dramatic shrinking of the earth by jet propulsion technology since 1960. The same degree of radical change could be brought about with eco-innovative technologies in the 21st century, in a post-industrial era.

Patterns of Production and Consumption

7 Dicken, P *Global Shift: The Internationalization of Economic Activity* London: Paul Chapman Publishing, 1992

8 Simai, M *The Future of Global Governance Managing Risk and Change in the Global System* Washington: United States Institute of Peace, 1994, p199

9 Mol, A P J; *The Refinement of Production: Ecological Modernization Theory and the Chemical Industry* Utrecht: van Arkel, 1995

10 Simai, op cit

From an historical basis, the technological restructuring of industry in modern times can be divided into eras defined by production and consumption processes. These eras are roughly defined by technologies which shape values, production and consumption systems, skill and employment patterns and investment needs.[8] They influence the style and the quality of life, and transform organisational systems and socio-political infrastructure and land-use patterns. They provide a framework within which entrepreneurs operate and influence the international division of labour and the functioning of global markets. The following is a list of the eras of industrial societies:

- *First modern era: industrial take-off* (1789–1848), with mechanical spinning and the steam engine as key technologies;[9]
- *Second modern era: the construction of industrial society* (1848–1980), in three phases: the age of railway construction (1848–1890), the age of electrification (1890–1940) and the age of mass motorisation (1945 to about 2010);
- *Emerging modern era: ecological transformation of the industrial system*, based on five generic, multipurpose technologies: microelectronics, information technology, materials science, biotechnology, power technology and propulsion technology;[10] these offer promise for delinking economic development from related resource inputs, resource use and emissions, and in monitoring processes of production and consumption in terms of their consequences for the environment.

Two points arise. First, if this view of shifts in production and consumption processes is reasonably correct, there is potential to reorganise production and consumption systems along sensible ecological lines. This is true, in particular, because the impact of change in these generic technologies is pervasive across a wide variety of production processes and in a large area of product families.[11] The technologies also have the potential to be self-reinforcing and interactive. Information technology can facilitate faster dissemination of knowledge and technical know-how on clean production and environmental management. Improvements in communication technology diffuse technological innovation. In the era of ecological transformation, or dematerialisation of the economy, the economic value of production can be embedded in computer memory rather than material things. Evidence suggests that dematerialised industries in the USA already have larger turnovers than do the defence and auto industries.[12] One conclusion is that the globalisation of an increasingly dematerialised economy at the onset of the 21st century is profoundly different from the growth of trade and overseas investment of the 20th century.[13]

Economies of scale based on massive capital investments, such as those in giant steel mills and vertically integrated production systems, are no longer the key to economic development. This means that small firms and creative individuals are put on a more equal competitive footing. For example, anyone with a computer is free to write new software or to break into journalism. This enhances opportunities for employment creation not linked to old-style industrial plant – for example, in freelance (or multitask, multi-employer) work. Although the location of educated workforces and high-tech communi-

Box 6.4 Good reasons for eco-innovation[14]

- *Less pollution and waste*: efficiency decreases pollution. Pollution is nothing but useful resources in the wrong place at the wrong time.
- *Increased quality of life*: eco-innovative technologies do not only reduce resource consumption but increase performance of services as well.
- *Equity and labour*: to increase the input of labour capital into the economy while decreasing the use of resources to avoid unemployment. Unemployment is an important factor that contributes to social destabilisation of persons and groups within societies.
- *Competitiveness* through the use of new and improved technologies in processes and products.
- *Marketability and good business*: efficient products and processes will achieve market penetration as they are cost-effective and do not entail government regulation. Improved public image is good for business.
- *Profitability*: resource savings on raw materials and energy is financially more attractive than buying and using resources; avoiding pollution is cheaper than end-of-pipe clean-up operations.
- *Less risk*: from on- and off-site treatment, storage and disposal of toxic wastes and improved health and safety of employees and consumers.
- *Efficient use of scarce development capital*: to build up an eco-innovative infrastructure. Instead of new power plants, factories can be bought that produce energy-efficient light bulbs.
- *International Security*: competition for scarce resources can sharpen international conflicts. Efficiency efforts can decrease the build-up of such tensions.

11 Simai, op cit, p202

12 Quah, D *The Invisible Hand and the Weightless Economy* London School of Economics, Centre for Economic Performance, 1996

13 Coyle, D 'Shrinking costs mean that anyone can be a star' *The Independent* 18 April 1996

14 von Weiszäcker et al op cit

cations equipment tends to reinforce the advantages of the computer literate in the developed world, this can change. This is because electronically based services, such as banking, data processing and electronic publishing, can be located wherever the human capital exists to carry out the functions. Countries and cities whose physical locations worked against them in the past may find they are no longer at a disadvantage. British Airways, for example, is shifting accounting functions from England to India, which has a well-trained professional workforce.

Secondly, it is clear that since the beginnings of the 1980s, many production processes and products, at least in developed countries, are already becoming cleaner per unit produced, and there is more recycling. The car is a good example of the gradual greening of technology – 75 per cent of the weight of cars in the European Union are now recycled. Of course, this is not enough as long the use of primary resources is increasing, but these type of developments support the view that some shift in technological development is underway.

Beyond this, there is not the space here to discuss the relationship of technology to human development except to say that cultural and political change can trigger technological innovation as well as be conditioned by it. It is important, therefore, to reinforce what we hope is an emerging wave of technological innovation. These eco-innovative products and processes are the next generation of environmental technology, complementing end-of-pipe technology. We also see the emergence of a new style of entrepreneurs, dedicated to using eco-innovation to achieve sustainable production and consumption systems. Within this context, it is important to reinforce the shift, and to search for the quantum leaps, in eco-innovation that are needed to supplement incremental change. Governments can adopt technology-forcing targets and policies which set standards ahead of existing best technology.

Product and Production: not Clean-up but Cleaner

In the past, environmental policy and practice have emphasised pollution control rather than pollution prevention.[15] Old-style environmental technologies generally treat waste by converting it to a comparatively less harmful form of pollution. But the emerging transformation is towards cleaner production processes that reduce problems at source. There is a powerful argument for moving beyond clean-up technology – it is a more efficient use of resources and thus, ultimately, more profitable for both business and society. Figure 6.4 shows that a full valuation of environmental costs in the life-cycle of a product or process promotes the use of cleaner technology over the more expensive option of clean-up technology. This recognises that, given externalities such as pollution, environmental improvement is achievable, but at a price.[16]

Starting at point 'x' in Figure 6.4, the environmental damage resulting from a product or process can be reduced by clean-up measures. However, expenditure on clean-up shows progressively decreasing returns. This means that a point will be reached where further expenditure on clean-up is unjustified because more environmental benefit can be achieved by other forms of investment which reduce both environmental damage and production costs. Competitive advantage and environment both benefit from this shift to the economics of cleaner technology.

15 Friends of the Earth, England, Wales and Northern Ireland *Working Future: Jobs and the Environment* London 1994

16 Engineering Council of Great Britain *Guidelines on Environmental Issues* London, 1994

Figure 6.4

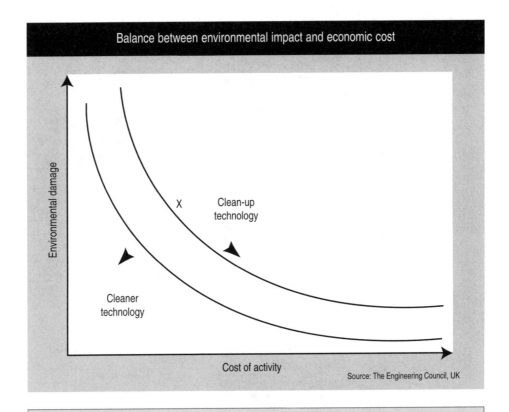

Balance between environmental impact and economic cost

Environmental damage

X   Clean-up
           technology

Cleaner
technology

Cost of activity

Source: The Engineering Council, UK

Box 6.5 New times, new questions, new technology

From a systems point of view, it is highly questionable whether attempts to 'ecologise' technology – which was invented and made operational and reliable under unecological economic conditions – is a promising approach. Entirely new technical answers must be found to hitherto unimportant economic questions: how much welfare can be produced from one litre of water or one tonne of steel? This situation can be compared to the 19th-century experience when legislation forced the internalisation of social costs into the price of labour and, as a consequence, a sharp increase in labour productivity was achieved.

F Schmidt-Bleek[17]

Product Life-Cycle Assessment

There is value in recycling but it can be relatively expensive and inefficient because of transport, energy and disposal costs; there are also opportunity costs in terms of lack of feedback on product improvement. For some products and materials, recycling may not be the best option. This is best assessed by emerging integrated, product life-cycle approaches in which management and audit schemes are

17 Schmidt-
Bleek, F op cit

Figure 6.5

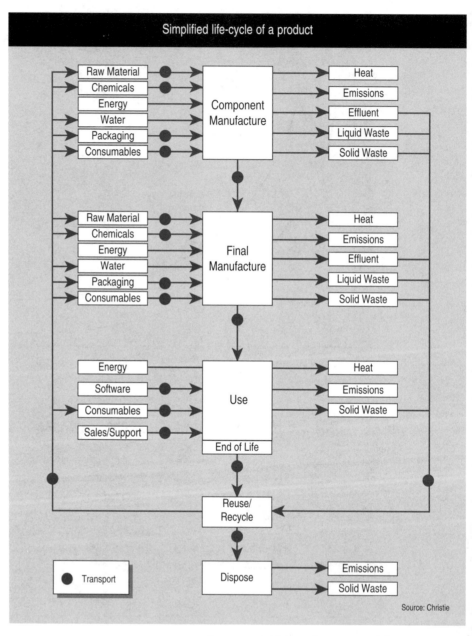

Simplified life-cycle of a product

Source: Christie

designed to reduce energy and material flows, emissions and wastes, and transport costs throughout the life-cycle of a product. The first step in eco-innovation, then, is to move to a full life-cycle assessment (LCA) of products and processes. Figure 6.5 shows a product life-cycle.

LCA, or cradle to grave assessment of products, processes and projects is intended to assess:

- all primary inputs of raw materials and energy, to ensure minimisation of material intensity per service unit;
- all emissions to the environment and solid residues, for reduction or zero emissions;
- all the inputs and waste associated with reuse, recycling and ultimate disposal, again for reduction and to ensure maximum service life.[18]

Life-cycle assessments can also contribute to the awareness of areas for improvement in the material- and energy-efficiency of products and processes. According to Russell, LCA is not just a scientific technique but 'an environmental improvement process that takes us outside our factory fence, our home or our business to look at the driving forces behind the products and services that society uses'.[19] Such LCAs should also extend to an assessment of the human condition related to raw materials extraction, processing and all the other steps in the production process. The recent attention drawn by campaigning organisations to the woeful conditions of employment in some developing country factories owned by multinationals is a case in point. The next step will be for such companies to include attention to the human conditions of employment in annual reports.

Monitoring of Resource Flows in the Production Process

If good decisions are to be made, there is no doubt that the information intensity of the management process underpinning cleaner production strategies will be high.[20] Strategic company decisions will benefit from monitoring the net use of resources in terms of material intensity per product or service unit (MIPS). Accurate monitoring systems can increase awareness of the wastage of materials and, with it, money, as well as other areas of potential improvement. The US-based optoelectronic firm EG&G, for example, established a 'materials balance accounting system' for its commercial divisions in 1995. Materials balance data collection started as part of an environmental-management planning process which emphasises self-assessment and goal setting at the division level. The new system was created out of a belief that material inputs had to be considered as well as wastes and emissions, in order to fully assess the environmental impacts of a plant's activities. Data elements include:

- beginning of year and end-of-year inventory, for each chemical used in production;
- amount acquired during the year;
- quantity consumed in the production process;
- quantity shipped in or out as product; and
- quantities emitted to air, discharged to water or disposed as waste.

As company divisions developed the necessary monitoring and tracking systems for hazardous materials, reporting became more uniform and standardised. The data revealed instances where reporting person-nel were not accounting for all materials – for example, air emissions were understated or quantities shipped in product had been overlooked. These cases suggested that materials accounting helped division managers to better understand their processes and how to make them more efficient.[21]

From a managerial point of view, the benefit of LCAs and resource-use monitoring consists in promot-

18 Engineering Council op cit

19 Cited in Fussler op cit

20 Christie, I et al *Cleaner Production in Industry* London: Policy Studies Institute, 1995

21 Wallace, A and Parker, W 'Measuring and reporting environmental performance in a global company: a case for materials accounting' unpublished paper, 1996

22 Material by
Harrison, M first
appeared in *The
Independent*

Box 6.6 Innovation in the firm: UK£20 million profits from waste

For the Tioxide company, the world's second biggest producer of white pigment, sales of waste recycled from the production process now outweigh those of the core product. In 1995, Tioxide recycled 0.77 million tonnes of gypsum, carbon dioxide and iron salts into agriculture, construction and water treatment. The next target is to double sales of recycled material to UK£40 million (US$60 million). Most of the waste, from plants in the UK, USA, Malaysia and South Africa, is packaged and resold locally. From its start in 1993, Tioxide's recycling division now employs 250 people, and is viewed as a leading edge division. Production processes are designed with recycling in mind so that waste comes off the line in a way which can be conveniently packaged.[22]

The director of Tioxide says:

We began the materials business because we faced ever tighter environmental standards, escalating costs of treatment and dumping and because the industry had a poor image of recycling which needed improving. But it has resulted in the whole company looking at the environment in a different light. We used to be focused on compliance with the law but we have moved beyond that and are working much more closely with local communities to look at ways of anticipating environmental problems and how best to tackle them.

ing the concept of material flow cycles and resource conservation. These are essential to achieve the kinds of reductions in material flows necessary to live within a fair share of environmental space. Although costs may rise in the short run, resource conservation and more integrated circuits in production permit cost reductions in the long run. End-of-pipe technologies, on the other hand, often raise operating costs, especially for energy and disposal. The introduction of resource, energy, and ecobalances will entail a high initial effort with regard to the collection and documentation of data, but will pay in the long run in the form of win–win opportunities for environmental improvement and company profitability.

Based on this, there are two broad areas of innovation required: the management of materials and energy use, to achieve reductions; and waste and pollution management.

Reducing Waste, Materials and Energy Use in Production

It is often said that there is no waste in nature. Completely closed industrial loops, or zero-emission factories together with full-product recycling, will be a big step towards sustainable development. But many industrial processes will continue to generate waste for some decades to come. Nevertheless,

Table 6.1

The principles of waste management	
Highest Priority	
Elimination	Complete elimination of waste.
Prevention	Prevention of waste production should be considered at the initial feasibility and design stage and may determine if the project should proceed.
Waste minimisation; source reduction	The avoidance, reduction or elimination of waste, generally within the confines of the production, through changes in industrial processes or procedures.
Recycling	The use, reuse and recycling of waste for original or some other purpose such as input material, materials recovery or energy production.
Treatment	The destruction, detoxification, neutralisation, etc of waste into less harmful substances.
Disposal	The discharge of waste to air, water or land in properly controlled or safe ways such that compliance is achieved; secure land disposal may involve volume reduction, encapsulation, leachate containment and monitoring techniques.
Lowest Priority	

Source: The Engineering Council (UK)

process efficiency is very often instigated by the drive to minimise waste production. Processes which use less materials and energy almost always produce less waste, a fundamental component of environmental space.[23] Consequently, waste minimisation is of key importance to ecoefficiency. But many companies are not aware of the extent or the costs of the waste they produce or of alternatives:

> *Today many companies are unaware of how much they are throwing away, or they think that existing processes are at maximum efficiency. Forty-four per cent of British companies do not know how much waste costs them.*[24]

23 Friends of the Earth op cit

24 Biffa Waste Services, 1994, quoted in Friends of the Earth op cit

Waste represents loss of valuable raw materials and requires significant investment in pollution control measures, both in terms of hardware and human resources. The Engineering Council of Great Britain notes that: 'Many such end-of-pipe waste treatment techniques do not actually eliminate waste but merely transfer it from one medium to another.'[25]

The council argues that there are few technical obstacles to waste minimisation – the barriers to improved practice are political, institutional and financial. They argue that shifting companies 'out of the waste production business' can generate substantial economic as well as environmental benefits. They propose the following principles of waste management, set out in Table 6.1, and suggest an appropriate range of techniques for achieving this.

Reductions in the materials and energy use of a production chain can be achieved by any or all of the following measures:

- use industrial design skills and miniaturisation to reduce product size and unnecessary functions without reducing the utility value of the product.
- Reduce wastage of materials during production.
- Substitute recycled for primary materials.
- Substitute goods or services with inherently low material intensity for those with high intensity.
- Increase the product's lifetime.
- Use products more intensively or more efficiently during their lifetime.[26]

Product Rethink and Redesign

To date, most eco-innovation of product and process design has been incremental. This has contributed to a decrease of some emissions, to less damaging emissions and to some efficiency improvements in energy and materials use. However, a more fundamental and effective approach to environmental innovation is the complete redesign of processes and products. For example, the ban on CFCs has lead to the use of completely new coolants and propellants. A modest but useful example is retail aerosol products propelled solely by compressed air. The development of this benign CFC-substitute contrasts with industry's opinion, only a few years ago, that CFCs were essential for the required task.

This example also demonstrates that the degree of innovation required to achieve a dematerialised economy cannot be left to the individual firm. Governments have an important role to play in establishing standards, guidelines and a level playing field for all competitors in an industrial sector. Government can (and should) also provide incentives for eco-innovation – for example, through tax reform. Under these conditions, industry has the capacity to generate real eco-innovation in a short period of time. The role of government in eco-innovation is taken up in Chapter 8.

Virtually all products and processes should be subject to a sustainability life-cycle audit. In some cases, major changes towards dematerialisation will be possible. A major challenge is to overcome the 'planned obsolescence' of products, which is: 'A symptom of modern consumer society in which demand for new products stimulates needless consumption and results in excessive resource depletion and waste production'.[27] One option is described as 'upgradability' in which a product contains core elements which are designed for long life and modules which can be upgraded to enhance function and performance. Another possibility is shared access to common products. In Germany, shared automobiles for non car-owning households are administered by non-profit cooperatives. In future, audio, video and computer

25 Engineering Council op cit p33

26 Hille, J *The Environmental Space Concept: Implications for environmental reporting, policies and assessments* Copenhagen: European Environmental Agency, 1996

27 Bayley, N 'Making the most of life: Upgradability' *UK CEED Bulletin* no 48, autumn 1996

GUEST ESSAY 6.2

Izaak L G Van Melle

The Corporate Challenge of Sustainability

In my position as managing director of an internationally expanding company, I have come to consider sustainability as our greatest corporate challenge. Being aware of the necessity of making our economic objectives balance with available natural resources and the health of the ecosystem can cause moral conflicts for me as far as the objectives of our company are concerned. This is especially the case when opportunities for corporate growth conflict with our company's objective to be sustainable in the year 2005.

To balance the effects of our company's consumption of fossil fuels, approximately 5000 hectares of newly planted or protected trees could compensate in terms of acting as a sink for carbon dioxide emissions. Under normal trading circumstances, it is financially feasible for our company to support this level of afforestation, and we are working towards this goal. At the moment we have planted, or are protecting, approximately 3000 hectares of trees. Given that forests have many more functions than just absorbing CO_2, we believe that, in this way, our company is at least able to compensate for any damage we inflict on the environment worldwide. Tree planting may not be the ultimate solution to excess CO_2 emissions for the world economy, but for the time being this is a good approach, given that every year a staggering amount of forest disappears.

We are also looking for energy savings in new factory construction. For example, on our new building in China, we have ensured that the roof faces the sun to achieve optimum benefit from solar gain and solar panels. Depending upon the location, wind energy can also be cost-effective.

At each plant location we strive to define the optimum in order to achieve sustainability. The mix of solutions ranges from cost-effective measures to expensive technology such as photo-voltaic panels. Everything on location which contributes to the realisation of our sustainability objectives must be utilised. A long-term investment programme leading towards sustainability and reduced energy and materials consumption is drawn up in which, in generally, the most effective environmental investments come first.

Izaak Van Melle is Managing Director of Van Melle International, a confectionery company with operating companies worldwide, for instance in The Netherlands, China, the Philippines, Brazil and other countries.

equipment on one site with duplicate functions could be replaced by one on-site monitor, with the rest of the hardware and software centrally located and accessed via a cable connection.

Products also include the offices we work in and the houses we live in. For example, the new offices of the South Tyneside Groundwork Trust in the UK are 90 to 95 per cent self-sufficient, for a capital outlay of only 10 per cent more than for a conventional building. The office consumes less than half the energy of a conventional building, nearly all of it produced sustainably on-site, and will export electricity to the national grid much of the time. There are similar examples in many countries.

> ## Box 6.7 Message on a can of aerosol cleaner
>
> This new process uses the natural strength of air as the only propellant. The air is pumped into the can in the same way as a bicycle tyre. The efficiency and practicality of the aerosol is maintained. This new generation of aerosols gives the same performance as traditional sprays while respecting the environment.

If we wish to reach the target of a tenfold increase in average ecoefficiency, more far-reaching improvements in current production techniques are also required. A strategy of redesign and rethink will place demands on the decision processes of companies. Cramer and Stevels of Philips Electronics, for example, emphasise the relationship of long-term company strategy to eco-innovation.

Contrary to incremental improvements, relatively little experience has been gained within industry with the development and implementation of far-reaching, longer-term environmental product improvements. When these improvements are at stake, choices should be made in the earlier phases of product development, strategy development and know-how planning. Similarly, the time horizon of product planning will be extended to three to 15 years and even beyond. As a result, environmental improvements of this kind require decisions at the strategic company level.[28]

Transport Intensity of Products

Rethinking to generate the same end-use benefits more efficiently must also mean rethinking of product transport. In the first instance, dematerialisation will mean less product mass to move. Furthermore, a criteria of nearness, which can be called the proximity principle, means that spatial economic arrangements or financial system boundaries have to be designed to avoid unnecessary long-term transport of both persons and goods. Transport must pay the full economic cost, including costing the relative contribution to greenhouse gas emissions.

Certainly, there must be a drastic curtailment of the transport intensity of many consumer products; a typical case is the little retail yoghurt containers which regularly travel 4000 kilometres around Europe by truck. Another involves trousers motored from Spain to the Ukraine for sewing, and back to Spain for packing, before being trucked again to European countries for sale. Governments (and the European Union) allow this kind of irrational situation to be economically advantageous for industrialists by subsidising road-building and by failing to incorporate the environmental and social costs of transport in pricing structures.

28 Cramer and Stevels, Greening of Industry Conference, November 1996, Heidelberg

Figure 6.6

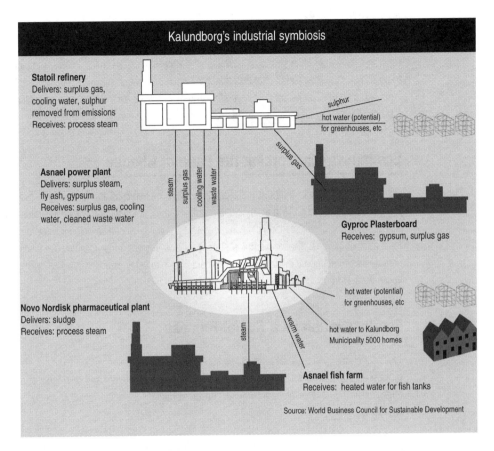

Kalundborg's industrial symbiosis

Statoil refinery
Delivers: surplus gas,
cooling water, sulphur
removed from emissions
Receives: process steam

sulphur
hot water (potential)
for greenhouses, etc

surplus gas

Asnael power plant
Delivers: surplus steam,
fly ash, gypsum
Receives: surplus gas, cooling
water, cleaned waste water

steam
surplus gas
cooling water
waste water

Gyproc Plasterboard
Receives: gypsum, surplus gas

Novo Nordisk pharmaceutical plant
Delivers: sludge
Receives: process steam

steam

warm water

hot water (potential)
for greenhouses, etc

hot water to Kalundborg
Municipality 5000 homes

Asnael fish farm
Receives: heated water for fish tanks

Source: World Business Council for Sustainable Development

On-Site Industrial Ecology

Reducing waste and material flows at the business level can be reinforced by on-site industrial ecology to increase material and energy efficiency. This approach is well known in European combined heat and light schemes, called cogeneration, where excess heat generated by an industrial process, such as a power plant, is used for heating offices or residential buildings. The power plant could also be burning waste materials, if this is more efficient than recycling or using primary fuel.

A more complex example is provided by the community of Kalundborg in Denmark, which has set out to be a prototype community for industrial development and cooperation. Here the wastes from industrial processes, such as hot water and excess energy, serve as inputs to other industrial processes, to agriculture in the form of fish farming and to the municipality. Figure 6.6 shows the interactions in Kalundborg.

Kalundborg evolved over time. A follow-on step is the development of purpose-built industrial estates where neighbouring companies use and reuse materials and the waste energy of their neighbours. Canada's new eco-industrial parks provide a good example. Here centralised 'utility islands' provide common services, including steam, electricity, hot or chilled water, industrial gases, compressed air, common effluent treatment facilities, heavy metal reclamation using reverse-osmosis, cogeneration, energy cascading, and the recycling of heat, water and other waste products. This common provision eliminates duplication of investment in technology and know-how in the resident industries, freeing resources for eco-innovation in the core business area.

The provision of utility islands is a profitable business in its own right; in turn, they enable companies to reduce substantially the capital expenditures required to set up new manufacturing or processing facilities. Eco-industrial parks are also a good way to attract new, clean industry to municipalities looking for inward investment with minimised ecological damage.

Eco-Innovation: Forcing the Pace of Change

With the growth of knowledge in materials science, a measure of delinking is already in progress – but there is a long way to go. The air-propelled aerosol mentioned above is not yet refillable, which would be a next step. The power station in Kalundborg is still burning coal, albeit cleanly, and thus contributing to fossil-fuel emissions. These examples show that eco-innovation is possible but also that a genuinely dematerialised economy will take time. If the process is to be encouraged, people must understand more about the nature of innovation and its unfolding.

Eco-Innovation as a Social Process

Just as technology is a social artefact, so eco-innovation is now understood to be the result of a complex process of social interaction as well as one of technical discovery and the application of new knowledge.[29] The process involves interaction and feedback in a social network, among different interest groups, between:

- different functional roles in the firm – not only research and development, technical and senior managerial, but other line areas such as personnel, marketing and purchasing departments;
- the firm and its industrial suppliers and customers;
- the firm and external sources of specialist knowledge, such as research institutes, universities, industry associations, other firms, regulators;
- the firm and other external stakeholders, such as sources of finance (shareholders, banks, insurance companies);
- the firm and the wider community, such as NGO pressure groups, local communities and individual customers; and
- the firm and levels of government or multilateral organisations.

The network-base process is described by Christie of Britain's Henley Centre for Forecasting:

29 Christie et al;
op cit p70–71

30 Christie et al
ibid

Innovation is driven not only by discoveries in research, nor simply by demands from the final customer, but also by a constant, more or less organised dialogue between the firm and groups at all points on the value chain. In short, innovation is a social process deriving from the development of a network of communications focused on the firm.[30]

Figure 6.7

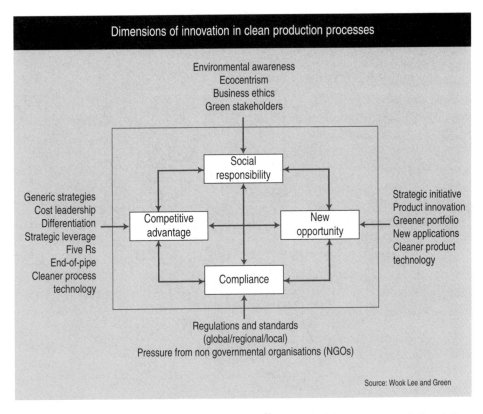

Dimensions of innovation in clean production processes

Environmental awareness
Ecocentrism
Business ethics
Green stakeholders

Social responsibility

Generic strategies
Cost leadership
Differentiation
Strategic leverage
Five Rs
End-of-pipe
Cleaner process
technology

Competitive advantage

New opportunity

Strategic initiative
Product innovation
Greener portfolio
New applications
Cleaner product
technology

Compliance

Regulations and standards
(global/regional/local)
Pressure from non governmental organisations (NGOs)

Source: Wook Lee and Green

31 Wook Lee, B and Green, K 'Towards commercial and environmental excellence: a green portfolio matrix' *Business Strategy and the Environment* vol 3:3, autumn 1994, p75

32 The diagram is influenced by Wiedner, H 'The capability of the capitalist state to "solve" environmental problems' paper presented at the World Congress of the International Political Science Association, Buenos Aires, 1991

The elements of the relationship are shown in Figure 6.7.[31] A particularly important aspect is the relationship of business to government, in terms of the use of regulation and incentives to drive innovation. This is discussed in the next section and we return to it again in the final chapter.

Eco-Innovation in the Political Interest Cycle

It took around 25 years from the first clear signs of environmental concern, such as Rachel Carson's seminal book on pesticides *The Silent Spring*, to achieve a broad consensus on environmental pollution and a level of reasonably functioning environmental institutions and policies. These institutions, many of which are effective in their own right, are nevertheless often marginalised from key decision structures in government and in society. A quantum leap in integrating environment and economic development needs to parallel the quantum leap in technology discussed here. The institutional prerequisites for embedding environmental space concepts in decision-making are discussed in Chapter 8.

How long will it take before eco-innovation becomes a core business activity for key economic actors, and governments, the world over? Can we expect positive developments by, say, the year 2010? If innovation is to be fostered, it helps to understand the process by which entrepreneurial innovation interacts with a growth of political interest on key policy issues. There are five phases of political interest and action, shown in Figure 6.8.[32] The first is one of ecological ignorance where only a few prescient people

Figure 6.8

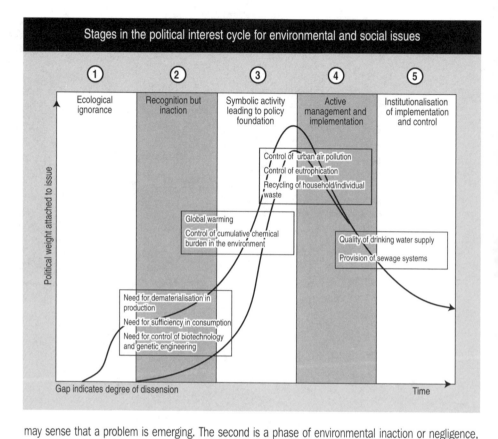

Stages in the political interest cycle for environmental and social issues

may sense that a problem is emerging. The second is a phase of environmental inaction or negligence, in which government remains passive in spite of growing proof of risks to health and the environment. Important information is usually ignored. Protest about the issue – for instance, from environmental organisations – is ignored or even suppressed. The third stage is one of symbolic activity, leading to policy formation. In the early part of this phase the problem is officially recognised and strategies are discussed, many of which will not be sufficient, or will be watered down to meet the perceived need of special interest groups and industry. There is still no full consensus over the nature of the problem, and some special interest groups will continue to argue that the problem is minor or does not exist. At the beginning of this phase large differences in opinion about the nature and extent of the problem and about its causes and effects usually exist. However, sooner or later responsible government reacts to the signals, often by gathering data on which to base a provisional view point as to the seriousness and extent of the problem, and by devising policy responses which can initially, or gradually, tackle the problem.[33] This provides a bridge to the fourth phase of active problem management. Here, a good degree of understanding and consensus about the particular problem is called for, alongside a partnership between government and business to develop solutions and efficient policies and practices. The final stage is institutionalisation of policy implementation and control, where the means of dealing with a problem become a routine function of governance and business management and refined and adjusted in a continuing process.

Of course, different problems rise up the political agenda at different times in different countries. This

33 Winsemius *Guests in Our Own Home; Thoughts on Environmental Management* McKinsey & Company, 1990. Winsemius provided the initial inspiration for Figure 6.8

dynamic flow is shown in Figure 6.8, which also gives current examples of key issues. The issue of sustainable production and consumption, for example, is only in phase two, with little attention or recognition beyond a few conferences and a mention in some specialised magazines and a few books. Concern about global warming is in the early symbolic period of phase three. There is a substantial amount of interest and debate, but some scientists associated with particular interest groups are still aggressively denying the emerging scientific proof, and governments have yet to take any real action to stem the problem beyond (mostly unmet) commitments not to let the problem spiral out of control. The problem of ozone depletion, on the other hand, is at phase four. Policies are increasingly effective, albeit with 50 years to go before problem resolution. Finally, in some countries, the monitoring and treatment of industrial effluents is at phase five – that is, a routine function of government and business. In other countries, things are not so far along and businesses routinely try to avoid regulation in this area.

This dynamic framework suggests, with moderate optimism, that the need for sustainable production and consumption will rise up the political agenda. It also suggests areas of action:

- basic and policy research on production and consumption issues and options for securing quality of life without ecological degradation;
- technological and business innovation by leading-edge companies;
- NGO campaigning to force the pace of change;
- communication among key stakeholders around the world to generate the process of mutual learning about the problem, which is a prerequisite for consensual action;
- quantitative indicators and targets, which address ecological, economic and social issues simultaneously; and
- government commitment to steady, long-term action.

But there are worries. Firstly, even at phase four, measures tend to ignore the interdependence of the ecosystem's components. For example, in addressing problems of fossil-fuel emissions which contribute to global warming, motor vehicle technology may be altered to control air pollution even while an irresponsible land-use planning system allows a low density urban sprawl of houses, shopping malls and offices which are unserviceable by public transport. These land-use patterns will promote car journeys many decades into the next century, and invariably the growth in traffic will overwhelm the degree of improvement achievable by changing vehicle technology. Even a quantum leap technology such as electric cars will not solve the overall problem, at least as long as electricity is produced by methods which contribute to global warming and the prices of electricity fail to encompass externalities. These methods, as noted in Chapter 3, include not only the obvious coal-fired power stations but imponded reservoirs for hydropower which release greenhouse gases.

A second problem is that inertia in the innovation process, and the relatively lengthy time it takes to marshal incontrovertible scientific evidence in challenging areas of science, means that problems are already serious before serious attention is directed towards them. For example, ozone depletion will remain a problem at least until the middle of the next century, and many of today's children will suffer additional skin cancers as a result. These types of cumulative impacts will continue to arise. For example, a recently documented rise in the incidence of brain tumours in the developed countries is hypothesised by American scientists to be related to one or more of the following factors or their interaction: occupational exposures to chlorinated hydrocarbons, organic solvents, paints and oils, pesticides, electromagnetic fields and chemical compounds used as artificial sweeteners, and, possibly, a history of dental x-rays.[34] Clearly, the amount of science required to untangle this issue will be substantial. This is typically the case where human–environment interactions are simultaneously interactive and dynamic.

One way forward is to institutionalise the precautionary principle, which argues that lack of scientific certainty is not a sufficient reason for postponing measures to prevent environmental degradation. This raises a host of issues about risk assessment in society, including the justification, need and benefit of technological development, the context of use, and public confidence in the trustworthiness of regulatory provisions and regulators and industry. The biggest problem is that there is tremendous pressure on regulatory mechanisms to take responsibility for wider social issues when the mechanisms in question are not an appropriate means for addressing key dimensions of such issues.[35] This is a common problem with environmental impact assessments, which can describe the effects of a new hydro dam or coal-fired power plant but can say nothing about whether energy conservation would not be a better option. Nor have regulatory mechanisms begun to deal with the cumulative, interactive risks of chemical pollution, because the science is still very weak. This reinforces the usefulness of environmental space which reduces toxic effects by reducing inputs at source, thus bypassing the problem.

Another step is to promote quantum leaps in sustainable production and consumption. These can result from technological breakthroughs as a result of research and development, but are even more likely when government and business combine forces to tackle serious issues. This happened at the end of the 1980s on the issue of ozone depletion. Both political attention and emissions of CFCs reached their peak. Well-aimed instruments were a result of both technological trial-and-error by industry and political commitment to the Montreal Protocol. A combination of levies, permissions and financial instruments and education have been used to reduce emissions. In the case of CFCs, the effects of those measures have resulted in a rapid decline in CFC consumption, at least in the countries that ratified the protocol. As CFCs ultimately proved relatively easy to replace, technological innovation was rapid.

Major technological developments are always possible. For example, a radical yet feasible technological shift will be that from a hydrocarbon-dominated global economy to one based upon solar energy and other renewable resources, a quantum leap which some scientists are already predicting.[36] Steady progress is important, too, because it creates the conditions which foster innovation, in business and by government.

The Role of Entrepreneurship in Eco-Innovation

The rate of technological change, and whether and when a quantum leap occurs, is related to factors such as the availability of capital, market operation and entrepreneurship. The attitudes of different key players regarding technological innovation is important for the speed of development and market penetration. The attitude depends both on the (self-) motivation of individuals and on the phase in the political interest cycle.

Midgely, Fussler and others propose a typology of entrepreneurs according to attitudes to innovation. Fussler proposes: innovators, early adaptors, majority adaptors and laggards.[37] Their involvement in technical and political aspects of environmental issues can be overlaid on the various phases of the

34 Hankey, B et al 'Brain and Other Nervous System Cancers' in Miller et al (eds) *Seer Cancer Statistics Review 1973–1990* Bethesda, Maryland: National Cancer Institute, 1993, ppIII.1-III.20

35 Mayer, S et al 'Uncertainty, Precaution and Decision Making' Brighton: ESRC Global Environmental Change Programme, *GEC Programme Briefings* no 8, 1996

36 Okkerse, C and Van Bekkum, H testimony to the Sustainable Technology Research Programme, The Netherlands

37 Fussler, C and James, P *Driving Eco-Innovation* London: Pitman, 1996

Figure 6.9

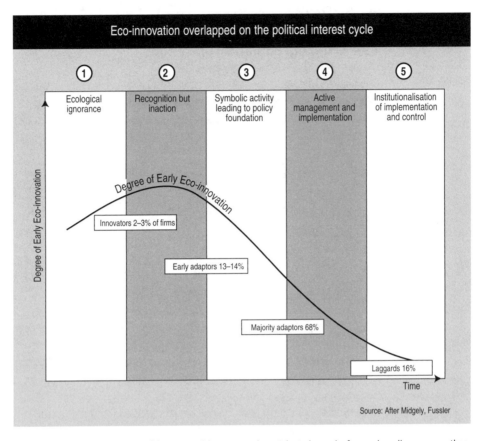

Eco-innovation overlapped on the political interest cycle

①	②	③	④	⑤
Ecological ignorance	Recognition but inaction	Symbolic activity leading to policy foundation	Active management and implementation	Institutionalisation of implementation and control

Degree of Early Eco-innovation

Innovators 2–3% of firms

Early adaptors 13–14%

Majority adaptors 68%

Laggards 16%

Time

Source: After Midgely, Fussler

policy cycle described above. Of course, this process is not just dynamic for each policy area; rather, there is a rolling dynamism to it, as the influence of innovators drives forward the process of both policy and eco-innovation in business. This is shown in Figure 6.9. One effect of innovation is to force the pace of change.

Innovation is not only good for the environment: it is good business to be ahead of competitors in tackling new markets. For example, Fussler asks:

> *How does this chaotic, turbulent world of value migration and ever-changing networks relate to sustainable development? One implication is that the status quo is not an option. Whether sustainable development happens or not, the world is not going to stay the same. The lesson for innovators is to understand what customers will need in future. This is where a sustainability perspective provides a bridge to the long term. One rail of this is the demographic drivers which are changing customer values and wants. The other is the likelihood that products will be reshaped by rising resource and environmental costs as we press against the limits of our planet.*[38]

38 Fussler, ibid

GUEST ESSAY 6.3

Claude Fussler

Can Eco-Innovation Be Legislated?

Eco-innovators decide to be part of the solution rather than defenders of the status quo. They look for unmet needs within the sustainability debate. They aim at a delicate balance – more quality of life for a larger number of people, at less environmental burden. But they don't forget the importance of positive financial returns. A bankrupt enterprise with a stranded initiative achieves nothing for society.

Eco-innovators need space and freedom. They are driven by their understanding of society's needs and an intuition of the things that shape the future. They build reality from a chance event and imagine the undreamt solution. They have tenacity and a passion for meeting their customers' needs.

Direct legislation can do little to foster eco-innovation and may even stifle creativity and enterprise. Legislation didn't invent the transistor, the laser, photo-voltaics or any of the other technologies that are changing life for the better at this turn of the century. Legislation comes after great ideas are born. But the hand of the legislator can help the process of change. It can shape markets, hasten or delay the adoption of new processes, reduce risk and ban obsolete, dangerous products and damaging consumer habits. Policy-makers who are sensitive to the dynamics of innovation will encourage sustainable consumption habits. This will reduce the risk of market failure when eco-innovators launch ultra-low-impact products and services.

Governments, therefore, can do much to encourage eco-innovation, such as:

- remove subsidies from resource-intensive processes and consumer habits;
- provide incentives to adopt eco-efficient solutions;
- facilitate access to venture capital for the innovators dedicated to breakthroughs in eco-efficiency; and
- sensitise consumers and entrepreneurs to the positive opportunities in sustainable development.

Claude Fussler is Vice President for Public Affairs, New Business and Environment of Dow Chemical Europe SA and the author of *Driving Eco-Innovation*.

The relationship between business innovation and government policy is potentially productive for eco-innovation. Because innovative companies invariably anticipate long-range global trends and their market impacts, business innovators are often steps ahead of government policy, which tends to be most influenced by the agenda set by early and late majority adaptors. This is not surprising, as these non-innovators are in the majority and government tends to respond to majority interests. One problem is that in the current political climate, it is difficult for governments to put the long-term interests of all citizens above short-term demands for lower taxes, etc, or for politicians to look beyond the next election. Therefore, political reform and democratic renewal are critical and intrinsic to sustainability reforms.

Where innovation is stifled by short-term interests, society, environment and business all lose out. We return to this issue in the final chapter, when we argue for government to promote debate on different options for achieving sustainable societies within the boundaries of environmental space.

Conclusion

Eco-innovation and entrepreneurship can make major contributions towards realising a sustainable, dematerialised economy. Although this chapter has reflected our enthusiasm for the potential benefits of technological development and eco-innovation, they are necessary but not sufficient for the changes in production and consumption patterns which must take place. This is for two reasons:

- human nature embodies a strong propensity towards overconsumption. Our genetic programming to secure life-supporting basic needs for oneself and one's family easily and unwittingly extends into a habit of overconsumption which is hard to break. As long as these habits exist as market opportunities, companies will be around to exploit those opportunities. Improvements in technological efficiency must be complemented by changes in social values, cultures and ethics towards sufficiency, and by legal, financial and economic mechanisms which will encourage us to live within the bounds of environmental space.
- Eco-innovation does not resolve the inherent socio-economic disadvantages of capitalism which, although it is recognised as the best game in town, is far from perfect. There are endemic constraints such as poverty, structural unemployment arising from the replacement of labour by capital, and a strong tendency for business to externalise environmental costs and to encourage overconsumption for short-term profitability. These constraints can substantially reduce quality of life, even while GDP is rising. The next chapter examines some of these issues.

This is not to suggest, however, that the business sector cannot also make an important contribution to these larger issues, which go beyond eco-efficiency. In particular, sophisticated, innovator companies genuinely concerned about sustainable production and consumption, and about the future world in which their markets will exist, will not only work within existing structural constraints, but will question them and propose constructive changes. They will use their capacity for trends analysis and strategic forecasting to assess the conditions under which global sustainable development, and sustainable profit-making, can be achieved – for the good of business and for the good of human life.

CHAPTER

7

Sufficiency: Rethinking the Consumer Society

Introduction

Like many things in life, consumerism is a two-edged sword. There is great virtue in competition and choice over goods and services. The consumer rights movement all over the world has empowered households to secure better value for money in the things they buy. Virtually no one would prefer the shoddy, outdated goods, and disdainful and inefficient services, which characterised those provided by monopolistic suppliers, either in the state or the private sector. Consumer power, too, has the potential to supplement regulation in promoting environmental stewardship by big business.

On the other side of the coin, consumerism is a transactional way of life: everything is reduced to a price and things which cannot be priced are often marginalised. We have argued that enough goods and services can quickly become too much 'stuff'. The continuing growth in production inputs caused by excess consumption is fuelled by economic and social pressures, and advertising causes confusion between needs and wants in consumer society. This growth outstrips gains from ecoefficiency, thus guaranteeing the rapid ecological deterioration which affects all countries. As Herman Daly explains, the cargo on the boat may be distributed with great efficiency, but the boat will still sink under too much weight. Efficiency without sufficiency is counterproductive; Wolfgang Sachs argues that the latter has to define the boundaries of the former.[1]

1 Sachs, W The Political Anatomy of Sustainable Development Wuppertal: Wuppertal Institute, no 35, 1995

Nor can economic growth be relied on anymore to increase the employment prospects or the household income of the average family. Economic growth is too often jobless growth, so its benefits are not spread around society. It can also be wealthless growth, when the real wealth of societies is measured by the quality of life enjoyed by its residents, young and old, rich and poor. Unsustainable economic growth reduces quality of life, rather than contributes to it. As we move into a new century, therefore, this is an ideal time to question the rationale of growth. We also need to examine the values that underpin consumer culture, and ask whether material values have taken precedence over what Ingeborg Refling Hagen calls 'life values'.[2] Material values, such as money, power and fame, decrease in value the more they are shared. Life values, such as love, hope, humour and community spirit, increase the more they are shared. We argue that to live within environmental space, ecoefficiency must be matched with a concern for the balance between material and life values, as well as sufficiency, which is living better on less.

It is a good time to raise these questions because consumer culture is spreading around the world, especially in the newly industrialising countries, as incomes rise, and because of global marketing, advertising and satellite TV. As with any two-edged sword, this spread of consumer culture, with its attendant value system which suggests that 'you are what you buy', brings benefits and costs. The costs of consumerism include: stressful inducements to consume more and more even if quality of life declines as a result; excessive individualism; a deterioration in the quality of time and rapid consumption of space; a deterioration of the public or civic realm and community life; and impacts on working life in terms of overwork by some and unemployment for others. Each area is discussed in turn.

Box 7.1 Defining efficiency and sufficiency

Efficiency = getting the same goods and services out of less material.
Sufficiency = getting the same welfare out of fewer goods and services.

Is More Always Better?

The first step is to question the potent but simplistic notion that more is always better. Many people around the world, faced with an onslaught of consumerism, or caught in a treadmill of overconsumption, are asking the same question. They realise that more and more goods is not always better. They wonder whether industrialism is still serving the human race, or whether the situation has somehow become reversed – too many people working harder and harder with less satisfaction and more insecurity to service a growth imperative that no longer makes sense. This means questioning the direction of modern life as it has evolved in the last half of the 20th century. Those who have asked important questions include Islamic thinkers in Asia, who are concerned with 'the social disintegration that comes as a package with consumer capitalism',[3] indigenous peoples in North and South America, the country teams of Sustainable Europe and the North–South Project, and millions of Americans who are choosing voluntary restraint, or downshifting, in favour of lower earnings, less stress and more quality time for family, community and the pursuit of genuine happiness.

Environmental space builds on this questioning. We do not argue that consumerism is inherently bad, because we all enjoy its obvious benefits. But experience tells that there must be more to life than material goods if it is to be worth living. It is important to question because, as human beings, we have an enormous advantage. We can alter our lifestyles, and we can achieve multiple goals in the socio-economic, cultural and spiritual realms of life. As we have suggested, the simplistic dictates of the

2 Discussed in Hareide, D 'Has Quality of Life Improved in Western Europe? The Quest for the Magic Message of Numbers' Oslo: unpublished paper, 1995

3 Habib Chirzin cited in Seabrook, J In the Cities of the South: Scenes from a Developing World London: Verso, 1995

> # Box 7.2 Redefining the American Dream
>
> For many years, North America has been dominated by a central economic and cultural principle: more is always better. This core tenet has largely defined our economic system, household behaviour and mass culture. Yet, in recent years, many people have begun to question and challenge this fundamental aspect of North American life. Faced with a dramatic gulf between those who have and those who have not, an environment increasingly degraded by urban sprawl and waste, and a civic society characterised more by consuming than by caring, many individuals are asking 'how much is enough?' Consumerism is not inherently bad, but when it reaches excessive levels and becomes our primary preoccupation as a people, it damages our moral, social and environmental fabric.
>
> Center for a New American Dream, 'Mission Statement', 1996

market economy may provide necessary, but not sufficient, aspirations for high quality of life. There is also substantial evidence that, in affluent societies, quality of life begins to decline once a certain level of material affluence is achieved.

Nevertheless, proconsumerist trends are strong and cannot be ignored when considering the relationship of the market economy to environmental space. Consumerism is fuelled by advertising, which equates overconsumption with a modern lifestyle. Consumerism exerts a powerful hold, nowhere more so than in the United States, and consumerism as a way of life is in danger of spreading worldwide to become one of the most powerful ideologies of the 21st century. Yet it is entirely possible that consumerism is an inadequate and inappropriate value system for a world facing mounting environmental crises. William Leiss argues that:

> *In a lifestyle that is dependent upon an endlessly rising level of consumption of material goods, individuals are led to misinterpret the nature of their needs and to misunderstand the relationship between their needs and the ways in which they may be satisfied.*[4]

The spread of Western-style consumerism across the globe is also in danger of eroding core values in traditional cultures. Deep-rooted cultures, such as those in China, India and Africa, are now facing fundamental changes because of the criss-crossing encounters of individuals, institutions, societies and cultures on an unknown scale, and because of the penetration of global communication and advertising which can initiate value change. Although new possibilities for synthesis and cooperation are opening up, this trend may also result in a severe loss of cultural diversity just at the point when we are questioning the dominant development paradigm. The Swedish sociologist Bertil Egero summarises the situation:

> *The post-industrial countries are facing the challenge of an ultimately necessary transition to ecologically sustainable economies. Today, however, when history is*

4 Leiss, W *The Limits to Satisfaction* Toronto: University of Toronto Press, 1986

said to have come to an end, there is not even a theory to guide our way to a realisa-
tion of such a transition. A similar uncertainty concerns the way forward for many
countries in the South. I believe I am justified in interpreting the crisis in these
countries as in no small part a cultural crisis, a result of West-supported develop-
ment strategies aimed to 'bypass history' and carry the country in a swift change to
a modern industrial society.[5]

From Sustainable to the Slippery Slope of Overconsumption

Sustainable consumption is the use of goods and services to meet basic needs and to bring a better quality of life, while minimising the use of natural resources, toxic materials and emissions of waste and pollution over the life-cycle, so as not to jeopardise the needs of future generations.

Certainly, consuming basic resources, such as freshwater, to stay alive is sustainable, at least when there is enough to go around. But when does sustainable consumption become unsustainable? The issue is difficult because the typical trajectory of a national economic development path, the early stages of GDP growth, encompasses two aims: meeting basic needs, which is necessary consumption, and providing for life-fulfilling additional consumption based on products from the marketplace, as well as opportunities for education, leisure and cultural enjoyment, which fulfill human potential. At the family level, acquiring consumer goods is an extension of this drive to satisfy basic needs and can bring substantial satisfaction and increases in quality of life – up to a point.

Beyond this optimum level of consumption lies what we might call the slippery slope of overconsumption. It is never clear where overconsumption begins – with one car per household or with three or four, as is now common for the middle classes in North America? The effects can vary for different households. There is also a strong social dimension in terms of what Americans call keeping up with the Joneses, or what Keynes called the shift from absolute to relative consumption. This describes the tendency to buttress our social status by achieving consumption rates which equal or better those of our neighbours. This happens even if family life and valuable time with children or other loved ones has to be given up to achieve the prevailing pattern of consumption.

While it may be difficult to say at what point overconsumption begins in any particular society, the debilitating effects are increasingly obvious. Certainly, globally, the richest one fifth of the world's population are not only well past the point of rising quality of life, but the pollution they are generating as a result of resource consumption is threatening the future of the planet. In Chapter 3 we documented how, in North America, alternative measures which focus on quality of life, rather than crude GDP, show a marked decline over the past 20 years. Other systems for assessing quality of life demonstrate how GDP ignores many key life-fulfilling aspects of community – for example, voluntary work for neighbourhood, church and civic groups – because they are unpaid aspects of life. In America, community activities are in decline as people spend more time shopping and watching television.[6] Other measures, such as the Index of Sustainable Economic Welfare (ISEW), show the folly of assuming quality of life is rising, as measured by GDP, when we are depleting the natural capital upon which future quality of life may depend.[7] If a forest is cut down, or farmland is turned into a carpark, GDP tells us that more money flows

5 Egero, B 'No Longer North and South – The New Challenges of Demographic-Economic Interrelations' paper presented to the International Conference on Human Ecology, Göteborg, 1991

6 Schor, J B *The Overworked American: The Unexpected Decline of Leisure* New York: Basic Books, 1991

7 New Economics Foundation *Growing Pains: An Index of Sustainable Economic Welfare for the United Kingdom* London: NEF, 1994

around the economy and we mistakenly think this is progress. Finally, GDP ignores the profound income inequality which characterises some developed, and many developing, countries. This taints aspirations by demonstrating, all too starkly, that the richest are the best off, and can lead to crime and ill-health which destabilises societies. GDP is silent here too.

Of course, the appropriate balance between market and public provision is an area where there is no ready answer. The market economy, and markets themselves – whether local places for trading or in terms of the global capitalism – are natural and exciting aspects of human life and serve powerful economic functions and social needs. Their role must be considered and built upon in a reexamination of consumerist values. New messages must be sent by consumers to the marketplace, rather than allow the marketplace to dictate the pattern of consumption. The Sustainable Europe Campaign is attempting to encourage such a critique by working with the grain of markets rather than against them. In other areas of life, however, such as education, health provision or public transport, purchasing power in the marketplace is a poor mechanism for distribution, particularly when the total framework of costs and benefits to both individuals and society is used to assess distribution mechanisms. In these cases, government, and the non-profit voluntary and service sectors of society, can have an important role in the allocation of goods.

The rest of this chapter initiates a programme for reconsidering the relationship between consumerism and quality of life, and for promoting sufficiency. This recognises that the way forward is to encourage a change of values towards a more sophisticated form of consumption and market mechanisms, based on better knowledge of potential dimensions of quality of life. The chapter looks at the impact of consumption on the household on what we call the public realm of social interaction and on working life.

Understanding Consumption and Quality of Life

Probably the most difficult aspect of criticising what has come to be called the consumer lifestyle is assessing when necessary and useful consumption stops and the slippery slope of overconsumption begins. A simple diagram (Figure 7.1) illustrates the problem. The beginning of the upward curve describes a low-consumption, non-industrial lifestyle – for example, farming or grazing in Sulawesi or Mali or the early days of North American farming, hunter-gatherers in the Brazilian rainforest, or agrarian peasants in 18th-century Scotland. Within this low-consumption lifestyle there may be inadequate basic needs: food, shelter, clothing, clean water and so on, and this is unsustainable. Conversely, many of these simpler lifestyles are, or were, sustainable. There are also unsustainable industrial lifestyles characterised by inadequate consumption, often within the context of a majority of society having adequate or more than adequate consumption.

The area towards the top of the curve ('S' to 'D') describes the transition to a sustainable, industrial lifestyle where the advantages of modern science, education and medicine generate the secure fulfilment of basic needs, maximise quality of life in a relatively sound environment, and lengthen life expectancy and reduce infant mortality. Problems associated with overconsumption surface on the downward slope, which represents an increasingly unsustainable lifestyle, and in which quality of life is decreasing despite rising income levels. Unfortunately it is never clear when we are on the downward

Figure 7.1

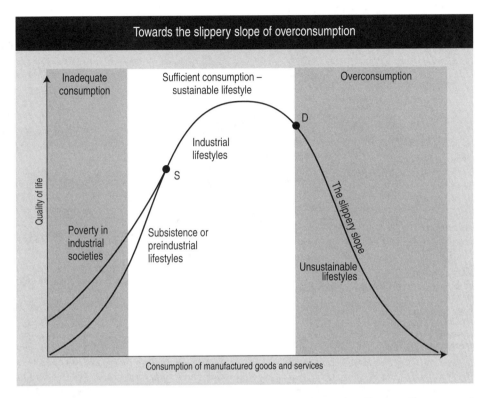

Towards the slippery slope of overconsumption

Inadequate consumption

Sufficient consumption – sustainable lifestyle

Overconsumption

Industrial lifestyles

D

S

Quality of life

Poverty in industrial societies

Subsistence or preindustrial lifestyles

The slippery slope

Unsustainable lifestyles

Consumption of manufactured goods and services

slope and therefore passing point 'D' into the realm of overconsumption. The beguiling nature of consumer goods makes it all the more difficult to make any detached assessment of their relative value, especially since these goods reinforce our sense of status in society. Furthermore, some households in society will already be living sustainable lifestyles, even while others, often the most prominent or powerful in society, are on the downward slope.

The location of point 'D' is the nub of political debate about sustainable development. Societies may pass well beyond point 'D' before becoming painfully aware of the environmental and social consequences of over-consumption. For example, the bioeconomist Georgescu-Roegen argued many years ago that humankind becomes addicted to all the technological devices which enhance our physical powers and provide us with increased comfort.[8] How many of us can say honestly that we do not enjoy flying off to an exotic location, whatever the effect on the atmosphere? It is this kind of addiction which drives our endless pursuit of natural resources, and takes us out of the zone of sustainable development. For many of the lower-income countries, including Eastern Europe and the former Soviet Union, as well as the Asian NICs, the question is whether they can design their emerging societies to remain within zone 'SD' while they still have the chance. Their scope for action offers both a risk and an opportunity.

Many lower-income regions around the world lie broadly within the sustainable part of the curve today, from Portugal to Kerala, given that their consumption levels are generally within the bounds of environmental space while their achievements on social indicators, such as education and infant mortality, are as high as many so-called developed countries. This suggests that one means of rethinking quality of life is to look at areas of the world that have a sustainable resource use and use low levels of non-

8 Georgescu-Roegen, N *Energy and Economic Myths: Institutional and Analytical Essays* Oxford: Pergamon, 1976

9 Sen, A 'What did you learn in the world today?' *American Behavioral Scientist* vol 34, pp530–548, 1991

References from p 141:

10 Durning, A in Brown, L (ed) *State of the World 1991* London: Earthscan, 1991

11 DeLillo, D *Mao II* London: Jonathan Cape, 1991

12 For a discussion, see Giddens, A *Modernity and Self-Identity: Self And Society In Late Modern Age* Cambridge: Polity Press, 1991; and Carley, M and Christie, I *Managing Sustainable Development* London: Earthscan, 1992

Table 7.1

Life expectancy and GDP per capita		
Country	Life expectancy at birth	GDP per capita (1993 US dollars)
Japan	79.6	20,680
Sweden	78.3	17,900
Greece	77.7	8,950
Spain	77.7	13,660
Netherlands	77.5	17,340
Costa Rica	76.4	5,680
USA	76.1	24,680
Barbados	75.7	10,570
Cuba	75.4	3,000
Portugal	74.7	10,720
Belize	73.7	4,610
Georgia	72.9	1,750
Sri Lanka	72.0	540

Source: UNDP, *Human Development Report 1996*

renewable energy, but also have a high quality of life, as measured by infant mortality, literacy and life expectancy. Sen, for example, suggests comparing GDP per capita and life expectancy at birth in different countries.[9] Table 7.1 does this for a number of countries. The difference in quality of life compared to GDP, and thus resource consumption, is paralleled by other indicators. Sen attributes the difference to well-coordinated government policies in health, education and social security.

In another example, Kerala State in southern India has been proposed as a model of sustainable development by Bill Alexander of the Food First Institute in California. In Kerala, a per capita GDP of around US$300 compared with US$29,000 in the United States indicates a very low throughput of industrial products and generation of pollution. Yet Kerala, for historical and political reasons, has a low birth rate, very near the American average; low infant mortality; a male life expectancy of 70 years, compared to 72 for an American; and an adult literacy rate of 100 per cent. To find similar indices of quality of life, one needs to look to European countries such as Spain and Portugal, themselves on the lower end of consumption on the European scale. Alexander suggests that Americans become ecotourists in Kerala to learn something of the true nature of sustainable development.

> Pursuit of economic success must be balanced by a healthy sense of values and concern for each other. An overemphasis on material well-being can warp a peoples' value system.
>
> Goh Chok Tong, Prime Minister of Singapore

At the other end of the spectrum, trends in consumer culture are best monitored in the USA – the undisputed leader in the per capita consumption of almost everything – where 5 per cent of the world's population consume, each year, one third of the Earth's resources traded in that year. Alan Durning notes that compared with the 1950s, Americans now own on average twice as many cars, drive 2.5 times as far, use 21 times as much plastic, and travel 25 times as much by air as their parents did.[10] But there is not a shred of evidence that Americans are happier than the Keralese as a result.

Indeed, the achievement of high levels of income and consumption often comes to seem empty or hollow. Many people admit to feeling confused and oppressed by what American novelist Don DeLillo calls the 'blur and glut...the too much of everything' of the consumer culture.[11] In overconsuming societies, the super abundance of consumer choices and media threaten the individual with sensory overload. Coupled with an erosion of religious belief in consumer societies, a feeling of personal meaning-lessness develops.[12]

Income and Happiness

There is no consistent correlation between national or individual income and happiness. A pioneering study in this area has been undertaken by Veenhoven, who initiated a global comparison of measures of happiness set against levels of income per capita.[13] The results are summarised in Figure 7.2. Although studies of this nature are methodologically difficult, Veenhoven demonstrates clearly that the richer the country, the smaller the correlation between income level and individual happiness.[14] He discovered that beyond a certain per capita income level, money no longer creates happiness, which derives from other non-material factors. These findings are borne out at the national level in a Norwegian study by Hareide, who found that current levels of perceived well-being were about the same in 1993 as in 1960, in spite of a trebling of GDP.[15]

Other studies in both Europe and North America confirm that, above the poverty line, say for some 80 per cent of the population, there is no correlation which can be found between increased income and increased happiness.[16] In part, this is because expectations, fuelled by advertising and social pressures, rise with income, but satisfactions do not. So there is always an element of dissatisfaction which increased income cannot cure. A survey of a large sample of Americans, reported in the next section, summarised its conclusions on happiness in this way: 'We are the richest people on earth and in history, and yet many of us are not happy. We are trying to meet non-material needs with material goods'.[17]

13 Veenhoven, R Happiness in Nations: The study of life satisfaction Rotterdam: Erasmus University, 1993; see also the discussion in Spangenberg et al Sustainable Europe: The Study Brussels: Friends of the Earth Europe, 1995

14 For a discussion of indicators of quality of life, see Carley, M Social Measurement and Social Indicators London: Allen and Unwin, 1981

15 Hareide, D The Good Norway Gyldenal, 1990

16 Bedell, J 'Life and Work in the Balance' The Independent 23 June 1996

17 Merck Family Fund Redefining the American Dream: The Search for Sustainable Consumption Conference Report, 1995, p6

Figure 7.2

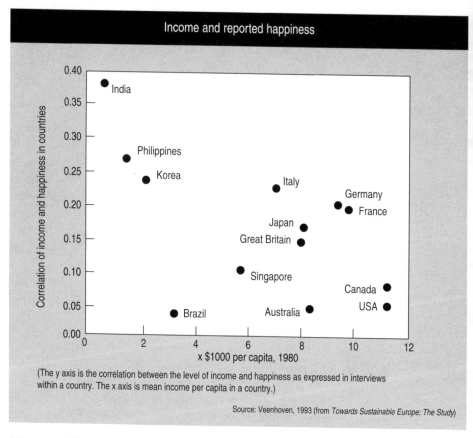

Income and reported happiness

(The y axis is the correlation between the level of income and happiness as expressed in interviews within a country. The x axis is mean income per capita in a country.)

Source: Veenhoven, 1993 (from *Towards Sustainable Europe: The Study*)

Material Values: Dissatisfaction as a Way of Life?

Dissatisfaction with high industrial wage rates in a capitalist society is nothing new. Charles Kettering of General Motors summed up the role of marketing and advertising in 1929 as 'the organised creation of dissatisfaction'. John Kenneth Galbraith said the same: 'Production has to create the wants it seeks to satisfy.' According to Juliet Schor: 'Advertising had to persuade consumers to acquire things they most certainly did not need.'

Industrialisation in the 19th and 20th centuries and the rise of market-dependent mass consumption have always been two sides of the same coin. Mass consumption also fuels individualism; on the one hand, it enables households to separate themselves from their historical social role of self-production, with consumption attempting to provide a sense of meaning and self-definition in life. Employers have real incentives to keep work hours long, and in Schor's words, 'one of capitalism's most enduring myths is that it has reduced human toil'.

Dissatisfaction is not the only cost. Modern materialist society extracts a high price for prosperity. For example, Schor has charted a 40 per cent decline of leisure time and the coincident rise of working time, and work-related stress and disease in America in the past 25 years.[18] This is due to what she calls the 'insidious cycle of work-and-spend' where a never-ending process of consumption must be paid for by

18 Schor op cit

long hours, which must be rewarded by more consumption, and so on. It is no accident: workers who are earning a lot of money because they work long hours provide the market for the very products they are producing, and never mind if they do not really need the goods in question. The consumption becomes the reward for the hard work and the long hours.

Nevertheless, it cannot be a very satisfying reward: the conditions of dissatisfaction must be maintained, or markets for useless products would disappear under a gale of common sense. We become addicted to consumption, which provides no lasting satisfaction. Schor calls this the work-and-spend disease:

> As people became accustomed to the material rewards of prosperity, desires for leisure time were eroded. They increasingly looked to consumption to give satisfaction, even meaning, to their lives. In both the workplace and the home, progress has been translated into more goods and services, rather than more free time. Consumerism traps us as we become habituated to the good life, emulating our neighbors, or just get caught up in the social pressures created by everyone else's choices. Work-and-spend has become a mutually reinforcing and powerful syndrome – a seamless web we somehow keep choosing, without even meaning to.

We have created a diagram which summarises the problem in Figure 7.3.

Although the growth of long work hours and the decline of leisure, at least in Anglo–American societies, has been marked in the past three decades, it represents more than a temporary phenomenon: it is the natural tendency of capitalism. This is because it is rational from the point of view of the profit-making firm, even if it locks workers into an irrational situation. The tendency lessened in the early 20th century, due to the rise of strong industrial unions, who secured reductions in working hours as a main policy plank. But the weakening of the unions since, and their near emasculation in the 1980s in many countries, accounts for the reestablishment of work-and-spend in the recent past.

The Lure of Positional Goods

The idea that there is something fundamentally self-defeating in modern patterns of overconsumption was identified by Fred Hirsch in his highly perceptive assessment *The Social Limits to Growth*. He analysed the widespread dissatisfaction that accompanies overconsumption and related it to the inevitable decline in the scarcity of what he called positional goods. These confer status or superiority only if they remain scarce, an unlikely proposition in the mass materialist culture of a full world economy. As positional goods become widely available, their value and the satisfactions they offer decline.

The car is a good example of a positional good – what freedom it must have given to those first drivers in the early part of the 20th century! Is it any wonder that car advertising almost always shows a lone car speeding through a spectacular remote countryside? Of course, the reality is profoundly different. Today, many people in the world from Manila to Minneapolis to Mauritius spend a good portion of their lives either trapped in traffic jams, or trying to figure out how to rearrange their lives to avoid them, for example by leaving for work at five in the morning. As automobile congestion spreads in space and

Figure 7.3

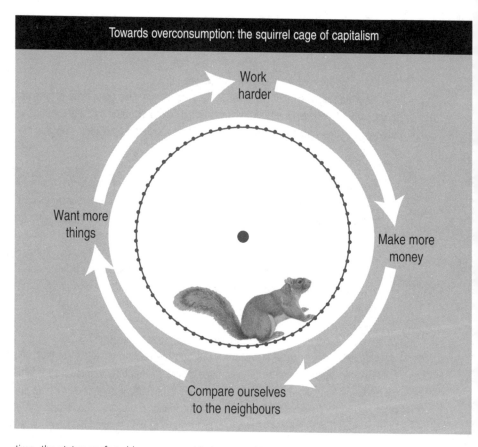

Towards overconsumption: the squirrel cage of capitalism

Work harder

Want more things

Make more money

Compare ourselves to the neighbours

time, the status conferred by car ownership becomes just a shadow of what it once was. For instance, rising car ownership fuels suburbanisation and suburban values, which reduces demand for public transport and gobbles up scarce farmland. Soon enough, car travel is not a positional good but a bare, and often unpleasant, necessity of life.

If pursuit of positional goods is a blind alley in terms of life satisfaction, why does it appear to remain so attractive to members of consumer societies? Our ability to perceive the futility of pursuing positional goods in a materialistic lifestyle, often at the expense of more valuable activities such as enjoyment of family life, is made doubly difficult by a number of factors. The first problem is that not only do people use goods to define their social status, but they become dependent on consumption because they substitute external goods for fulfilment of inner needs. And the more an individual uses consumption to satisfy inner needs, the more importance they are likely to attach to the use of material goods as an indication of social standing. The result is a consumerist society in which the overconsumption of material goods becomes the pinnacle of achievement. Here, too, for the majority of people, mass consumption is achieved but at a price where labour becomes more and more stressful and controlled, a point we return to below.

The second problem is the pervasive influence of advertising. This, even in spite of our knowledge of what is happening, structures values systems in favour of materialism. World advertising expenditure is

Figure 7.4

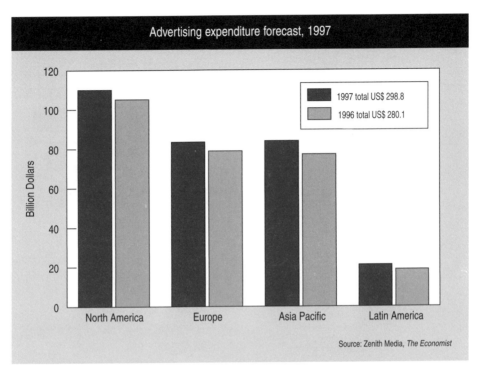

Advertising expenditure forecast, 1997

Source: Zenith Media, *The Economist*

expected to reach US$299 billion per year in 1997, of which US$110 billion will be spent in encouraging North Americans to consume yet more. Advertising expenditure is growing by about 6 per cent per year (see Figure 7.4).

Another powerful constraint is the steady process of reorganising society in a way which favours consumption of positional goods. This is caused by the tendency, in most societies, for the most politically and economically powerful to be the first to acquire those goods, or to benefit from their consumption. We mentioned the restructuring of Western societies around the car and the impact of mass tourism. For example, the appropriation (consumption) of 50 of the 52 beaches of the island of Mauritius by hotels owned by wealthy domestic and overseas business interests confines local people to

> Holidays and access to desirable places are also positional goods, and their value to the consumer is diminished once they become widely available. Exotic locations fill up with Western tourists and native cultures become more and more like the ones back home. Unspoilt landscapes attract more and more visitors, whose presence requires the construction of more roads, car parks and other facilities, thus rapidly spoiling the scenery and the atmosphere. The syndrome is increasingly familiar: the devaluation and destruction by tourism of the very thing which the tourist comes to see.
>
> Michael Carley and Ian Christie[19]

19 Carley, M and Christie, I op cit

Figure 7.5

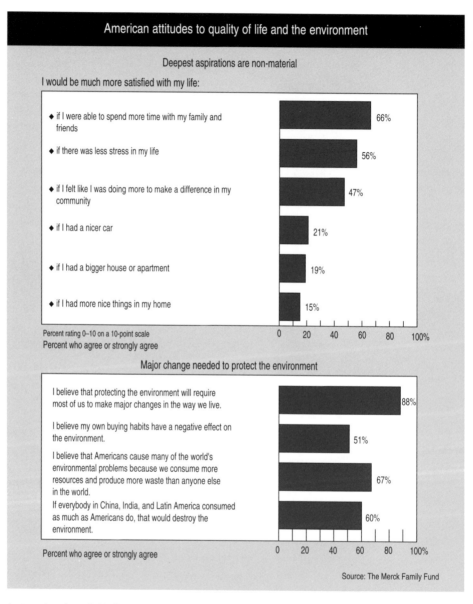

American attitudes to quality of life and the environment

Deepest aspirations are non-material

I would be much more satisfied with my life:

- ◆ if I were able to spend more time with my family and friends — 66%
- ◆ if there was less stress in my life — 56%
- ◆ if I felt like I was doing more to make a difference in my community — 47%
- ◆ if I had a nicer car — 21%
- ◆ if I had a bigger house or apartment — 19%
- ◆ if I had more nice things in my home — 15%

Percent rating 0–10 on a 10-point scale
Percent who agree or strongly agree

Major change needed to protect the environment

- I believe that protecting the environment will require most of us to make major changes in the way we live. — 88%
- I believe my own buying habits have a negative effect on the environment. — 51%
- I believe that Americans cause many of the world's environmental problems because we consume more resources and produce more waste than anyone else in the world. — 67%
- If everybody in China, India, and Latin America consumed as much as Americans do, that would destroy the environment. — 60%

Percent who agree or strongly agree

Source: The Merck Family Fund

just two locations. Aside from the inequality of the situation, which evolved in the space of a few decades, it confirms that package tourism is the favoured form of 'beach consumption'.

What Americans Feel about Overconsumption

A recent survey of around 4000 Americans, in four very different cities and towns, bears this out and gives a more detailed picture of the effects of work-and-spend. This was initiated by the Merck Family

Figure 7.6

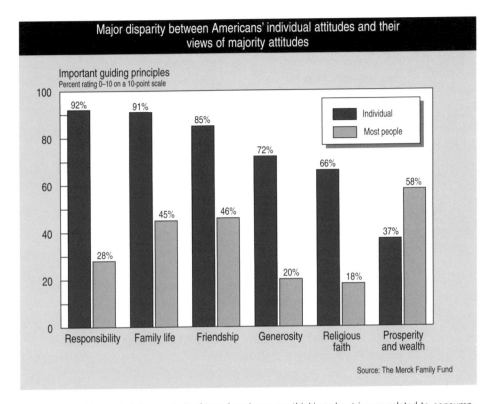

Major disparity between Americans' individual attitudes and their views of majority attitudes

Important guiding principles
Percent rating 0–10 on a 10-point scale

Legend:
- Individual
- Most people

Responsibility: 92%, 28%
Family life: 91%, 45%
Friendship: 85%, 46%
Generosity: 72%, 20%
Religious faith: 66%, 18%
Prosperity and wealth: 37%, 58%

Source: The Merck Family Fund

Fund and provides a statistical portrait of how Americans are thinking about issues related to consumption, environment and quality of life (see Figure 7.5). The feelings of Americans are instructive. In the Merck survey, 89 per cent of Americans agreed that 'buying and consuming is the American way'. But the survey also revealed a deep concern about excessive materialism: 82 per cent felt that most Americans 'buy and consume far more than we need' and 86 per cent felt that 'today's youth are too focused on buying and consuming things'. One commentary from the Merck survey states: 'When they look at the condition of American life today, people from all walks of life – rich and poor, men and women, all ages, all races – reach a remarkably similar conclusion: things are seriously out of whack.'[20] A great majority of those surveyed felt dissatisfied with their lives and felt that their non-material aspirations were unfulfilled. Sixty-six per cent wanted to spend more time with family and friends, and 56 per cent wanted less stress in their lives. Many people felt stuck on a treadmill of conspicuous consumption, with relentless pressures to keep up with their neighbours' level of consumption. Most realised that these levels of consumption had a negative effect on the environment and were unsustainable, both for Americans and the rest of the world. But they felt trapped in the squirrel cage. One man said, 'If the Joneses get a new car, I've got to go out and buy one... The Joneses are killing me.' Others linked excess materialism with loss of community, family breakdown and crime. One respondent said: 'Things have become so important to us that things, and the acquisition of things, run our lives and our relations with others.'[21] Another speaks of a 'lust for wealth and power that we've been taught to worship' and a third: 'I think we value things more than people... the relations people used to have among each other have broken down.'

20 Reported in
Yes: A Journal of
Positive Futures
Spring/Summer,
1996

21 ibid

Interestingly, a majority of the surveyed Americans ranked non-material, or life, values (responsibility, family life, friendship, generosity and religious faith) as more important than wealth. But most also felt that American society, described as 'most other people', ranked wealth above all else and attached little importance to life values. In fact, most people shared a concern for life values. Figure 7.6 shows this disparity between what Americans feel and what they think their neighbours feel. This rather startling finding suggests that many Americans believe that their own value systems, which give rightful emphasis to life values, diverge from an overall, highly materialist set of values embodied by the majority of society; this is not the case.

This suggests that, in this advanced industrial society, pressure to overconsume is dictated not by the feelings and aspirations of a majority of individual households, but by some combination of:

- social pressure to conform to ever-rising consumption patterns;
- the economic power structure dictated by America's large corporations; and
- the influence of advertising agencies and the media, particularly television and film.

These corporate interests benefit most directly from overconsumption and influence the direction of society. According the to Merck Family Survey, this is despite the feelings of a majority of individual American households. The survey also reveals that individual American households would like to take action to change their lives: to use possessions longer, to shop less, to spend less money, to drive cars less and to spend more time with neighbours. But there is a big constraint on action: the Joneses. In a fragmented, atomised, capitalist society people have trouble envisioning how collective change away from materialism could take place. And the change needs to be collective, to be accomplished as a society; how else will the majority be absolved from maintaining consumption levels like those of their neighbours, or aspiring to what they see on television?

The survey revealed that American households cannot see a way to initiating the necessary change that will relieve them of the need to keep up consumption levels. The will is there – a recent study by Schor at a large American telecommunications firm found that 73 per cent thought they could spend less and live more simply. Certainly some Americans are downshifting – making do with less money. But they are still a small minority in a country where the pressure to consume is great indeed.

Advertising, marketing, even packaging aim at shaping people's preferences rather than, as *laissez-faire* theory holds, merely responding to them. Unsure of what they stand for, people increasingly rely on money as the criterion of value. What is more expensive is considered better. What used to be a medium of exchange has usurped the place of fundamental values, reversing the relationship postulated by economic theory. The cult of success has replaced a belief in principles. Society has lost its anchor.

George Soros[22]

22 Soros, G 'The Capitalist Threat' *Atlantic Monthly* February 1997

The Impact of Excessive Individualism

Americans clearly want to downshift from a position of overconsumption and excessive materialism. However, they are hampered not only by corporate interests which promote overconsumption, but also by what has been called excessive individualism. This tendency was first identified 150 years ago by De Tocqueville in his book *Democracy in America*. In a recent examination of the role of individualism in American society, Lane distinguishes between two types: utilitarian individualism, which maximises economic self-interest, and expressive individualism, which is self-actualisation in terms of feeling, intuition and experience.[23] He identifies a serious problem in American society of aggressive utilitarian individualism, which generates rapid economic growth but has resulted in a fundamental decline of a sense of community and a degradation of public life. Lane sees this as 'the most important unresolved problem in America'.

The current trend of overconsumption is summed up by American economists Frank and Cook in their description of what they term a winner takes all society: 'more and more Americans are competing for ever fewer and bigger prizes, encouraging economic waste, income inequality and an impoverished cultural life'.[24] That the winners in America are taking all is indicated by economist Edward Luttwak, who argues that the top 2 percent of American households have been the only beneficiaries of all the economic growth during the past quarter of a century.[25] If Americans are to take up a role among the world's leaders in implementing sustainable development, and to use their tremendous ingenuity and the freedom of their society for sustainable purposes, they will need to strengthen opportunities for collective action on the problems of overconsumption and excessive individualism. A first step is to recognise that this is a serious problem. They have begun doing that. The growing interest in downshifting, now encompassing about 3.5 million Americans, a Canadian campaign for an annual 'Buy Nothing Day' and the strategic campaign of the Center for a New American Dream, whose mission statement was cited above, are all evidence that perceptions are changing. But the task will not be easy.

The Acceleration of Time and the Shrinkage of Space

There is one other stressful area in human life: the acceleration of time and the shrinkage of space. Like positional goods, the costs and benefits of these are mixed, but there are both; somehow, a little bit is a

23 Lane, L M 'Individualism, civic virtue and public administration' *Administration and Society* vol 20:30–45, 1988

24 Frank, R and Cook, P *The Winner Take All Society* New York: Free Press, 1996

25 Quoted in Bedell, op cit

26 United Nations Development Programme *Human Development Report 1996* New York and Oxford: Oxford University Press, 1996

> When we juxtapose the current debate on economic growth with the notion of human development, the first impression is that the concepts belong in two different worlds – that they don't connect. The economy reigns supreme, determining political choices and the limits of social action. And the free market emerges as the leading ideology, fostering competition and an exaggerated narcissistic individualism that equates the realm of values with the dictates of efficiency.
>
> Fernando Henrique Cardoso, President of Brazil[26]

Figure 7.7

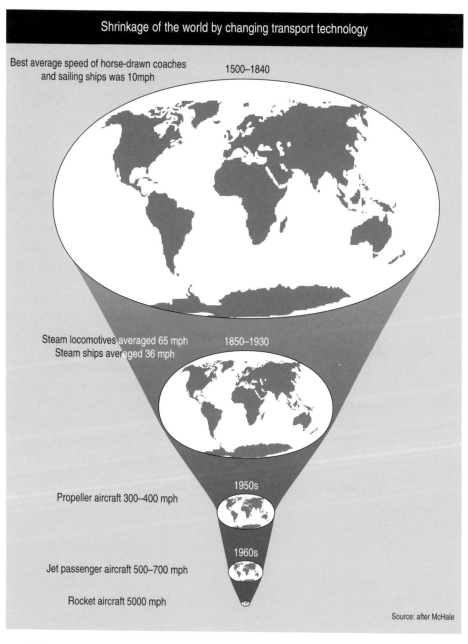

Shrinkage of the world by changing transport technology

Best average speed of horse-drawn coaches
and sailing ships was 10mph   1500–1840

Steam locomotives averaged 65 mph   1850–1930
Steam ships averaged 36 mph

1950s

Propeller aircraft 300–400 mph

1960s

Jet passenger aircraft 500–700 mph

Rocket aircraft 5000 mph

Source: after McHale

27 Original
graphic from
McHale, J *The
Future of the
Future* New
York: George
Braziller, 1969

good thing but more and more is not.

Three aspects of time and motion define modern life. One is speed – we live in a world where people, resources and human thoughts and ideas speed around a world which seems ever smaller; this is touted as the essence of modernity. Figure 7.7 indicates the shrinking of the globe by jet propulsion: New York is now closer to Tokyo than it was to Philadelphia at the time of American Independence.[27] One-hour plane trips from London to Sydney are now proposed, and distance will have nearly vanished.

Speed defines our way of life and is embedded in the current version of modern culture. But are the benefits all they are intended to be? Are we aware of the losses? Is life improved by masses of people speeding ever more quickly to the Earth's beauty spots, so that they are beautiful no longer? Is faster always better, or is there a price to be paid for a constant acceleration of production, information and daily life?[28]

A second factor is that, although we are speeding ever more, there never seems to be enough time left over to really enjoy the most important things in life, such as family, friends, nature, study and reflection. It would seem that getting there faster should mean we could spend less time travelling, but the opposite seems to be the case. In the long run, faster transport has not resulted in time savings, but in increased travel distances for business, recreation and shopping, whether by car or by air, with an attendant environmental impact.[29] Of course, much speed is only technological illusion. We can fly from Tokyo to Manila, or New York to Chicago, in two hours, but we will certainly spend three or four hours getting to and from airports, and another hour shopping in those airports. A car will do 160 kilometres per hour on the open road, but in most cities from London to Mexico City to Manila the average pace of a car journey is exactly the same as the pace of a horse journey 200 years ago.

A third factor is that speed and lack of time breed stress – the enemy of modern man. On the highway, road rage is more common as drivers become intensely frustrated by their inability to move at the speed the vehicle is designed for and to arrive in time. People leave for work (or the airport) earlier and earlier because, in the modern city, congestion spreads in time and space. Time is cramped by the need to work more and to live less; this is made worse, in turn, by the information overload generated by rapid-fire communications of undifferentiated information. A recent study of 1300 managers for the news agency Reuters confirmed the stressful nature of information caused by the proliferation of faxes, voice mail, electronic mail, junk mail and the internet. Symptoms include a 'feeling of inability to cope with incoming data as it piles up, resulting in mental stress and even physical illness'.

Moving On: Steady State or Steady Flow?

A recent conference in Amsterdam asked:

> But what about the future? Is it time to build a 'selective slowness' into the design of our lives? Might a combination of ultra-fast information and slowed-down movement be a sound strategy for sustainable design?[30]

At least until we live forever, time is a valuable resource – just as fresh air, clean water or the world's forests are. The pacing of time and speed is part and parcel of the need to consume less and enjoy more. At the societal level, one possibility is to draw on Herman Daly's concept of the steady state society, and to ask whether things could not remain as they are with much higher quality of life as the intended social goal, rather than quantity of goods and rapidity of change. Daly describes the conditions – zone 'SD' in Figure 7.1's slippery slope diagram – of the steady-state economy: limited throughput of industrial goods and inequality and population numbers.[31] The steady-state economy is ecological; physical growth is

28 *Doors of Perception 4* Amsterdam: Final Conference Programme, 1996

29 Bleijenberg, A and van Swigchem, J 'Efficiency and Sufficiency: Towards sustainable energy and transport' Delft: report by Energy Conservation and Environmental Technology for Sustainable Europe Campaign, 1997

30 *Doors of Perception 4* op cit

31 Daly, H E *Steady State Economics* (second edition) London: Earthscan, 1992; Daly, H E 'The Steady State Economy: Towards a Political Economy of Biophysical Equilibrium and Moral Growth' in Daly and Townsend, K N (eds) *Valuing the Earth* Cambridge: Mass: MIT Press, 1992

economically viable only as long as the marginal benefits of growth exceed the marginal costs.

Daly gives an analogy of the steady state: a library with a constant stock of books limited, say, by storage space or a maintenance budget. For every new book acquired, an old one must be recycled, and no book would be replaced unless the new one was qualitatively better. The quality of the library steadily improves although the quantity of the books it contains remains constant. He suggests that 'a steady-state economy, far from being static, is a strategy for forcing qualitative improvement and sustainability'. The idea of the steady-state economy is not new. Daly cites his inspiration as John Stuart Mill's chapter 'On the Stationary State' in *Principles of Political Economy*. He also notes that for most of the history of mankind, near steady-state conditions were maintained. Only in the past two centuries in the West has growth become the norm.

The steady-state economy is an attractive concept. Other authors have taken it up – for example, Alexander, who prefers the term steady-flow for its dynamic implications:

> *Steady-flow means movement and process. Steady-flow is like a dependable river or stream. Flowing merrily along, many interesting things happen, sometimes in unexpected and exciting ways. The size of the stream flow, the quantitative aspects change little. Quantitative limitations on the use of the earth's resources allow the regenerative capacity of Gaia to remain constant or to increase.*

Treasuring the Public Realm: A Renaissance of Community and Place

Too often, an increasing tendency to elevate private consumption over public life in consumer society results in the damaging or even outright destruction of the public realm. These are the places where we come together with our neighbours in recognising that humans, like most of the rest of the animal kingdom, are intensely social beings. The erosion of the social realm, or its disappearance in face of the onslaught of excessive individualism and privatisation, is all too common. The following is a description which applies to urban America and Canada, and a growing number of other places around the world:

> *Our 'second-hand' America has been reduced to a kind of teenage wasteland as the predominant setting for our lives: a place of strips and malls and interchanges and vast parking lots; of signs and overhead wires and dying trees in concrete pots; of toothless main streets and decaying empty areas at the center of our cities, and equally bleak new but half empty areas at their periphery.*[32]

32 Robertson, K in *American Planning Association Journal* Spring 1987

This occurs not only in America. In Britain, too, once thriving high streets which provided the focus of community life have become characterised by boarded-up shops and rubbish-strewn pavements – victims of a supposed retail revolution of out-of-town shopping malls. Such malls force people to travel by car and marginalise car-free households. In the grocery sector, around a quarter of a million small shops have disappeared, due in part to predatory pricing, and the giant supermarkets of five companies now control 60 per cent of retail sales. Some people love them, but more and more are loathed by many customers for their scale and impersonality.[33] This loathing is seized on as another marketing opportunity – home food shopping through the internet is the current market favourite, turning a social process into a private one and undermining social places, some with a history going back to medieval times. Of course, prices *are* lower, but the net costs and benefits need to be viewed more widely.

This is part of a broader process where social interactions are privatised or turned into commodities to be bought and sold: a shifting of human functions from the public to the private realm. The difference is between sitting with friends in the park or in a city centre café and staying at home to watch a movie on the VCR. There is nothing wrong with either, but when the balance shifts too much, when the park or the city centre becomes empty and dangerous, something valuable is lost. Some people are aware of the problem. Britain has a 'save local shops campaign' to fight the deterioration caused by out-of-town shopping. Americans are trying to recreate the lost sense of community in new small towns, such as the Disney-owned Celebration in Florida. But these are likely to be minuscule substitutes for the enormous structural changes which take place in our societies when market considerations alone dictate land use and patterns of social interaction.

Unfortunately, the very process of dematerialisation discussed in the previous chapter can also contribute to these changes: here, the digital revolution becomes the 21st-century version of the 19th-century industrial revolution. We interact with an automatic teller machine (ATM) instead of walking to a local high street bank. The neighbourhood banks close, and by then we are into internet banking and we do not even need to leave the house. Other proposals are for on-line bookstores, internet newspapers, and virtual shopping areas, each diminishing the opportunities for face-to-face human interaction. Of course, they are convenient, so their growth seems inevitable even if the cost is larger than it might seem.

At the extreme, a 'virtual world' is at our fingertips, public space is compressed into digital bits, and we are invited to interact on an increasingly superficial basis with a vast number of people over a flickering screen. All of this can contribute to a decline in the quality of local neighbourhoods and town centres, combined with the disastrous effects of out-of-town shopping malls to undermine urban vitality at the very time when sustainable development seems to require the re-urbanisation of human interaction. Nevertheless, there are no easy answers on how to recreate social spaces which are not economically functional, as the branch bank once was.

One possibility is to share, rather than own, the advantages of technology. For example, the ecological backpack of a desktop computer is around 16 to 20 tons of material (about half that of a car), and the average daily use is about an hour a day.[34] Computers could be available in local public libraries, accessible on foot or by bike, and the library could be a local neighbourhood centre, with information on employment, childcare, public events, recreation and local environmental and planning issues. Similarly, in Europe there is a spreading movement towards non-profit car sharing organised by local government, resulting in car-free households and neighbourhoods. From its origins in Germany, this initiative has spread across Northern Europe. Central and local government, working with community groups, have an important role to play in such efforts, which aim to dematerialise society and promote the community.

In some countries, however, the loss of traditional community bonds, under the impact of excessive individualism, television, global advertising and consumer culture, produces sharper reactions. The rise of Islamic and Christian fundamentalism, and the resurgence of Orthodox Judaism, are all due in part to a

33 Carley, M
*Sustainable
Transport and
Retail Vitality*
Edinburgh:
Historic Burghs
Association of
Scotland and
Transport 2000,
1997

34 Private
communication
from Joachim
Spangenberg,
Wuppertal
Institute

> We are learning very fast that the belief that a free market is all it takes to have a functioning society – or even a functioning economy – is pure delusion. Unless there is a functioning civil society, the market can produce economic results for a very short time – maybe three to five years. For anything beyond that, a functioning civil society is needed for the market to function in its economic role, let alone its social role.
>
> Peter Drucker, 87-year-old US management guru

distaste for the secular materialism and loss of community which threatens to squeeze the spiritual dimension out of daily life. While these are extreme reactions, the protection of the public realm needs to become part of a mass movement for sustainable production and consumption.

Getting a Balance between Public and Private Consumption

A related factor, which varies from country to country, is the provision of goods and services for public and private consumption. Where high-quality public goods are readily available, such as education, health services, public transport, public safety or parks and leisure services, these are good, and often better, substitutes for private consumption in contributing to quality of life. For example, where widespread, high-quality education is provided by the state, parents are under much less pressure to earn the high fees associated with private education; the benefits of education for the next generation are thus assured without reference to income. In some cases, such as a national park, private consumption, however grand, remains a poor substitute for public goods.

One of the saddest outcomes of the transition to a market economy in Russia is the rapid decline in the quality, and even the provision, of state primary education, and the rise of fee-paying primary schools. The fees charged are in excess of average yearly incomes for many ordinary Russian households. Some state schools, on the other hand, cannot even afford to open. This situation can only mean deterioration of future quality of life, at the personal and social level, and may reinforce a stark income inequality which will be reinforced through coming generations.

Some economists suggest that providing certain public goods will initiate sustainable economic

35 McLaren, D et al *Tomorrow's World: Britain's Share in a Sustainable Future* London: Earthscan, 1997

> Not only are many of the things that make our lives better not material goods – but many of them have no price. We don't have to pay for the air we breathe or our experience of nature. The pleasure of seeing our children grow up is priceless. For many people, simply the knowledge that our children will be able to enjoy their lives is the most important thing in the world. The existence of such non-monetary factors in the quality of our lives means that it is possible to reduce material consumption to increase well-being, at least at the individual level.
>
> Friends of the Earth, *Tomorrow's World*[35]

growth, where private consumption generates negative externalities or inefficiencies.[36] Take, for example, the private car, which obviously pollutes, damages health and so on – private automobile ownership is at the social limits to growth, requiring the expenditure of 10–20 megajoules of energy to roll one tonne one mile. A three-tonne tram carrying 40 passengers will be around 13 times as energy efficient, and the negative externalities will be far less. Would it not be better for the economy, the environment and urban mobility if some combination of private and public initiative provided this public good, rather than encouraged the production of yet more cars?

Finally, whatever the apparent inroads of Thatcherism and Reaganomics, it should not be assumed that people resent paying taxes for high-quality public services that are efficiently delivered. A recent Gallup survey of British attitudes, reported in *The Economist*, showed that fully 73 per cent of Britons say they want more government services, even if that means paying more taxes.[37] Only 10 per cent want tax cuts and 17 per cent are content with current tax levels. These views might not accord with those of 'American taxophobes', but they do demonstrate the British and European concern for the public dimension of quality of life – which is, no doubt, mirrored in most countries.

Armed Quality of Life?

It may also be important to extend our definition of public goods to reflect the range of factors which influence quality of life. Inequality and public safety are two related examples. There is growing evidence that too much inequality in society lessens quality of life – for the haves as well as the have-nots. At minimum, inequality causes deterioration of health and increased incidence of disease. This situation is found by researchers comparing inequality and health in different states in the USA.[38]

More alarming are cases in some countries in South America and Africa, and some regions of the USA, where city streets are highly dangerous, cars are likely to be hijacked and wealthy residents live barricaded in walled, barbwired compounds patrolled by armed guards. In these situations, insufficient household income, dramatic income inequality and the widespread presence of firearms destroy the quality and safety of the public realm and reinforce the need for private consumption to substitute for public life and to buy security. The security comes at a high price in terms of household stress and in sheer cost. The publication *Business Week* estimates that 7 per cent of the American economy is devoted to coping with crime, which is investment foregone in areas such as education or childcare.[39]

The world is more or less divided into countries where it is safe to walk down the street and those where it is not. Where it is not, private cars are often the only relatively safe means of travel, marginalising the poor and anyone committed to sustainable transport. Countries which are headed down the latter road would do well to re-examine their priorities, and their income distribution patterns, to see whether wiser options exist. In another 10 or 20 years the alternative may be too depressing to contemplate.

Reassessing the Nature of Work

In the previous section we have discussed the impact of overconsumption on the household and on the public realm. Here we look at a third aspect of most people's lives, the workplace. At a global level, the proportion of the world's population of working age (15 to 64) is increasing. Between 1970 and 1990,

36 Quah, D T 'Discarding non-stick frying pans for economic growth' paper of the Centre for Economic Performance London School of Economics, 1966

37 The Economist *The World in 1997*

38 *The Independent* 14 September 1996

39 Cited in Rowe, J 'Honey, We Shrunk the Economy!' in *Yes! A Journal of Positive Futures* vol 1 Spring/Summer, 1996

Box 7.3 No joking matter – *The Economist* on the decline of real wages in America

'The economy is creating tens of thousands of new jobs, that's the good news', says a man, looking up from his newspaper. 'So what's the bad news?' he is asked. 'To support a family you'll need three!'[40]

---

around 1140 million people joined the labour force, and another 1360 million will join between 1990 and 2010.[41] Of these, 95 per cent will be in the developing world.

The conditions of work and household income have a major impact on quality of life and hence sustainable development the world over. As industrialisation continues in NICs, and the influence of what Charles Handy calls 'supra-national' corporations gurus, the evolving conditions of work in developed countries will influence global employment patterns. Main concerns are the labour market impacts of changes in the way modern economies function, particularly with regard to the balance between labour and capital investment in production, conditions of work, unemployment and the effects of globalisation in creating an international labour market.

Market Reform and Social Justice: What Balance?

A major concern is the impacts of the recent market revolution – the relentless drive to economic efficiency, downsizing of workforces, labour market flexibility and privatisation of state activities. This has its origins in Thatcherism and Reagonomics, set against a background of the rapid restructuring of national economies away from manufacturing. In the USA, for example, the manufacturing contribution to corporate profits dropped from 52 per cent in 1965 to 25 per cent in 1995. Interest in what might be called an Anglo–American version of market capitalism has spread around the globe since the 1990s, with the message taken into the Eastern transition countries and the developing countries by the World Bank and the IMF, in the latter as part of structural adjustment programmes (SAPs). Argentina, for example, is just one of many countries to have carried out radical market reforms, including extensive privatisation (although unemployment remains high at 18 per cent). Nor are traditional party politics a good guide to any government's approach – traditional left-of-centre parties, such as in Canada and the USA, often carry on with market reform after sweeping Conservative parties from office.

The contribution of these market reforms to short-term economic efficiency is real, but in many cases the social costs have been high in terms of increased income inequality, poverty for those out of work or in low-paid jobs, and work-related stress for those disadvantaged by the labour market. The key question which many people are asking is whether the benefits of these reforms can be retained without extensive social costs? The general hope is that an alternative to this extreme version of capitalism is available, with economic efficiency balanced against a concern for social justice for all citizens. Here Anglo–American examples give us an idea of how the trend unfolds; these can be set against Western European and other social democratic models to opt for less market reform and higher levels of social

40 19 October 1996

41 Simai, M *The Future of Global Governance: Managing Risk and Change in the Global System* Washington: The United States Institute of Peace, 1994

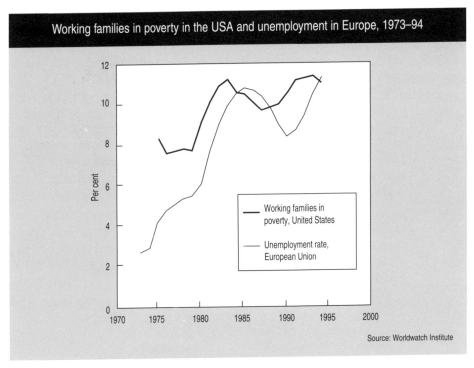

Figure 7.8

Working families in poverty in the USA and unemployment in Europe, 1973–94

Per cent

Working families in poverty, United States

Unemployment rate, European Union

Source: Worldwatch Institute

subsidy, such as for the unemployed. Some developing countries have also resisted market reforms, doing away with subsidies on basic foodstuffs, for fear of social destabilisation, although many other countries have embraced them.

The appropriate balance between economic reform and social justice, however, is made unclear by the fact that the Anglo–American model appears to create jobs, and thus reduce unemployment, at a faster rate than the social democratic approach. This makes market reform a matter of considerable interest in countries with high unemployment rates. It is certainly the case that outright unemployment in Europe, for example, is around twice the Anglo–American average, but also the case that in the latter real poverty, even of people in work, is not uncommon (Figure 7.8). It is also the case that in the most flexible labour markets, employers may hire workers on the economic upswing, but, equally, will lay off workers *en masse* on the inevitable downswing, thereby transferring the social costs of regular market fluctuations to the least-paid members of society. Whatever the appropriate balance, the quantity, quality and security of employment opportunities must be assessed in considering how structural processes can be adjusted so that employment opportunity and decent work conditions are available to all.

Changing Conditions of Work

An obvious impact of market reforms is that corporations are producing increasing amounts of goods and services with ever smaller, downsized workforces, with the result that unemployment and underemployment are profound social challenges in virtually all countries. In the USA, recent research shows that chief executives who fire the most employees have been rewarded with the highest levels of compensation for the past four years up to and including 1996, suggesting little slowing in this trend.[42]

This downsizing signals a permanent change in employment conditions, dictated mainly by employers – who have more latitude of action now that the power of unions has shrunk in many countries. Under this new framework, workers are now individual free agents, with no job security and no right to collective representation, but with a high degree of mobility and able to pick and choose employers and locations. Some workers, with highly marketable skills, thrive on these freelance conditions. For others, part time instead of full time jobs, lower pay, longer working hours, increased stress, less time with family, and lack of job security is the norm. More are on short-term contracts or even zero hours contracts, meaning there is no guarantee of pay. The chairman of computer chip giant Intel, Andy Grove, sums up the new conditions of work: 'No matter where you work, you are not an employee. You are in business with one employer – yourself – in competition with millions of similar businesses worldwide.'[43]

The workforces in developed countries and NICs will be increasingly polarised between those who can take advantage of, and thrive on, these new employment conditions and a large number of people increasingly caught in low-paid 'McJobs', without health or holiday benefits. These are the people who will cycle frequently in and out of unemployment, with those over 40 years of age tending to drop out of the labour market on a permanent basis. The result in countries with flexible labour markets is that income inequality is increasing, a point to which we will return. In Britain, for example, low wages are the single most important cause of poverty, with one third of households in poverty even while one person is working.

The other side of the coin is unemployment. Even while an increasing number of people are locked into long hours and a diminished family life, millions of others have no choice but to accept unemployment, with insufficient income to enjoy or even secure the essentials of life. The system may make sense from the company and the shareholder point of view, but it makes little sense from the viewpoint of workers, or from that of society at large. This situation holds even in the prosperous USA, with its highly flexible labour markets. The Economic Policy Institute reports that around 13.5 million Americans, 10 per cent of the labour force, are now underemployed, in that they have only part time work when full time is required.[44] Eight per cent of the nation's permanent jobs were lost every two years, between 1989 and 1995. Since 1985, real wages fell by 10 per cent. Six million US workers do not expect their jobs to last one year. This contingent workforce is growing as more companies use temporary in place of regular employees. The institute sees a continuing shift in the US labor market towards low-paid, part time jobs. In the UK, research suggests that more than 90 per cent of the jobs which will be created in the next

42 Research by the Institute for Policy Studies reported in the *Financial Times*, 2 May 1997

43 Quoted in S Caulkin 'You scratch my back – I'll keep my skills up to date' *The Observer*, 11 May 1997

44 Economic Policy Institute *The State of Working America* Washington, 1996

45 Rifkin, J 'Now the robots are after your job, too' *The Independent* 26 February 1996

Box 7.4 Whatever happened to the leisure revolution?

It is, perhaps, predictable that not a single leading advocate of information age technologies has even hinted at the possibility that we might benefit from the array of new labour-saving technologies with a radically reduced working week. Instead of shortening the working week, employers are shortening the workforce – effectively preventing millions of workers from enjoying any of the benefits of the technology revolution.

Jeremy Rifkin[45]

decade will be part time jobs.[46] This loss of income security for households makes it more difficult for families to feel confident about life-long prospects, engendering feelings of permanent unease.

Pessimists such as Rifkin, the author of *The End of Work*, think the situation will only get worse. He predicts that by 2020 less than 2 per cent of the global workforce will be engaged in factory work and suggests that 'redefining the role of the individual in a society without mass formal work is perhaps the seminal issue of the coming age'. It is not just blue collar jobs which are hit. The service sector is also automating, eliminating vast numbers of white collar jobs. As a result, in his view, we are moving into an era of near workerless production which could generate massive unemployment.[47]

The emerging knowledge-based economy will provide well-paid jobs for a small elite of scientists, professionals, business leaders and entertainers, including sports personalities, but fewer and fewer for a mass workforce. Some jobs will be transferred to lower-cost locations on a global basis. British Airways, for example, is sacking 5000 employees in Britain and sending the accounting work to India where well-trained staff can be hired at one tenth the wages. This is good for the Indians, bad for the British and pits workers in one country against those in another. Back in Britain, another 17,000 airline staff are being required to accept pay cuts of up to one third, a three-year wage freeze or a five-hour increase in the working week as a condition of remaining in employment.[48] Pay rates for new staff are expected to be 20 per cent lower than at present.

Insecure underemployment, familiar to workers in Third World countries, is spreading, as is the attempt by local economies to stave off the problem by a spiral of lower wages relative to international competition. Workers in the former coal-mining valleys of South Wales and industrial areas of Scotland, for example, now assemble video recorders, TVs and other electronic goods for lower wages than do South Koreans. An increasing trend reported by the UK's Henley Centre for Forecasting is for employees to work for a temporary period of up to three months for nothing in the hopes of securing employment.[49] This has a knock-on effect on wages and hours worked: the lowest-paid manual workers in Britain now earn less, relative to the average, than workers in 1886 when statistics were first collected. In Britain, the number of employees working more than 50 hours per week has grown by one third to 25 per cent of the workforce, with one in 59 people working more than 70 hours per week. A study by the Rowntree Foundation indicates that quality of family life deteriorates when one or both parents work more than 48 hours per week.[50] A survey by the Institute of Management shows that 61 per cent of British male managers would like to spend less time at work and more time with family and friends. This is the downside of the much vaunted market revolution.

Work, Income and Inequality

For most people in work, there is ample evidence that the dissatisfaction we are made to feel with our income levels – Kettering's 'organised dissatisfaction' – which drives us to work-and-spend, is not with our absolute circumstances but with our relative position vis-à-vis our neighbours, the Joneses. Dissatisfaction is, therefore, fuelled by income inequality in society and, perhaps increasingly in a globalised economy, by inequalities between societies.

Inequality is a fact of life in a world where 447 billionaires enjoy an amount of wealth which exceeds the combined annual income of 2.75 billion people in the lower one half of the world's income distribu-

46 Business Strategies *Occupations in the Future* 1996

47 Rifkin, J *The End of Work: The Decline of the Global Labor Force and the Dawn of the Post-Market Era* New York: Putnam's Sons, 1995

48 *The Independent* 15 October 1996

49 *Independent on Sunday* 17 October 1996

50 Ferri, E and Smith, K *Parenting in the 1990s* London: Family Policy Studies Centre and the Joseph Rowntree Foundation, 1996

Figure 7.9

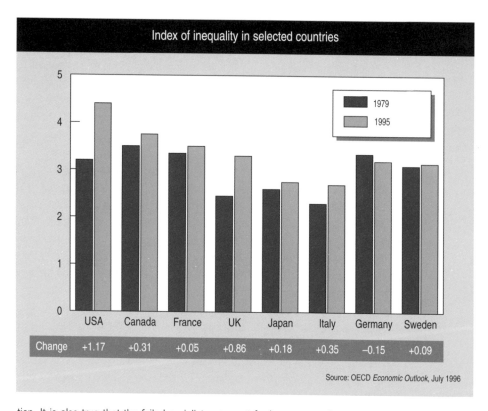

Index of inequality in selected countries

| Change | +1.17 | +0.31 | +0.05 | +0.86 | +0.18 | +0.35 | −0.15 | +0.09 |

Source: OECD *Economic Outlook*, July 1996

tion. It is also true that the failed socialist argument for income equality regardless of achievement or social contribution did not work – nice in theory but not in practice. So, inequality is something to be managed but not done away with. Nevertheless, as with radical market reform, it does not follow that because a little good, more is better. Inequality is increasing in many countries (see Figure 7.9). In the West there has been an uncoupling of income and GDP growth during the 1980s, resulting in a stagnation of average incomes and increasing wage differentials.[51] In the USA, for example, the *Wall Street Journal* reports that the pay of top-earners is now 212 times higher than that of average employees, up from a multiple of 44 in 1965.[52] During 1995, salaries and bonuses of chief executives in the US rose by 10.4 per cent compared to a 2.9 increase in average earnings. Globally, the collective profits of the world's top 500 companies (the Fortune 500) rose by 15 per cent to US$323 billion, while the size of their workforces remained approximately constant.

In the developed world, there has been a tendency for this wage inequality to grow. The Economic Policy Institute suggests that wage inequality in the USA is fostered by a 'weakening of labour market institutions [that is, trade unions, collective bargaining and the national minimum wage], the impact of globalisation and the move into low-wage service industries'.[53] The USA and Britain may have been notable for a substantial rise in income inequality in the 1980s and 1990s, but there is pressure on other governments in developed countries to cut away at employee security and benefits to allow domestic employers to compete better on a world stage where fewer and fewer may benefit from well-paid work. Trends towards inequality are mirrored in the world as a whole. Chapter 3 showed that the share of global

51 Spangenberg et al, op cit

52 *Wall Street Journal* 26 June 1996

53 Economic Policy Institute op cit

Figure 7.10

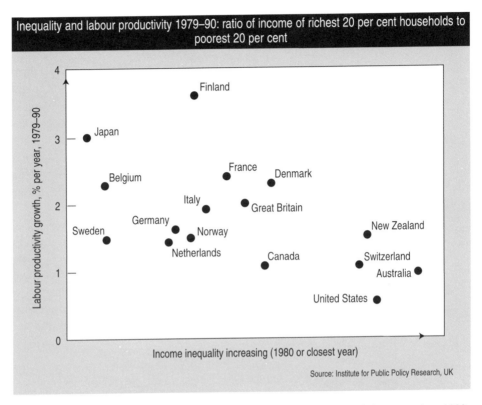

Inequality and labour productivity 1979–90: ratio of income of richest 20 per cent households to poorest 20 per cent

Source: Institute for Public Policy Research, UK

wealth owned by the poorest one fifth of the population decreased from 2.3 to 1.4 per cent since 1980, while the share of the richest fifth increased from 70 per cent to 83 per cent. One outcome is increasing polarisation between rich and poor or, as the OECD puts it, widening wage gaps 'fuelling social tensions and swelling the ranks of the working poor'. In addition to the social trauma, this dramatic wage inequality fuels consumption aspirations which cannot be fulfilled for the vast majority of the world's population.

A recent study by the World Bank suggests that economies with very unequal income distributions pay a price: they grow more slowly than those whose income is more evenly spread.[54] The bank suggests that the link between high inequality and low growth lies largely in the inability of the poor to borrow. For any given level of GDP per person, a country with an unequal distribution of income or wealth will have a higher proportion of poor people who cannot borrow to finance, say, education or business, start up, and the economy will grow more slowly. Another study makes similar findings – that reducing inequality contributes to growth, again due to the contribution of equality to educational attainment and lowered fertility rates as people invest in higher levels of education for fewer children.[55] Interestingly, this study also suggests that countries with a more equal income distribution, and thus a larger middle class, tend to have fewer violent changes of government and more political stability. Finally, there is a tendency to assume that income inequality may contribute to labour productivity by encouraging the poor to work. The evidence tends to be the opposite, however, as shown in Figure 7.10.

54 Deininger, K and Squire, L 'Measuring Income Inequality: A New Database' *World Bank Economic Review* September 1996

55 Perotti, R 'Growth, Income Distribution and Democracy: What the Data Say' *Journal of Economic Growth* June 1996

Table 7.2[56]

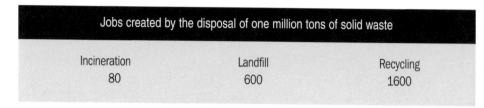

Jobs created by the disposal of one million tons of solid waste		
Incineration	Landfill	Recycling
80	600	1600

News Ways of Thinking About Work

Because of the number of people marginalised by unemployment and working poverty, and the stress associated with new conditions of work, the current situation is unsustainable. Therefore, a core target for the Sustainable Europe Project has been to initiate discussion on political, economic, and social options 'to limit the use of natural resources, while at the same time providing new chances for job creation, reliable social security and satisfying ways of consuming'.

A first step is to change the perception that efficiency in production comes about from eliminating humans from the workplace. Beyond this, we do not pretend to have the magic answer to the problem of work in the modern society. However, three ways forward are examined: green jobs, derived from ecoefficiency applications; the relationship of education to work in a dematerialised economy; and promotion of what has come to be called the intermediate labour market, the third sector or the social economy. Each is discussed briefly.

Green Jobs

Ecologically sound industrial processes can generate work: this is shown in Table 7.2. There is also growing evidence that tax changes can trigger environmental improvements and job creation. This supports the move towards ecotaxation: the reduction of taxes on labour and the substitution of taxes on unsustainable natural-resource consumption and pollution: a win–win situation. This forces us to think more about the productivity of resources. Ecotaxes can be 'revenue-neutral' – there is no need for a reduction or an increase in tax flows.

A variety of scenarios supports the win–win view. In the UK, a study proposing an increased escalatory tax on road fuel of 17.6 per cent per annum suggests that with the revenue being recycled through a decrease in employers' national insurance contributions, employment could increase by 1.275 million in about ten years. More conservative modelling suggests a gain to the UK economy of 400,000 to 700,000 jobs which could reduce unemployment by a quarter.[57] For Belgium, a CO_2-reduction energy scenario foresees a growth in employment of 27 per cent in 2000 and a reduction in the consumption of energy and CO_2 emissions of 8.5 per cent. Reducing value-added tax on products that are not energy-intensive would encourage their use at the cost of energy intensive products (public transport instead of private, for example). Furthermore, the compensation of the tax on labour would favour substituting energy with labour.

In Austria, a scenario for a tax on end-use energy envisages, for the first year, an additional taxation of approximately 80 groschen per litre of petrol, five groschen per kilowatt hour for gas, heating-oil, coal and coke and about 10 groschen per kilowatt hour for electricity. Renewable energy carriers are exempt. Apart from considerable long-term reductions in fossil-fuel inputs, cuts in labour costs and a consistent policy of promoting energy-saving technologies would result in an additional 11,000 jobs after five years.

56 Young, J E and Sachs, A *The Next Efficiency Revolution: Creating a Sustainable Materials Economy* Washington: Worldwatch Paper no 121, 1994

57 Jacobs, M *Green Jobs? The Employment Implications of Environmental Policy* Brussels: World Wide Fund for Nature, 1994

Joachim Spangenberg and Odile Bonniot

Towards a Corporate Human Development Index

Any consideration of corporate sustainability quickly moves beyond obvious measures of economic vitality to human capital – the basis of any company's success. But it is not quantifiable at this level of generality. To provide some measurability, a corporate human development index (CHDI) is proposed, based on the criteria the UNDP developed for its human development index (HDI) of nation states, modified to suit the firm. Like the HDI, the CHDI is derived from a limited number of indicators.

The three main components of the HDI are longevity, knowledge and material standard of living. Equivalent criteria for the firm could be durability of the relationship between the employee and firm, education levels and distribution of remuneration. These variables can be assessed as follows.

The relationship between employees and firms consists of:

- quality of industrial relations and labour conditions;
- personnel rotation (fluctuation of personnel, average duration of employment), indicators of the reliability of employment for employees;
- amount of regular work hours annually lost due to consequences of labour conditions (for instance, accidents, job-induced diseases, early retirements).

Education input and maintenance of human capital comprises:

- amount of 'embodied education' brought into the firm by employees;
- maintenance or improvement of human capital: hours invested in education and formation of skills per year and capita.

Distribution of remuneration consists of:

- minimum income paid by the company as a multiple of the national social aid standard;
- relative size of CEO or board member income compared to shop-floor average.

Like the HDI, there could be adjusted versions. An obvious adjustment is a gender adjusted CHDI, taking into account income inequities and female representation in decision-making positions. An environmental adjustment would assess the resource and transport intensity of the firm. This adjusted CHDI could then characterise the non-monetary dimensions of a company's sustainability.

Joachim Spangenberg and Odile Bonniot are researchers at the Wuppertal Institute for Climate, Environment and Energy in Germany.

Education and Work in a Dematerialised Economy

Green jobs are one way to create employment. Another is to focus national development strategies on the emerging global knowledge industry, which tends to emphasise the value of human intellect over inputs of financial capital. According to Quah, it is 'in the dematerialised sectors that economies show the greatest capacity for growth'.[58] To take advantage of the opportunities offered by dematerialisation, a high-skill base is critical, otherwise in Quah's words, the 'skill-deprived segment of the population becomes roadkill on the information superhighway'.

By the end of the 20th century, children under 15 will make up more than one third of the global population. This suggests that, perhaps more than any other factor, education could be a powerful tool for achieving sustainable development in the dematerialised economy. Broadly based, adaptable skills are also more relevant than narrow, highly technical skills. Companies will expect their employees to be more holistic, that is, to be able to fill a number of related roles or tasks in an efficient and versatile manner. While employment cannot be guaranteed, people having a broad range of skills are likely to have security of employment in that they will be more confident about switching from job to job. Changes towards a more independent and responsible labour force may also be important, and highly innovative companies are characterised by having simple hierarchies and encouraging employee participation in production and quality-control decisions. Another aspect of this positive approach is that levels of education and the quality of professional training are likely to prove significant in developing sustainable consumption behaviour and social responsibility. We believe that long-range and lifelong education needs to be stimulated to develop understanding of, and concern for, sustainablility issues beginning in primary school.

There are also important implications for work in dematerialised, developing societies. One implication is that countries in areas such as Asia and Africa can enjoy the opportunity of development leapfrogs to dematerialised, information-based economies. For example, they can go straight to the most modern telecommunications systems, without the costly and inefficient step of building land-lines, and straight to computer-based systems or the most efficient forms of transport. These leapfrogs are already happening – China, for example, is buying computer chips as fast as the USA.[59]

Finally, there are interesting implications for social equity. As Quah notes, when one segment of the population consumes dematerialised, knowledge-based goods (say, the benefits of a software programme, or participation in adult education), its benefits are not diminished, even if many more people also partake. This is quite different from the car in the traffic jam, to use an earlier example – where increasing rates of consumption decrease the individual utility. It is quite the opposite from most kinds of physical machinery, land or property. This suggests that movement towards the dematerialised economy can generate social as well as economic and environmental benefits.

Sharing Work

58 Quah, op cit
59 *Financial Times* 17 May 1997

Our notions of work are very much culturally conditioned. Schor notes, for example, that in many so-called primative societies, people would expect to spend at least half of all waking time on leisure activities – the Kapauku of Papua New Guinea never work two days in a row! This can be compared with the Anglo–American tendency to work longer and longer hours, in conditions of greater stress and insecurity. Economic progress has given us more things and less time to enjoy them. In Schor's words, 'We have paid a price for prosperity.'

A radical rethink of work time could be a useful way forward, particularly in combination with moves towards knowledge-based work. The latter will be increasingly based on portfolio-style working practices, where people turn their hands to a variety of tasks, some paid, others unpaid, such as educational upgrading or voluntary work, but all of which are stimulating and rewarding. There are various options for sharing paid work. The most obvious is a reduced working week, to share out the jobs, and probably reduced unsustainable consumption in the bargain. In the USA, for example, cutting back the average workweek to 40 hours could create seven million additional jobs.[60] This would still be a long week compared to European norms. The Dutch, for example, manage to generate one of the highest GDPs in Europe, and one of the most complete range of public and social services, on an average 32-hour work week. An increasing number of Dutch prefer to work just four days per week, which allows additional relaxation time, reduces stress, and also allows childcare to be shared more equitably among working couples.

We could even switch to part time work for all members of society, and we would probably be no less satisfied or, quite possibly, more satisfied with life. But there are enormous barriers to this common-sense approach. The main barrier is the influence of the social norm of work-and-spend. Change will not come about, therefore, from individual action or downshifting alone, but only from concerted intervention on a social level – action by government, voluntary organisations, political parties and other collective organisations.

Redefining Work: the Intermediate Labour Market

Although many people will benefit from knowledge-based work, it is unlikely that the emerging economic system will ever again create the conditions of full employment, which politicians in many countries still pretend they can deliver. To move the agenda forward, the New Economics Foundation points out the importance of acknowledging rewarding work which does not fit into conventional perceptions:

> *Enclosure of work as 'employment' has meant that the labour market exclusively defines work within society, where those out of work are dismissed as 'economically inactive'. The results? We have twin evils – mass unemployment on the one hand and a large amount of socially useful work remaining undone on the other. It is hard to imagine a worse outcome.*[61]

Various experiments are emerging in Britain, such as intermediate labour market for the unemployed which involves options of a modest wage, training and socially useful community work. This helps lower the barrier between unemployment and employment, and the risk of unemployment benefit encouraging long-term unemployment. At a larger scale, researchers have recently calculated that one million socially useful jobs could be created in Britain at a cost of only 0.02 per cent of total public expenditure. These jobs would be in housing, health, education, environmental projects, energy conservation and care in the community.[62] This reflects the possibility of creating what Prime Minister Aznar of Spain calls a new sector of employment, geared to meeting social needs in environment, education, home repairs and

60 Rifkin, op cit, p230

61 Cited in Bedell, op cit

62 Reported in Merry, P *Why Work? The Human Ecology of Work and Employment* Edinburgh: Centre for Human Ecology, 1997

home help, culture and heritage, security and support and local development.[63]

Rifkin also calls for empowering a third sector that is not part of business or government but is a voluntary or NGO sector providing meaningful, socially useful work. The three sectors each have their role in creating capital for building quality of life: business (market capital), government (public capital) and the voluntary sector (social capital). To fund the development of social capital and to create employment, Rifkin suggests:

- shadow wages in the form of tax-relief benefits related to voluntary work;
- social wages; one possibility is for a negative income tax which establishes a minimum income for all members of society; and
- a company tax credit plan for any firm willing to voluntarily reduce its working week; implement profit-sharing for employees; and agree to a formula where compensation to top managers is not disproportionate to employees' wages.

63 Aznar, G
'L'emploi du
troisième type'
*Transversales
Science Culture*
no 39, 1996

64 ibid, p294

65 See, for
example,
ECOTEC
Research and
Consulting Ltd
*The Potential for
Employment
Opportunities
from Pursuing
Sustainable
Development*
Dublin:
European
Foundation for
the Improvement
of Living and
Working
Conditions,
1994; Erskine, A
'Sustainability,
Incomes and
Equity' in
proceedings of
the OECD
Seminar *Towards
an Ecological
City* Glasgow,
November 1995

66 O'Riordan, T
'The radical
agenda of
localism and
democracy' *Town
and Country
Planning* July
1995

One advantage of the social wage proposals would be to reduce the enormous cost of means-tested benefits and to do away with the stigma of unemployment. The company agreements are entirely feasible. The Dutch, for example, with one of Europe's most successful economies, have a high level of job sharing. In Britain, a company owned by its employees, John Lewis Department Stores, already sets a 40:1 ratio as the maximum salary difference between the chief executive and the lowest paid employee. Rifkin's overall vision is also worth reflection:

> *Taxing a percentage of the wealth generated by the new information age economy and redirecting it into the neighbourhoods and communities of the country, and toward the creation of jobs and the rebuilding of the social commons, provides a new agenda and a powerful vision of what life could be like in the 21st century.*[64]

This is part of an emerging argument for linking tax reform to economic development and income redistribution.[65] For example, O'Riordan suggests that if Britain is to genuinely implement sustainable development it will need to develop 'a radical agenda of localism and democracy' with new sources of 'civic income' to fund local development. He suggests that ecological levies on polluting industrial processes could raise UK£40 to 50 billion annually for local economic development, training and urban regeneration initiatives.[66] At the world level are suggestions such as the Tobin tax which would exert a minuscule levy on the billions of dollars of daily global transactions for currency speculation, with the proceeds used for global development. This is discussed in the next chapter.

Conclusion: Changing Consumption Patterns through Social Organisation

An important fact about overconsumption, excessive individualism, declining public space and the changing nature of work is that deeply ingrained materialistic lifestyles and values, reinforced by massive expenditures on global advertising, cannot be changed solely by moral appeals to the individual or the household. Certainly, this cannot be done as long as social status, household autonomy and perceptions of security are enhanced by unsustainable consumption.

The spread of life values including dematerialistic attitudes and habits, in which acquisition of goods becomes less important to life fulfilment, can only come about through social organisation. This requires the development of a strong feeling of community or participation in the sustainability project. To paraphrase the American term, we must work with the Joneses to build a more healthy society, rather than try to exceed their level of consumption. Solving the dilemmas of overconsumption, and restoring the public realm to its rightful and rewarding place, is mainly a social and political, rather than a household, project.

What are the elements of this project? Firstly, the way to organise such a large endeavour is what Carley and Christie describe as action networking, which can be thought of as community development at national and global levels to develop organisations committed to a common agenda.[67] For example, the Sustainable Switzerland campaign has drawn together 11 national organisations, including the Swiss League for Nature Protection, the Swiss Energy Foundation, WWF Switzerland, Greenpeace, the working group for development organisations, and others. Such action networks are open and non-hierarchical, but they are also focused on practical step-by-step achievements and are driven forward by a 'linking pin' organisation with a mandate, resources and a clear sense of purpose. There is already an emerging international network on sustainable production and consumption issues, but it still needs to build towards a broadly based social movement. Such a movement needs to link the interests of developed and developing countries, which must have a common agenda for reforming production and consumption to mutual benefit. It must also work with other initiatives on development, economic reform, the amelioration of poverty and the reorganisation of employment.

Secondly, the goals of sustainable production and consumption need to be translated into a series of practical steps which can be achieved internationally and, in a revised form, can be locally determined by each country; such steps need to form a lobbying package if they are to be presented to politicians. Environmental space analysis and debate, linked to national sustainable development strategies, are a good place to start.

Thirdly, civil society, including churches, unions, NGOs, trade associations and so on, needs to come together to confront the issue of unsustainable consumption. This means questioning materialistic values and the interests of large corporations, including marketing and advertising priorities. It needs to be said that it is okay to question the direction of capitalism and industrial society in a constructive way – it is not a God-given system, or a system of ethical values, and it does not evolve in a beneficial way without human guidance. The market economy is an efficient means of organising the transaction of goods and services, but it is not all there is to life.

We have argued that the economic market is necessary but not sufficient for quality of life. If we want our children and grandchildren to live happy and fulfilling lives, then it is important to discuss these issues. The alternative is to remain trapped in work-and-spend routines which we know are neither satisfactory nor what we genuinely want out of life. If that continues to be the case in the rich, developed countries, then there will be enormous social pressure for NICs to follow down the route of materialism. Options that will take forward a programme of sustainable production and consumption based on environmental space are discussed in the next chapter.

67 Carley and
Christie op cit

CHAPTER 8

Sustainable Production and Consumption – Towards a Global Framework

Introduction

In the new millennium, there is a vital need to promote sustainable production and consumption, shifting steadily towards a position where each country is living within its available environmental space by the middle of the 21st century. This will require dramatic change in Northern consumption habits and values, a reassessment of North–South relationships based on the equity principle, and a revision of the policy framework of multi and bilateral aid and technical assistance towards a mutually beneficial agenda for sustainable development.

Given the usefulness of market mechanisms and their obvious limitations, an important challenge is to mount a constructive critique of the workings of global and national market economies, and the *laissez-faire* approach to capitalism. This must be done so that we can retain the main advantages of economic markets while keeping within the bounds of environmental space. This process of constructive critique must also become a mass movement based on discussion and debate, rather than just the intellectual project of a select few. This is the only way to move towards national and even global consensus on managing markets for overall human benefit.

The idea of market management and regulation is nothing new. Business already relies on a framework of laws and rules to guarantee the rights of capital and property, put in place and administered by national governments and, increasingly, by multilateral organisations such as the World Trade Organisation, the North American Free Trade Agreement, the European Union and others. However, the current framework of regulation is primarily focused on making trade grow, without assessing the broader costs and benefits of that growth or its quality. Simplistic *laissez-faire* ideology, based on intensive competition, does not recognise or foster development in vital areas of life where cooperation is necessary to secure the common good.

The time is right, therefore, to build and extend a global framework of market regulation that encompasses key social and environmental concerns, such as the amelioration of poverty and the reduction of global warming. This must be done within the context of equitable resource access and by creating a level playing field for countries and firms in order to compete globally. A campaign, linking government, business and voluntary groups needs to link top-down and bottom-up initiatives in an overall action framework. This kind of linkage is essential to the task.

In this final chapter, we suggest practical steps towards a framework for an international programme on sustainable production and consumption – which can help us achieve this vital goal of sustainable market economies.

Linking Top-Down and Bottom-Up

Sustainable consumption initiatives, such as recycling, are often undertaken by individuals, households or firms, or within the context of Agenda 21 by local towns. Such bottom-up initiatives are important and necessary, and there are many inspiring examples which are documented.[1] But they are not enough. They are not sufficient to change global production and consumption processes, and the drive to consumerism or materialism, without complementary attention to macro-social processes. In the words of a participant in the Sustainable Austria process:

> *The actions of a single company or even decisions taken in a national parliament are only drops in the bucket. The dynamics of world markets must be understood, because this is the way to influence things deeply.*

There are a number of reasons why micro-initiatives are not enough. Firstly, in terms of production, innovation by a single firm does not address the need to alter production in entire industrial sectors, such as the chemical sector, or to change national industrial policies, for example by rewarding ecoefficiency with tax benefits. This is important in order to ensure that sustainability initiatives do not undermine the relative competitiveness of any individual firm vis-à-vis its competitors in the sector; as a result, managers will have the confidence to alter production processes. Business, government and the scientific community need to work together in this area, both nationally and in the global marketplace. Sophisticated transnational companies can assist in reorienting attitudes at the international level.

Secondly, micro-initiatives cannot provide the collective public goods (such as an efficient public transport system) which underpin quality of life. Thirdly, in terms of changing consumption values, for the majority of households in any country, an altered lifestyle will only be possible as an overall social project involving a majority of households, locally and nationally. Otherwise, as we saw in the last chapter, there is immense pressure to keep up with the neighbours, reinforced by the media, marketing and advertising. Fourthly, sustainability also requires that important changes are made in the organisation of society, for example, altering land-use patterns and curtailing suburbanisation to lessen the need to travel by private

1 See, for example, Juffermans, J *Sustainable Lifestyles: Strengthening the Global Dimension to Local Agenda 21 – a Guide to Good Practice* The Hague: Towns and Development, 1995

car. Such policies are politically contentious, and politicians are seldom responsible to scientific evidence or rational argument alone. Change can only be achieved by generating widespread public support and political pressure.

A final difficulty is in challenging the perceived orthodoxy of the inevitability of overconsumption. There is sometimes a misalignment between values at the household level, even across many nations, and the values which win out in decision-making because of the influence of powerful lobbies and pressure groups acting on behalf of vested interests. For example, a recent survey of more than 13,000 Europeans discovered that the great majority of respondents (around 80 per cent) wanted fairly draconian control of the automobile in Europe's cities and towns, including banning almost all traffic from city centres.[2] The same survey discovered that politicians at national and municipal levels in all countries grossly underestimated this strength of feeling, identifying this as a minority view held by less than a third of the population. A reasonable hypothesis is that politicians have allowed themselves to be more influenced by the road lobby industries than by the views of their individual constituents. At the strategic European level, the continued promotion by the European Commission of new highway and motorway construction in so-called Trans-European Networks (55,000 kilometres of new roads) is identified by Friends of the Earth Sweden as directly related to powerful lobbying by European industrialists.[3] This gives rise to a ludicrous amount of road transport containing European goods: the costs of road transport are subsidised by European taxpayers, the majority of which probably would not agree to the programme if asked.

For these kinds of reasons, sustainable production and consumption will only succeed as the joint responsibility of stakeholders among government, business and voluntary organisations engaged in what has been called 'the rational planning of planetary conditions, not the defence of a restricted empire'.[4] What is required in each country is, firstly, a process of participation and mutual learning about the challenge of sustainability. Environmental space provides a framework for the required dialogue and debate among key stakeholders and social leaders, on the one hand, and for widening the debate to include a broad spectrum of citizens, through the media. Secondly, this drive towards national consensus is buttressed by local action and good practice, in the town, the neighbourhood and the household. Thirdly, an international support programme for sustainable production and consumption must involve international agencies and regulatory mechanisms which interject new messages into market pricing.

For our part, the Sustainable Europe Campaign has now broadened in scope and membership to implement a Sustainable Societies Programme which is an action network linking organisations in 56 countries. However, in terms of achieving sustainable development, this network is only as valuable as its ability to network further – that is, to build a network of networks, or a global coalition, creating, in effect, a broad social movement committed to a dematerialised global economy.[5] Here the Sustainable Societies Programme challenges groups and individuals around the world to join in this important effort. This involves three related areas of action:

- reorientation of the international development framework, and the objectives of its constituent organisations, to create more appropriate conditions for development in the South to reduce inequality and initiate the process of sustainable development;
- development of a series of international 'carrots and sticks' to foster sustainable production and consumption, such as labour, environmental and social regulations within trade agreements, and tax incentives for sustainable production and consumption; and

2 Reported in Blessington, H K 'Approaches to changing modal split: a strategy and a policy context' *Traffic Engineering and Control* pp63–67, February 1994

3 Nyberg, M *Green Capitalism* Göteborg: Friends of the Earth Sweden, 1996; available from Box 7048, 402 31; English version

4 Sachs, W 'The political anatomy of sustainable development' Wuppertal: Wuppertal Institute, no 35, 1995

5 For a discussion of this approach, see Carley, M and Christie, I *Managing Sustainable Development* London: Earthscan, 1992

■ an international effort promoting national sustainable development initiatives which link economic development to environmental and social goals, and create the conditions for public debate and participation in altering consumption patterns; national sustainable development strategies, prepared by national governments but linked in a global effort through the United Nations, could provide a framework for integrating local, national and international action on sustainable production and consumption.

Innovation at the Local Level

Within this context, we have not focused on local innovation or Agenda 21 because there are already many good sources of information on local initiatives, and because it is at national and international levels where progress needs to be made to support local action.[6] Of course, it goes without saying that NGOs, voluntary organisations, trade unions, church groups and other organisations in civil society can, by mobilising people and public opinion, play an influential role in accelerating the switch from business-as-usual to sustainable production and consumption. For example, the Environmental Home Guard (*Miljö heime vernet*) is a joint effort by Norwegian voluntary organisations to motivate and educate people away from the position of spectator and towards the role of participant in the struggle to protect the environment. There are 80,000 individual participants and a large number of schools, offices, housing coops and local municipalities involved in the initiative. There are many more equally important initiatives in Europe and around the world. However inspiring their work, these organisations cannot, nevertheless, achieve sustainable production and consumption without partnership with government and business, and an enabling international and national framework which is the focus of the remainder of this chapter.

With the Asia–Pacific region fast becoming a global, market-oriented, economic growth centre, issues of social equity, ecological sustainability, participatory policy-making, community cohesion and survival, and the democratisation of political power will determine the future of more than half of the world's people.

Letter from 35 Asian NGOs to the President of the Asian Development Bank, 1996

An Integrated Spatial Framework for Sustainable Development

The kind of vertical integration of development efforts required for sustainable development is shown in Figure 8.1. In Europe, this integration is referred to as subsidiarity; essentially, this principle argues that responsibility for development should be handed down, or decentralised, to the lowest feasible spatial, democratic or administrative level. Conversely, functions which are best carried out at higher levels, or which are necessary to enable lower-level action, are the responsibility of the appropriate higher level. A key point is that no one level is superior to another – all are of equal importance in the achievement of sustainable development, like the links of a chain. The different levels can also identify communities of common interest, varying from the household or the neighbourhood to the national or international sphere. Each individual may, by choice, be a member of one, more or all communities.

6 See, for example *Community Works! A guide to community economic action* London: New Economics Foundation, nd

Figure 8.1

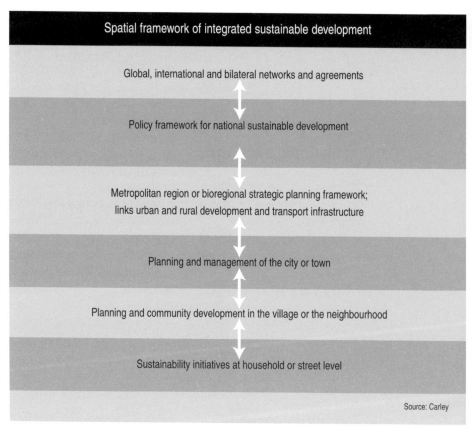

Spatial framework of integrated sustainable development

Global, international and bilateral networks and agreements

Policy framework for national sustainable development

Metropolitan region or bioregional strategic planning framework; links urban and rural development and transport infrastructure

Planning and management of the city or town

Planning and community development in the village or the neighbourhood

Sustainability initiatives at household or street level

Source: Carley

7 The regional development banks are the Asian Development Bank, the African Development Bank, the Inter-American Development Bank, the European Bank for Reconstruction and Development and the European Investment Bank

8 *Link*, issue on International Financial Institutions, no 74, September/ October 1996

The Role of Multilateral Organisations

The World Bank, the IMF, the WTO, the United Nations, and the five regional development banks, directed by national governments, can play a vital role in establishing an overall global framework for working towards sustainable production and consumption by the year 2050.[7] The International Financial Institutions programme of Friends of the Earth International sets out some priorities for a new development framework which could underpin such a transition.[8] The elements include the following:

Rethinking Development Aid

A great deal of multi and bilateral aid is intended to encourage the growth of national resource and materials consumption to promote macro-economic development. This supply-side approach results in a far from optimum use of natural resources as a tool for sustainable development, with many opportunities foregone in terms of future options. Sustainability for poor countries requires a development policy based on demand-side management: the genuine needs of people should come first, after which policy-makers must determine how maximum output (productivity) can be obtained through minimum inputs of natural resources and maximum creativity in development strategy. For example, in many countries a far more efficient use of sustainably produced electricity would be more sensible than building large hydropower plants, when the full range of economic and social dislocations are assessed, including the full opportunity costs of destroying natural resources, which could have served other development functions.

To gradually reduce global inequalities and address the needs of the poorest 20 per cent of the world's population, multilateral development banks and specialised agencies such as the UNDP should give more systematic financial support to primary education, health care, access to basic services and environmental protection.

Meeting Earth Summit and Social Summit Commitments

There is a deep gulf between the well-meaning commitments made at summit meetings and the failure to develop practical programmes for implementation. Agreements on, for example, biodiversity, climate change and desertification, should form the basis of establishing minimum criteria by which all downstream investments are evaluated to assess their compliance with these requirements. Moves should be made towards establishing a Sustainable Production and Consumption Summit in recognition of the need to tackle global problems at their source.

Stop Promoting and Funding Unsustainable Development

World Bank and IMF activities such as conventional Structural Adjustment Programmes (SAPs) and large-scale infrastructure investments, such as massive dams and road-building programmes, often dramatically undercut objectives of poverty reduction, social development and environmental improvement. For example, the World Bank is investing US1.75 billion of public funds in the massive Yacyreta Dam which will affect 109,000 hectares in Paraguay and Argentina, threatening the livelihoods of the area's indigenous peoples and the unique ecosystem of one of the world's largest water basins. At least 50,000 people will have to be relocated. And yet this project pales in size beside the World Bank's US$8 billion, 607-feet-high dam (185 metres) in the small African country of Lesotho, which will benefit mainly wealthy South African consumers in and around Johannesburg. Many of these megaprojects represent an outdated and unsophisticated development paradigm. More sophisticated methods of analysis are needed to assess the flows and distributional impacts of benefits and costs. The World Bank Inspection Panel should be further strengthened in this regard.

Beyond the impact of 'white elephant' megaprojects and the erroneous messages they send about the nature of modernisation and development, the multilateral organisations, particularly the IMF, have come to exert an enormous influence on the policies of developing countries. Structural Adjustment Programmes (SAPs) force indebted countries to restructure their economies by internal budget cuts and improvements in their export position in order to free up resources for debt reduction. But from an environment and development perspective, SAP policies have many negative effects.[9] The promotion of hard-currency exports as prescribed by the IMF results in an increase in the supply of raw materials on world markets, often to the point of surplus. When the balance of supply and demand is thrown off, the prices of raw materials drop, with the result that the income of the SAP recipient country eventually dwindles in relative terms. Since the lion's share of the raw material market is in the rich industrialised

9 Friends of the Earth Netherlands *Sustainable Consumption: A Global Perspective* Amsterdam: Vereniging Milieudefensie, 1996

Claude Martin

Costing Economic Growth

GDP measures the gross value created by economic activities in a given time. It indicates the monetary level of economic activities, but it often is used mistakenly as an indicator of welfare. Using GDP as an indicator of economic performance has a major flaw because it fails to include the loss of natural assets, such as land and soil, forests, species and minerals. The inaccuracy in the existing indicators tend to encourage economic expansion at the cost of the environment and quality of life. GDP should be adjusted for natural asset loss. The end result is environmentally adjusted net domestic product or EDP, which should be used by policy-makers, decision-takers and the media to indicate real progress.

A System of Integrated Environmental and Economic Accounting (IEEA) has been established by the UN as required by Agenda 21. The methodologies are there and have been tested mainly in developing countries. There are substantial benefits from the IEEA approach. It is more than an accounting exercise. It requires the formation of a stakeholder group, including government agencies, non-governmental sectors and external institutions. The existence of such a group can foster participation in decision-making, enable integration of environmental, social and economic considerations into development policy and raise environmental awareness in society. In addition to assessing the interaction between environment and economy, IEEA can support policies to ensure equitable distribution of natural assets, poverty reduction and as a basis for decisions on intergenerational equity – how much natural assets should be left to future generations.

However, the industrialised OECD countries have not accepted IEEA and major international development institutions such as the World Bank and IMF have not applied IEEA to their operations and policy formulation. Developing countries have become discouraged by this state of affairs. The inaction of industrialised countries and hesitation of major development institutions have lead to questions on the international applicability of IEEA. Concerned that environmentally adjusted economic indicators may be used unfairly in an international context – which will carry unfavourable political implications – developing countries are often unwilling to publish the results of IEEA and apply IEEA to their economic decision-making.

A system of information such as IEEA is essential. Environmental space analysis could inform that system. A new international momentum must be generated to cost economic growth and to integrate the environment into economic decision-making.

Claude Martin is Director General of the World Wide Fund for Nature, whose headquarters is in Geneva.

---

countries, this policy contradicts the need to reorganise production and consumption in wealthy countries in order to reduce their material flows and use of natural resources.

Finally, in the SAP country, land is invariably taken from local food production to grow export crops and, as discussed in Chapter 4, this constitutes an export of a valuable resource from the poor to the rich countries in an unsustainable manner. There is a related effect of export orientation which is that fewer financial reserves are available for increasing resource productivity for fulfilling domestic needs, and incentives for sustainable management of resources is eroded.

Resolving the International Debt Crisis

Until this is achieved there is little likelihood that the poorest countries can genuinely engage in a process of sustainable development. Since 1984, for example, sub-Saharan Africa has transferred US$150 billion to rich creditors in the North, and yet the total burden of debt still stands at US$135 billion – 2.5 times the area's annual export earnings. A third of this net transfer was to the IMF. In 1993, these countries paid US$306 million more to the IMF than they received from it.[10] This makes a mockery of aid and development programmes in those countries: for example, 70 per cent of aid to Zambia goes to repay debt.

The consequences of debt include the neglect of spending on health, sanitation, housing, education and water provision, which particularly impact on the world's poorest people. It also means cutbacks in infrastructure investments, which undermine productivity, and an inability to change the structure of production from primary products to those with greater added value. Debt also forces governments to accept ecologically destructive projects, such as a proposed mineral sands project in Madagascar which will destroy 6300 hectares of unique coastal forests and traditional fishing villages. It is no coincidence that Madagascar's international debt stands at US$4.3 billion.

In the debtor countries, the World Bank and the IMF have become the key economic policy advisors. In terms of resolving the debt crisis, therefore, they should set up a special development fund process which would not be conditional on SAPs or on enhanced SAPs. At the same time, debt burdens should be written off. This could take the form of a full write-off, or at least a partial write-off with the remainder reduced to the level which allows nations to service debt using their own resources and without necessitating social or ecological instability.

Broadening the Development Framework of the World Bank, IMF and World Trade Organisation

In the multilateral and bilateral sphere, as with national development, a major problem is the recurring failure to integrate environmental and social objectives with economic and trade objectives. The latter objectives continue on a narrowly focused path towards quantitative growth, often undermining other equally important objectives and development that are defined in a more holistic manner. An immediate step is to incorporate reasonable labour and environmental standards related to resource use within global trade agreements in order to ensure a higher quality of environment and development rather than the reduction of standards to the lowest common denominator in the short-term interests of trade. These standards should be refined and developed to preserve civil society and the quality of public life. However, there appears to be a real risk that the emergence of standards necessary for sustainability will be blocked by the OECD's Multilateral Agreement on Investment (MAI), under negotiation as of this writing by 29 industrial nations. Among other things, the MAI could restrict government regulation of corporate investment and behaviour, and prohibit the establishment of labour, environmental and human rights standards.

10 Pettifor, A 'The HIPC Initiative: treating the cancer of debt' London: Jubilee 2000/Debt Crisis Network, 1997

Work in Partnership with National Governments to Achieve Sustainable Development

National governments and financial institutions, such as the World Bank and the IMF, can only provide a fraction of necessary development aid and private money now accounts for 70 per cent of financial development. Given this situation, there is a real risk that vital development projects will fall by the wayside simply because they are not the most profitable short-term option.

So that private finance is not allowed to drive the development agenda on its own, multilateral organisations should assist national governments in devising appropriate, long-term sustainable development frameworks, and then decide which elements can be financed privately and which can be financed with an injection of public funding. Furthermore, the same high development standards, such as for the environment, basic civil rights for people and communities, gender analyses and indigenous peoples' policies, should apply to private financing guaranteed by the World Bank and IMF.

Regional development banks can play an important role in providing 'microcredit' to poor entrepreneurs if private financial markets fail. These development banks can take a broader social view of lending operations than do private banks. A flood of small loans could do more to achieve regional economic development than the massive injections of finance into dubious large projects. Think how far the US$1.75 billion invested in the Yacyreta Dam might have gone in US$500 loans to budding local entrepreneurs. The objectives of multilateral development organisations, and bilaterial aid, should be total quality of life rather than narrow economic growth objectives. Accomplishing this will require a more sophisticated understanding of the basic dimensions of quality of life, even if such dimensions cannot be quantified. Multilateral organisations must also broaden the participatory base in their policy-making to include civil society rather than just governments and become much more open, transparent and publicly accountable.

Providing a Flow of Public Information on Regional and National Development Options

Achieving the right balance of economic and social development without environmental damage is a difficult task. Ostensibly neutral, multilateral organisations should take on a major role in providing the public with good information on the costs and benefits and long-term implications of sustainable development options. National and regional resource accounting frameworks could be extended further to include consumption and production factors based on environmental space analysis.

Giving the United Nations a Firm Mandate to Promote Sustainable Production and Consumption

There is potential for the United Nations, working through the Commission on Sustainable Development (CSD), UNDP and UNEP to make a major global contribution to sustainable production and consumption. But the current approach is very weak, and there is a big gulf between the targeted approach embodied in environmental space and the current soft approach which is without clear commitments and recommendations in the field of international trade policies, coordination of economic instruments, and in

GUEST ESSAY 8.2

Anil Agarwal and Sunita Narain

The Sharing of Environmental Space on a Global Basis

The idea that global environmental space should be equitably shared amongst all human beings was first indicated in the Centre for Science and Environment's (CSE) critique of the World Resources Institute's (WRI) *World Resources Report 1990*. This report tried to apportion responsibility for the problem of global warming. Though apportionment of the carbon dioxide and methane sinks was inherent in the WRI model, it was not made explicit. When this apportionment was unravelled it was found that countries which produced larger quantities of CO_2 or methane had been given a larger share of the sinks. CSE questioned these calculations as these sinks are largely global common property. They should be equitably shared by all human beings on earth. Once this value assumption was built into the WRI model, the distribution of responsibilities for global warming changed dramatically across the nations of the earth.

Later, CSE's 'Statement on Global Environmental Democracy' pointed out that the South needs ecological space to grow but that this space has already been colonised by the North. The poor are not even using a small share of their legitimate portion of the global commons, such as the atmosphere, thus permitting the North to pollute at little cost and to build up their industrial base cheaply and rapidly. In the post Rio period, Friends of the Earth has launched a vigorous campaign to push nations towards sustainable consumption – an objective set by the Rio conference – by focusing on the equitable sharing of environmental space. FoE's campaign has rightly evoked debate and discussion in Europe.

The existing property rights regime covering the entire global environmental space is extremely complex. While certain components such as forests, grasslands and farmlands are private, corporate or national property, others such as the oceans and the atmosphere are global common property. Equitable sharing of environmental space will come about through two different economic approaches.

For products that emerge from individual, corporate or national property, the market pricing mechanism should be modified through public policy so that ecological costs incurred in production and consumption are internalised in consumer prices. Financial benefits accruing from this internalisation should accrue to the producing countries on the condition they use this income to move towards sustainable production systems. On the other hand, the sustainable use of global common property should be encouraged through equitable entitlements. To ensure these are used in a sustainable manner by each country, appropriate economic agents should be identified in each country and incentives provided by setting up opportunities for trading their unused entitlements on a periodic basis. Within a globalised economy, those who consume more than their fair share of the world's environmental space must be asked to buy the extra space from those who do not consume their share. And those who consume beyond their own share should pay economic penalties to a global fund which would compensate those affected by the resulting environmental damage, and underwrite a prevention programme.

Anil Agarwal is Director and **Sunita Narain** is Deputy Director of the Centre for Science and Environment, New Delhi.

managing the life-cycle impact of goods and services. UNEP and other bodies could also promote information flows on certain products to enable consumers to make more informed choices in the marketplace.

Given a strengthened CSD and UNEP committed to targeted change in trade and the environment, discussions could be shifted from the WTO into a broader framework which encompasses sustainable production and consumption, international commodity issues, multilateral efforts for employment creation in business and social spheres, the social negotiation of work conditions and working time, climate change and transport, and technology transfer. This should be carried out as part of a comprehensive review of WTO and the Bretton Woods institutions, and a consolidation of policy-making efforts of the international community on production and consumption issues within the UN.

One option would be the establishment of an Intergovernmental Panel on Trade, Environment and Sustainability (IPTES) to take on some of these tasks, where the WTO might not be fully competent. An IPTES would set environmental, social and general labour standards, the latter in collaboration with the International Labour Organization (ILO), which might then by applied by the WTO. These would include minimum labour standards applicable globally to protect workers from exploitation in the context of a level playing field applicable to all firms. In time, such minimum standards would become entrenched and a real achievement would be made, which would be both socially and economically sound. Broader sustainable production and consumption policies could be promoted at the regional level by the regional development banks and the regional agencies of the UN, such as the Economic Commissions for Africa and Latin America.

Finding New Mechanisms for Funding Development

A genuine commitment to development requires both political will and resources, given that a lot can be accomplished with modest amounts but that little is achieved with nothing. There are two challenges. One is to raise funds internationally for development and reduction of poverty; the other is to devise management mechanisms for promoting sustainable production, sustainable consumption and global equity, internationally and nationally, which could include international financial transfers. The first is touched on briefly here, the second is the focus of the remainder of this chapter.

A regular international source of development funds is an idea first floated in the Brandt Report of 1980 and taken up again by the UNDP in the *1994 Human Development Report*. It is particularly important as the squeeze on national aid budgets tightens. One option is a global flat tax – for example, a modest tax on the daily US$1.23 trillion of currency movements, such as first proposed by Nobel laureate James Tobin in 1972. This tax is based on the idea that since money is now a commodity to be bought and sold, there is no reason why it should not carry a modest sales tax. A small levy, say of 0.1 per cent, would have virtually no effect on capital flows but would be large enough to generate substantial resources (say, US$300 billion) each year for development purposes. Even a figure of 0.01 per cent of turnover would raise half as much as the present level of bilateral aid flows.[11] This is fair because all companies would be treated the same (the level playing field) and because those who benefit most from world trade and investment – large corporations and global investors – would pay the greatest share of

11 For a discussion, see Overseas Development Institute *New Sources of Finance for Development* Briefing Paper, London, 1996 (1)

Table 8.1

Options for raising global revenue for development
(a)	A tax on all or some international financial transactions (the Tobin tax). Variants include a tax on bond turnover, or on derivatives.
(b)	A general surcharge on international trade.
(c)	Taxes on specified traded commodities such as fuel.
(d)	A tax on the international arms trade.
(e)	Surcharges on post and telecommunications revenue.
(f)	An international lottery.
(g	A surcharge on domestic taxation (usually expressed as a progressive share of income tax).
(h)	Dedication of some part of national or local taxes, for intance on luxuries (or surcharges on them).
(i)	Parking charges for satellites placed in geostationary orbits.
(j)	Royalties on minerals mined in international waters.
(k)	Charges for exploration in or exploitation of Antarctica.
(l)	Charges for fishing in international waters.
(m)	Charges for use of the electromagnetic spectrum.
(n)	A tax or charge on international flights (or, alternatively, on flights in congested sectors). A variant is tax on aviation kerosene.
(o)	A tax or charge on international shipping.
(p)	Pollution charges (for example for dumping at sea).
(q)	A tax on traded pollution permits.
(r)	A voluntary local tax paid to a central global agency.
(s)	A new issue of IMF Special Drawing Rights (SDRs), distributed to the poorer developing countries (or used for peacekeeping or other global public goods).
(t)	Sale of part of the IMF gold stock.

Source: Overseas Development Institute

the tax. It need not be expensive to collect, although it would be necessary to prevent countries from freeriding and setting themselves up as tax-havens.

There are many other possibilities, some of which are listed in Table 8.1. Some, such as (l) to (m), involve a surcharge on the use of the global commons. Others, such as (d) and (n) to (q), operationalise the polluter-pays principle, with proceeds which could be used to help developing countries install pollution-control equipment or to enhance ecologically sound activities such as the preservation of the rainforest. In this respect they mirror the intended purpose of the Global Environmental Facility (GEF), an environmental improvement grant, although some of that funding may well have been diverted from traditional aid.

The assumption, in this section, has been that an efficient and enduring system of international cooperation linking South and North in a common effort towards sustainable development is a prerequisite to living within global environmental space. In the next section we consider ways in which the market can be adjusted to promote these ends in an efficient manner, and how government and civil society can come together to discuss, debate and plan national frameworks for sustainable development.

Promoting Sustainable Production and Consumption within the Context of the Market Economy

During roundtable debates organised within the Sustainable Europe Campaign, it is often mentioned by people from many different backgrounds and countries that the prices of natural resources are far too low. These inaccurate prices send out weak or non-existent messages to the marketplace on the long-term costs to human societies (and the biosphere) of excess resource consumption, waste and pollution. In order to reverse this situation within the bounds of the market economy, a fundamental step is to price natural resources appropriately. One of the major advantages of reducing consumption via the price mechanism, rather than through regulation, is that target groups are given more freedom and flexibility to devise their own methods of reduction and to be committed to their achievement. In this context, civil society and government also play a vital role in developing consensual goals and objectives for sustainable societies; this gives guidance to debates on appropriate resource pricing, on tax structures and on appropriate levels of provision of public goods.

There are four steps towards making markets work for sustainable production and consumption:

■ do away with government subsidies for unsustainable production and consumption activities.
■ Promote ecological tax reform and the reduction of externalities by making sure that polluter-pays and energy taxes are in place.
■ Develop equitable international tradeable emission rights, particularly for CO_2, which account for existing pollution and the ecological debt of industrialised nations.
■ Work towards political and scientific policies for genuinely dematerialised economies based on environmental space criteria, within the context of both international cooperation and national sustainable development strategies.

Unsustainable State Subsidies

Without interfering with the workings of the market, all national governments can make an immediate move towards sustainability by doing away with all state subsidies to unsustainable production and consumption, and those which damage global equity. The range of unsustainable state subsidies include those in favour of:

■ energy production;
■ resource extraction;
■ private transport and the infrastructure it requires;
■ waste disposal;
■ agriculture and forestry; and
■ investments designed to eliminate labour from production processes.[12]

12 Factor 10 Club *Carnoules Déclarations* Wuppertal Institute, 1995

Such state subsidies have been termed 'wealthfare' in the USA, where the subsidy regime consists of: discounted user fees for public resources; direct grants; corporate tax reductions and loopholes; subsidy of research and development (R&D) to benefit private companies; and tax breaks for wealthy individuals. In the USA, for example, the timber and livestock industries benefit from major give-aways which damage water quality and harm the commercial and sport fishing industries.

In the European Union, agricultural subsidies have meant the ploughing-up of traditional landscapes into grain deserts from which all vestiges of natural plant and animal life have been wiped clean. One result is that the songbird populations of Europe have gone into precipitous decline since 1980. Another is that underground water supplies in some areas have become so nitrate-loaded that they are unfit to drink. All of this is heavily subsidised by European taxpayers, insofar as agricultural subsidies consume one half of the entire annual budget of the European Union. Much of this unwanted food is then stock-piled at additional expense. There is little political will as yet to confront the powerful agricultural lobbies over the subsidy issue.

With the advent of the latest General Agreement on Tariffs and Trade (GATT) regime, agricultural subsidies in many OECD countries are also used to undermine agricultural economies and household livelihoods in the world's poorest countries by undercutting agricultural product prices. This suggests that current subsidy arrangements are unsustainable from every point of view.[13] The total amount of agricultural subsidies in the OECD countries is about US$175 billion, compared to the total agricultural aid to developing countries of about US$10 billion.

A good example of undoing this irrational situation is the USA's Green Scissors Coalition, an unusual alliance of environmental groups led by Friends of the Earth and conservative tax cutters, such as the National Taxpayers Union. Green Scissors has found that US$33 billion could be saved over the next ten years by cutting American subsidies which are wasteful and environmentally damaging. These include worthless water projects and subsidies for the unsustainable use of public land, highways and agricultural programmes.

Ecological Tax Reform

13 Oxfam *Trade Liberalization as a Threat to Livelihoods: the corn sector in the Philippines* London, 1996

14 Friends of the Earth *Working Future: Jobs and the Environment* London, 1994

15 Tindale, S and Holtham, G *Green Tax Reform* London, Institute of Public Policy Research, 1996

Ecological tax reform is an obvious second step, encompassing the polluter-pays principle for pricing and taxing of externalities and higher taxes on limited energy supplies and raw materials. Revenues can then be used to lower taxes on human labour, creating a win–win relationship between environmental improvement and job creation. The price of labour would decrease compared with energy prices and material inputs and waste disposal. The result is beneficial impact for economic employment levels, normally depressed by taxes on wages, without stimulating inflation.[14] For example, Sweden recently introduced a tax on sulphur dioxide emissions, which has resulted in a 40 per cent reduction in the sulphur product content of fuels in just two years. In the UK, it has recently been estimated that more than UK£20 billion (US$30 billion) per year could be raised by a package of ecotaxes which would then be used to reduce national insurance contribution by employees, business taxes (rates) and value-added (sales) tax. At least 500,000 jobs could be created by the year 2005, given immediate implementation.[15] The Sustainable Ireland study suggests an energy tax would create 9000 jobs in the first year of implementation.

For the State of Minnesota in the USA, an analysis suggests that shifting US$1 billion of tax burden onto pollution could generate the following reductions in taxes: 30 per cent on property taxes, 15 per cent on residential property taxes, 30 per cent reduction in worker compensation payments, and abolition of state income taxes for incomes below US$20,000.[16] Finally, an analysis of the six largest EU economies found that internalising all adverse environmental externalities could generate environmental tax revenues equal to 1.7 per cent of the collective GDP.[17] This could reduce labour taxes by the same magnitude and create 2.2 million additional jobs by the year 2010.

Ecotaxes, for all their potential benefits, however, do not prevent increasing economic activity from augmenting the absolute level of resource use even if the relative use of resources per unit of output decreases. The development of environmental policies during the last five to ten years in the OECD countries demonstrates the problem. Although environmental policies and rising ecotaxes, such as fuel tax in Britain, have been relatively successful in decreasing levels of emissions, use of fossil fuels and non-renewable resources is predicted to continue to rise. When cheap options for reducing the impacts of ecotaxes have been exhausted, it will become harder and harder for (inter)national governments to force entrepreneurs and citizens to decrease their emissions or resource use to sustainable levels. There is a need, therefore, for a solid ceiling on the use of resources. This ceiling is defined by available environmental space but cannot be enforced by setting targets alone.

Tradeable Rights

Systems of tradeable emission or resource-use rights offer the possibility of market-based steering within sustainable limits. The goal of tradeable rights is to bring the emissions of certain substances, such as SO_2 or CO_2, within ecologically acceptable boundaries in a market-oriented manner. The basic condition of such a system is that a national government or international body sets a maximum to the amount of emissions, or consumption of key non-renewable resources, measured in units consumed. Businesses within a national framework and governments within an international framework then purchase a quota from a clearing-house or an auctionary body. After a first distribution of the quota, market forces determine increase or decrease of price. For example, when – through economic growth – the demand for CO_2 units increases, then the price will increase. This stimulates efficiency increases in production and consumption systems.

The advantage of such a system over pure regulation is that the increase in efficiency will take place where it is the most cost effective. Industrial plants or countries with high rates of resource consumption or pollution will 'feel' price increases, and will therefore have an incentive to alter production technologies, products or services, or to shift economic growth, to less-polluting economic activities. The consumption and emission ceilings can be lowered step-by-step over time according to a clear reduction path to guarantee that entrepreneurs know well in advance what to expect. In this way, a positive drive is added to the dynamics of economic development.

The Importance of Equity Considerations in Tradeable Rights

An essential, but too often ignored, question concerning the implementation of any system of tradeable emission rights is the implicit social justice criteria and future impact of allocating these rights. There are a variety of options. UNCTAD (the UN Commission on Trade and Development), for example, distinguishes no fewer than ten criteria which can serve as the basis for allocation, ranging from pure

16 Blackwelder, B *Sustainable USA* Washington: Friends of the Earth, nd

17 DRI *The Potential Benefits of Integration of Environmental and Economic Policies – An Incentive-Based Approach to Policy Integration* Brussels: Report to the European Comission, Directorate General for Environment, Nuclear Safety and Civil Protection, 1994

grandfathering (based on current emissions) to size of national population (equivalent to the equity principle). Each option has advantages and disadvantages. Grandfathering, for example, is unacceptable to many developing countries because it takes no account of the cumulative environmental impacts of past pollution loads, sometimes called accumulated environmental debt.

A main reason for confusion between the various options is that not only must the ecoefficiency of the proposed trading permit system be assessed, but also the historical, ecological debt and equity implications. It is because the latter has been ignored, or glossed over, that many developing countries are against proposals for tradeable emission rights. The assumption within environmental space rights – of equally distributing tradeable permits at the initiation of the system – deviates from many conventional proposals for base-period emission rights awarded in proportion to existing emission patterns, and not according to a formula for intergenerational per capita (person–year) equity.[18] On the latter system, UNCTAD concludes:

> Countries buying permits are able to meet their abatement obligations more cheaply while those selling permits are compensated for their abatement expenses by revenues from permit sales. In fact, countries selling permits are better off than if there had been no agreement in the first place; they would therefore be keen to participate in such a scheme even if it had no environmental benefits. It follows that…the higher the environmental benefits that are set as targets, the keener will be the developing countries to participate, since the resources transferred to them will be greater.[19]

Pure grandfathering would mean that North Americans would be entitled to 19 tonnes of CO_2 emissions per capita, while Africans would only get emission rights worth one tonne per capita. This makes no sense from an equity point of view and would be unacceptable to a majority of the world's countries. A reasonable alternative is redistributing current global CO_2 emissions on the basis of population size. If this were effectively the basis of distributing emission rights, rich countries would have to buy enormous amounts of emission rights from poor countries.

The extent to which resources could be transferred from rich to poor countries is indicated by assuming a nominal price of US$30 per ton of carbon, a base assumption of both UNCTAD and OECD analyses. At this level, the distribution of emission rights on the basis of population size would trigger a transfer of US$285 billion from industrialised and transition countries to the South. Clearly, this might prove difficult even for the world's rich countries, so a transitional arrangement could be expected. Even given such an arrangement, it is reasonable to expect that the rich countries will make every effort to avoid spending more money than necessary for emission rights. This could trigger a quantum leap in emission control at source.

In this example, quotas are calculated under the condition of a ceiling presented by current CO_2 emissions, which are patently unsustainable. For a system of tradeable environmental space rights, this could only provide an initial starting point. In the long term, however, it is clear that the ceiling has to be lowered to a level of approximately half the current CO_2 emissions. A variation of the equity argument is that historical CO_2 emissions should also be accounted for, since they are the causative factor in current climate change. Krause, for example, calculates an initial capitalisation for cumulative emissions between

18 Krause, F, Bach, W and Koomey, J Energy Policy in the Greenhouse; Vol 1 From Warming Fate to Warming Limit: Benchmarks For a Global Climate Convention El Cerrito, CA: International Project for Sustainable Energy Paths, 1989

19 UNCTD, Controlling Carbon Dioxide Emissions: The Tradeable Permit System Geneva, 1995

1950 and the present to be some US$100 billion (at a price of US$1 per ton of CO_2) for the developed countries taken together.[20] Krause also suggests that, to avoid reinforcing existing relationships based on economic dominance, the amount of fossil carbon release rights that would be tradeable in any year should be limited to a small percentage of each country's or region's total, or to a fraction of annual increments derived from long-term reduction targets. Emission rights, therefore, would likely be no more than one of several elements in an overall redistribution and fossil fuel carbon reduction strategy.

Finally, it is important to note that although CO_2 emissions are used here by way of example, an extended environmental space rights system would need to focus mainly on volume of resource use, rather than on pollution per se, with the ecological backpack and environmental space calculations as part of the analysis of limits on consumption. This is also important because, while many rich countries have low levels of pollution per unit of GDP, it is their very high resource use per capita which is at the root of many problems, as we have stressed throughout this book. Poor countries may have high rates of pollution per unit of (often very low) GDP, but low resource use per capita. In this sense, a focus on CO_2 emissions is the exception to the environmental space rule. This is important because many people in the South correctly view historic overconsumption in the North as the major cause of environmental degradation.

In conclusion, a system of tradeable environmental space rights would stimulate eco-innovation within sustainable boundaries in both developed and developing countries. In addition to the ecological benefits, a major advantage is that even the world's poorest countries would become partners with equal rights in pollution control and sustainable production and consumption processes. This would both empower those countries and ensure the development of regulatory and trading systems which are genuinely global.

National Strategies for Sustainable Production and Consumption

Because of the complexity of sustainable development, and its essentially political and social nature, it can only come about by the development of forward-looking national strategy built on broadly based participation. As we have suggested in this book, the strategy is only relevant if it moves towards genuine targets for reduction of resource consumption with target years, and towards dematerialisation. Environmental space provides the policy guidance and analytic framework for considering the appropriate steps over time, but within a national political and cultural context. Strategy and participation are the chicken and egg – it is clear that the process of participation is as important as the scientific aspects of the strategy. Government can play a key initiating role in taking forward the national sustainable development strategy (NSDS). This in turn provides:

- a framework for local action;
- a means for developing national human-resource capacity around sustainable production and consumption; and
- a platform for international discussion and negotiation.

20 op cit   As for the scientific side, we need only reiterate that the environmental space approach considers subsidy

reduction, ecological taxes and (possibly) emission rights as steps on the road to dematerialisation, based on reductions of key inputs to production. These key indicators, which define around 90 per cent of global material flows, were described in Chapter 5. They will become more sophisticated over time. This operationalises key aspects of the concept of sustainable development, and gives rise to the possibility (and necessity) of factor eight to ten increases in resource productivity in developed economies. Further development of our knowledge of the material flows analysis, and the resource efficiency measure mentioned earlier, material input per unit of service (MIPS) – is a promising way forward on the scientific side of environmental space analysis.[21] Material flows analysis would fit well in a broader framework of sustainable human development analysis.

As stressed in this chapter, it is essential that an international framework develops. A negative reason is that decreasing intensities of materials usage may only reflect the displacement of material-intensive production, typical of the earlier stages of industrialisation, to industrialising countries.[22] There are, of course, many positive reasons, ranging from the satisfactions which come from cross-cultural endeavours to those stemming from the handing-on of an ecologically sound world to future generations.

Perhaps first and foremost, sustainable development is a national task. Are our governments up to the job? There has been much talk about the weakening of the nation state, particularly in the face of the rise of what Charles Handy calls supranational corporations. There are certainly a growing number of large corporations, anchored in no one particular country and answerable to no particular government, with annual turnover well in excess of the GDP of many developing countries. Whatever their current allegiances, these companies, such as General Motors, have achieved their size partly because of the support and intervention of their original national governments. At the same time, some nation states are at risk of destabilisation from armed and ethnic conflict, ecological crisis, such as impending water shortages, and social risks, such as large-scale movements of refugees. However, in spite of these developments (or because of them), the nation state, above all other institutions, needs to remain in a pivotal position in order to influence sustainable development, nationally and internationally, for the 50-year time frame of this discussion. Since current changes in the operation of the nation state are evolutionary, there is little likelihood of their disappearance. This also suggests the importance of building national competence, both within government and within partnership between government, business and civil society.

At the national level, no other organisation can support local initiatives with a national policy framework which links together different policy streams, such as economy, health, transport, land use and so on, and their downstream impacts. On the other side of the coin, local initiatives are very often undermined when the nation state is not committed to sustainable development, or only pays lip service to the concept without a clear commitment to implementation. In those cases, it is hard for local initiatives to make lasting achievements when swimming against a river of unsustainable national development. We argue below for the importance of a visionary, integrating national sustainable development strategy (NSDS) for each nation, around which to foster discussion and debate, and to institutionalise a process of setting targets for living within the boundaries of environmental space.

In the international arena, nation states are in a position to influence the directions and policies of multilateral organisations, and in combination with other nation states can act as a counterbalance to the growing power of supranational corporations. Interconnectedness in the global economy requires skill in coordinating national policies and national actions in many areas.[23] These include issues such

21 Hinterberger, F, Luks, F and Schmidt-Bleek, F 'Material flows vs "natural capital": What makes an economy sustainable?' *Ecological Economies*, forthcoming. Readers with an interest in material flow analysis should contact the Wuppertal Institute at the address in Appendix B

22 Spangenberg, J 'Concepts for Sustainability: Environmental Space and Material Flows' paper presented at the International ICLEI Seminar, Munster, 1996

23 Simai, M *The Future of Global Governance: Managing Risk and Change in the International System* Washington: United States Institute of Peace, 1994

as the management of the global commons, transboundary pollution and the regional and global implications of national policies. Sustainable consumption policies can directly reduce international tension over scarce resources. In all of these areas, the authority and competence of the nation state in achieving sustainable development is essential, as a basis for networking and for partnership with other nation states in formal and informal arrangements. Globalisation requires integrated policy-making at regional and international levels.

This integration is also necessary to promote diffusion of eco-innovation by leading-edge companies without undermining their competitiveness, and to ensure that the market is regulated nationally and internationally to deliver sustainable quality of life and not just the fruits of unregulated greed. Large corporations themselves will need to incorporate moves towards greater organisational democracy, listening to the concerns of their staff and shareholders. This is beginning to happen: a court in Canada, for example, has ruled that shareholders are entitled to table motions on the management of companies at annual general meetings. Governments, and the multilateral organisations through which they work, will need to encourage this trend.

A pivotal role for government is not to deny that healthy societies are like a three-legged stool: government, private enterprise and civil society interacting in partnership. This is particularly true since the modern state has downsized and privatised in many areas, shedding the functions which can be more efficiently carried out in other sectors. For example, the last chapter noted that many people see an emerging role for the voluntary sector in fostering constructive employment schemes. In Britain, evidence has emerged that the voluntary sector, if calculated at average wages, contributes the equivalent of UK£41 billion to the national economy, the third largest component of GDP.[24] In spite of this positive trend towards partnership, however, and recognising the complexity of governance and economy in the modern state, government must play a key role in promoting the common good.

National Competence from Decentralised Authority

The state is also in a position to foster the necessary top-down and bottom-up linkage. One of the main authorities often given to the state is the power to devolve that authority to other levels, spatially and sectorally. Given the complexity of the challenge of sustainable development, it has been common knowledge since the Brundtland report that the state cannot achieve sustainability on its own. Therefore, decentralising power, for example, to local government and from there to community groups active in local neighbourhoods, strengthens the capacity of societies to achieve sustainability objectives locally, national and internationally. A good example of capacity building is provided by Sustainable Austria which has built on its environmental space analysis by establishing the Academy of Sustainability Moderators. These are 'catalyst' people who receive 24 days of training in community organisation and media skills around sustainability issues. They are selected from each of the country's regions, and include not only representatives of voluntary organisations but those from central and local government and business.

In the circumstances of globalisation, decentralisation (as well as regulation) can be an essential tactic for achieving common objectives and retaining the competitive creativity of an open society. Power needs to be shared, not hoarded by centralisation. Within this context of decentralised authority and initiative, there are a number of areas in which national governments must be active to promote sustainable production and consumption; these are listed in Box 8.1.

24 Gaskin, K and Dobson, B *The Economic Equation of Volunteering: A Pilot Study* Loughborough: Centre for Research in Social Policy, 1997

Svend Auken

Environmental Space in Denmark's Policy Framework

Given the present ways of production, the world's ecosystems will quite simply not survive if the Third World attains the living standards of present-day Western industrial societies. This is, of course, unacceptable. The Third World has the same claim to affluence and welfare as those who happened to be first in line. That is why the crisis relates not only to those threatening single problems, but seriously calls into question our way of life.

There are limits to the growth of material use, which is large in Denmark and other advanced economies. For many of us who have reached a reasonable living standard, it is totally superfluous to have yet more money or to buy a bigger house. All countries have discussed sustainable development, but there is a great need to specify and quantify it to identify clearly the challenges facing us. One way to do this is by means of the concept of environmental space, which we call ecological scope. Therefore, the Danish Government introduced the ecological scope approach in Danish national policy in 1995. We did this because it could be a useful instrument in quantifying part of the sustainable development concept and improving our ability to move more quickly in this direction.

The ecological crisis will only be solved through a joint effort by the entire global community – and only if the economically strongest powers and groupings are determined to do so. Whatever Denmark chooses to do, it is evident that an isolated Danish initiative will have but limited impact. There is great need to promote international understanding in governments and among the general public of the importance of sustainable development and reduced resource use. I believe that all actors in the society, including NGOs, can play a critical role in this process. I want Denmark to be in the forefront of sustainable development – the right conditions are present. A densely populated society with limited social disparities, a good educational system and the Danish tradition of general enlightenment and broad public debate open up opportunities for making a valuable contribution to the development of a sustainable world. The opportunities for activating the unemployed within this task should be exploited.

There is every indication that the Danish people have started this process. Grass roots activities and dramatic changes in consumer patterns point in this direction. The business community is introducing environmental management on its own initiative. Denmark could be a pilot project for a new lifestyle which combines modern industrial production and welfare with ecological responsibility. This calls for determination to give high priority to research and technological innovation, but it may also be necessary to develop new management models and forms of organisation.

Svend Auken is Minister of Environment and Energy in Denmark.

The Role of Government in Eco-Innovation

Chapter 6 stressed that eco-innovation is a social process. One part of the process is strict regulation, which promotes innovation by the majority of companies and ensures minimum environmental compliance by laggard companies. A survey of engineering companies in Britain, for example, found only one company which felt that regulation was not a driving force for innovation. Leading-edge companies anticipated legislation and influenced its development.

The coherence of the general policy framework is also essential. It is clear that a stable, coherent and effective long-term policy is crucial for business to anticipate the possibilities for eco-innovation. It is also important for government to focus innovation where it is most needed from an ecological point of view. In the USA, for example, 71 per cent of all toxic emissions from industry arise from just four sectors: paper, plastics, chemicals and metals.[25]

Developing Consensus around the National Sustainable Development Strategy

Agenda 21 called for national sustainable development strategies (NSDS) to provide an overall framework for policy and institutional integration and to act:

- as a forum and a context for dialogue and debate, emphasising longer-term visions for societies and the values of those societies as they influence sustainable production and consumption;
- as a means of identifying key national issues, and the priorities for action and investment;
- as a way of focusing policy and research on those issues; and
- as a means of encouraging capacity building and strengthened institutional arrangements, which are the foundation of sustainable development.[26]

Although for the most part still in their infancy in terms of sophistication, these NSDS have the potential to make a major contribution to sustainable production and consumption in four ways.

1   NSDS foster widespread participation of government, business and civil society, both top-down and bottom-up in the rolling process of their preparation, often coordinated by national councils for sustainable development or a similar organisation. Because of the politically contentious issues addressed, a measure of national consensus is vital to their effective implementation.
2   NSDS promote the integration of economic development policies with social development and environmental policies. This helps to overcome one of the foremost policy constraints on sustainable development in most countries.
3   NSDS provide a framework for integrating environmental space analysis and targets on resource consumption into the framework of national policy.
4   NSDS could provide a real means of linking national efforts at sustainable production and consumption in an overall global movement through the coordination of the United Nations Commission for Sustainable Development (CSD). The CSD, with the full support of the General Assembly, in turn enables and rewards national initiatives, as well as integrates multilateral efforts by development banks and other organisations.

There is a solid literature emerging on NSDS, including a handbook for national governments developed by IUCN and a recent review of 20 such plans.[27] Considerable further development is required before the

25 Young, J E and Sachs, A *The Next Efficiency Revolution: Creating a Sustainable Materials Economy* Washington: Worldwatch Paper 121, 1994

26 Dalal-Clayton, B *Getting to Grips with Green Plans: National Level Experience in Industrial Countries* London: Earthscan, 1996

27 ibid, see also Carew-Reid, J et al *Strategies for National Sustainable Development: A Handbook for their Planning and Implementation* Gland: IUCN and IIED, 1994

strategies start living up to their potential; however, they have a real advantage in that they allow each country to devise their own national strategy for sustainable production and consumption, which takes into account local history, values and visions for future quality of life.

When NSDS are integrated with environmental space analysis, there is real potential to move from laudable intentions to genuine action; this can be monitored and assessed to ensure that societies are really moving in the direction of sustainable development. Without genuine targets, there is a real risk that the NSDS process can be abused if it amounts no more than superficial public relations. For example, too many current NSDS simply promote business-as-usual by interpreting sustainable development as economic growth with 'bolt-on' environmental protection measures. These fail to grapple with limits to economic activity or to address the social aspects of sustainability. Environmental space analysis could move these strategies from empty promises to phased, targeted action.

Finally, we have emphasised sustainable development strategies at the national level, but they could be just as important at the international level. For example, the European Commission's multistakeholder advisory council on sustainable development (the General Consultative Forum) has recommended for the European Union: a sustainability task force to develop innovative strategies, a regular sustainable development report for Europe; R&D on sustainability issues, promotion of sustainable lifestyles; and a think-tank on long-term policy called the House of the Future.[28]

Similar initiatives could be taken forward by other regional trading or economic organisations, such as NAFTA, ASEAN or the regional development banks. The notion of subsidiarity, discussed earlier, suggests that the chain of sustainable development efforts becomes stronger as links are added and strengthened. Within this context, powerful entities, such as the EU, should screen their foreign relations policies according to sustainability criteria, equivalent to a broadened environmental audit.

Environmental Space – Guide to Sustainable Societies

Because the long-range achievement of sustainable production and consumption will require many steps and actions over many decades, development of a coherent global framework is essential. This framework needs to provide us with:

- a means for developing a global understanding of production and consumption issues, both quantitatively and qualitatively;
- a means to set out real targets for moving in the direction of sustainability, rather than away from it, and for measuring the degree of our achievements.

28 General Consultative Forum *Vision 2020: Scenarios for a Sustainable Europe* Brussels: European Commission, Directorate General XI, Environment, Nuclear Safety and Civil Protection, 1997

Here the concept of environmental space, based on equal access to all crucial resources and their sustainable use, can bring a number of advantages to the link between production and consumption and national sustainable development strategies. Firstly, environmental space can provide a unifying element to assist in the vertical integration of policy from project-level analysis, such as environmental impact assessment, to the bioregional, programme or national policy level (strategic assessment and indicator systems), and finally to the international level, such as the European Union or the CSD. Over time, this type of integration could help generate a more unified and coherent policy approach to sustainable development within the context of linking top-down and bottom-up initiatives.

Box 8.1 National actions to achieve sustainable production and consumption

Immediate Steps

■ Stop subsidies to environmentally and socially damaging activities, such as unsustainable agricultural practices and road transport.

■ Ensure that externalities, including health damage, are fully costed in pricing structures.

■ Promote increasingly stringent ecological tax reform, transferring tax burdens from labour to resource consumption and pollution.

■ Develop, with business, financial and tax incentives (carrots) and regulatory mechanisms (sticks) to promote eco-innovation and resource efficiency.

■ Support public spaces and public functions, in the most efficient manner, to contribute to quality of life without encouraging private consumption.

The National Development Process

■ Develop a sense of national vision on what kind of society should be handed on to future generations; and a clear and honest assessment of existing and future challenges to economic and social development and environmental quality.

■ Encourage national debate on production and consumption, and long-range options for a sophisticated, dematerialised society.

■ Within this context, initiate a national sustainable development strategy (NSDS) process, which must formally integrate national economic development planning with environmental and social policy streams; integrate physical development with human resource development.

■ Decentralise authority and resources wherever appropriate closer to the bottom-up locus of development or to civil society.

National Sustainable Development Strategy

■ Review all policies and structural arrangements, such as land-use, transport and energy policies, for sustainability and policy coherence.

■ Assess existing consumption of environmental space for key indicators, and set targets for 2010 and 2050 in order to meet environmental space criteria.

■ Develop strategies for achieving targets which integrate local, regional and national action.

■ Set options for more stringent policies, better incentives and tighter regulation if interim targets are not met.

■ Report annually on key indicators, including those of environmental space.

■ Institutionalise consultation procedures and regular upgrading of the national strategy.

> *Environmental space is a guide*
> *in our journey towards more sustainable societies.*

Secondly, the concept of environmental space has the potential to influence production processes in different sectors, such as industry and agriculture, and to help build a broader public constituency around issues of sustainable production and consumption, fostering beneficial changes in consumption patterns. Thirdly, as stressed in Chapter 4, environmental space analysis provides, if not a completely hard and fast measurement entirely grounded in empirical science, a correct directional policy guidance – propelling the policy framework of national governments and of multilateral organisations in the right direction towards sustainability, rather than away from it.

Finally, the participants in the Sustainable Europe Campaign and the North–South Project who inspired this book are convinced that the countries and peoples at the forefront of sustainable development will also be at the leading edge of economic and social development, and will have the highest quality of life in the 21st century. The principles of living within the boundaries of environmental space, and the firm commitment to global equity, provide an equality of opportunity for all countries to participate in a process of mutual learning and action on sustainable development.

Appendix A: List of National Studies and Other Publications of the Sustainable Europe Campaign

1 These titles have been translated from the original languages. In some cases, there is also a summary translation of the national report in English. Please contact the national group for further information. Contact information is listed in Appendix B. There is also summary information on environmental space available in Japanese, Mandarin, Slovenian and Lithuanian. Please contact the national group listed or Friends of the Earth Netherlands for further information.

National Studies[1]

Amici della Terra, *Italy: National Data and Inventory, Towards a Sustainable Europe*, ENEA/Amici della Terra, Rome, 1995

Amigos de la Tierra, *Sustainable Europe, Sustainable Spain*, Madrid, 1996

BUND – Friends of the Earth Germany and MISEREOR, *Sustainable Germany: A Contribution to Global Sustainable Development*, A Study of the Wuppertal Institute for BUND and MISEREOR, 1996.

Coalition for Environment and Development, *Sustainable Finland*, Helsinki, 1995

Ecologists' Movement of Macedonia, *Sustainable Development of Republic of Macedonia*, Skopje, 1995

Friends of the Earth Austria, *Sustainable Austria*, Phase 2 Sustainable Europe Campaign, Vienna, 1996

Friends of the Earth Cyprus, *National Data and Inventory: Towards a Sustainable Cyprus*, Nicosia, 1996

Friends of the Earth Estonia, *Towards Sustainable Estonia, National Report to the Friends of the Earth Campaign on Sustainable Europe, Phase II*, Tallinn, 1995

Friends of the Earth for England, Wales and Northern Ireland, *Tomorrow's World: Britain's Share in a Sustainable Future*, London: Earthscan, 1997

Friends of the Earth Georgia, *National Study Georgia*, Tbilisi, 1996

Friends of the Earth Ireland *Sustainable Ireland*, Earthwatch, Dublin, 1997

Friends of the Earth Malta, *Sustainable Malta, Towards Sustainable Europe*, Valletta, 1996

Friends of the Earth Netherlands, *Sustainable Netherlands Revised: Sustainable Development in a*

European Perspective, Amsterdam, 1996

Friends of the Earth Scotland, *Towards a Sustainable Scotland*, Edinburgh, 1996

Friends of the Earth Sweden, *Transforming Society for Fair Shares of Environmental Space: Targets and Calculations for a Sustainable Sweden*, Göteborg, 1997

Hnuti DUHA/Friends of the Earth – Czech Republic, *Sustainable Czech Republic*, Prague, 1996

Institute for Sustainable Development, *Results of the Polish Study, FoEE-Campaign Sustainable Europe*, Warsaw, 1996

International Institute for Environmental Studies: Nea Ecologia, *National Report: Sustainable Greece in a Sustainable Europe*, Athens, 1995

Les Amis de la Terre de Midi-Pyrénées, *Results of the FRENCH Study, Phase II of the FoEE Campaign Towards a Sustainable Europe*, Puylaurens, Tarn, 1995

Les Amis de la Terre, *Towards Sustainable Europe: Report of the Study in Belgium*, Brussels, 1996

National Movement Ecoglasnost – Bulgaria, *National Study, Sustainable Europe Campaign*, Sofia, 1995

National Society of Conservationists, *Towards Sustainable Europe, Use of Environmental Space Expressed In Numbers For Hungary*, Budapest, 1996.

NOAH, *Sustainable Denmark, The National Report*, Copenhagen 1996

Rhododendron, *Sustainable Romania: Results of the Romanian Study*, Bucharest, 1996

Society for Sustainable Living in the Slovak Republic (STUZ/SR) *Towards Sustainable SLOVAKIA, The National Study*, English version, second edition, Bratislava, 1996

Swiss League for Nature Protection (SLNP), *Sustainable Switzerland: Results of the Swiss Study* Common Framework for the National Studies Phase 2 of the Sustainable Europe Campaign, Basel, 1996

The Project for an Alternative Future, the Norwegian Forum for Environment and Development (FORUM), *Sustainable Norway, Probling the limits and equity of environmental space*, Oslo, 1995

Ukrainian Environmental Association 'Zelenyi Svit', *Towards Sustainable Ukraine, Commission on Sustainable Development: The National Study*, Dnipropetzovsk, 1996

From the North–South Project

Friends of the Earth Netherlands, *Sustainable Consumption, A Global Perspective*, Amsterdam, 1997

From the Sustainable Europe Campaign

Hille, J., *The Environmental Space Concept: Implications for Environmental Reporting, Policies and Assessments*, Copenhagen: European Environmental Agency, 1997

Spangenberg, J. (ed.), *Towards Sustainable Europe: The Study*, Brussels: Friends of the Earth Europe, 1995

Spangenberg, J. (ed.), *Towards Sustainable Europe: The Handbook*, Brussels: Friends of the Earth Europe, 1995

Spapens, P. and R. Vervoordeldonk (eds.), *Towards Sustainable Europe: A Summary*, Brussels: Friends of the Earth Europe, 1995

Appendix B: Contact Points for Sustainable Europe Campaign and North–South Project Participating Organisations

AIDRom-Rhododendron
P.O. Box 48–41
Str. Halmeu nr. 12
Bucharest 2
ROMANIA
office@aidrom.eunet.ro

Amici della Terra
Via di Torre Argentina 18
00186 Rome
ITALY
foeitaly@gn.apc.org

Amigos da Terra
Calcada Margues de Abrantes, 10 – 3 Esq.
1200 Lisboa
PORTUGAL
foeportugal@gn.apc.org

Amigos de La Tierra
C/San Bernardo 24, 3rd floor
28015 Madrid
SPAIN
foespain@nodo50.gn.apc.org

Bond Beter Leefmilieu
Overwinningstraat 26
1060 Brussels
BELGIUM
bblv@pophost.euronet.be

BUND
Postfach 300251
53182 Bonn
GERMANY
Bund-bn@oln.comlink.apc.org

Centre for Environment and Human Settlements
School of Planning and Housing
Heriot-Watt University
79 Grassmarket
Edinburgh EH4 1ND
SCOTLAND
Michael.Carley@ed.ac.uk

Centre for Science and Environment
41, Tughlakabad Institutional Area
New Delhi 110 062
INDIA
cse@unv.ernet.in, cse@gn.apc.org

Chikyu no Tomo
4–8–15 Nakameguro Meguro-ku
Tokyo 153
JAPAN
foejapan@igc.apc.org

Coalition for Environment and Development
Nekalantie 17 B 4
33100 Tampere
FINLAND
marko.ulvila@uta.fi

DEM
Ul 'Vasil Gorgov' BB baraka 2
9100 Skopje
FYR OF MACEDONIA
dem@soros.mk

Earthwatch
31 Castle Street
Dublin 2
IRELAND
foeireland@toppsi.gn.apc.org

Ecoglasnost
PO Box 548
1000 Sofia
BULGARIA
ekogl@bulnet.bg

ENDA (Environmental Development Action in the Third World) Dakar
PO Box 3370
Dakar
SENEGAL
Masselo@endadak.gn.apc.org,
BVassent@endadak.gn.apc.org

Estonian Green Movement
Box 318,
EE 2400 Tartu
ESTONIA
oja@erl.tartu.ee

Federaçâo de órgâos para Assistência Social e Educacional (FASE)
Rua das Palmeiras 90 (Botafogo)
BR 22270–070 Rio De Janeiro
BRAZIL
fase@ax.apc.org

Friends of the Earth Austria
Alserstrasse 21/1/5
A–1080 Vienna
AUSTRIA
malko.allhau@signale.comlink.apc.org

Friends of the Earth Cyprus
P.O. Box 3411
Limassol
CYPRUS
foearth@spidernet.com.cy

Friends of the Earth England, Wales and Northern Ireland
26–28 Underwood St.
London N1 7JQ
ENGLAND
susdev@foe.co.uk

Friends of the Earth Europe (CEAT)
Rue Blanche 29
1050 Brussels
BELGIUM
foeeurop@foe.knooppunt.be

Friends of the Earth Ghana
PO Box 3794
Accra
GHANA
Theo_K_Anderson@foeghana.gn.apc.org

Friends of the Earth Netherlands
Postbus 19199
1000 GD Amsterdam
THE NETHERLANDS
susteur@foenl.antenna.nl

Friends of the Earth Scotland
70–72 New Haven Rd.
Edinburgh EH6 5QG
SCOTLAND
foescotland@gn.apc.org

Friends of the Earth Sweden
Box 7048
S–402 3l Göteborg
SWEDEN
foesweden@nn.apc.org

Georgia Green Movement
David Aghmashenebeli Ave., 182
Mushthaid Park, Green House
380012 Tbilisi
GEORGIA
irisi@gmep.kheta.ge
tactic@sustain.org.ge

HNUTI DUHA Praha
Lubianska 18
12 000 Praha 2
CZECH REPUBLIC
org.hduha@ecn.gn.apc.org

Institute for Sustainable Development
31 Lowicka Street
02–502 Warsaw
POLAND
ine@ikp.atm.com.pl

Les Amies de la Terre de Midi-Pyrénées
48 Rue Foulimou
81700 Puylaurens, Tarn
FRANCE
amiterre@micronet.fr

Les Amis de la Terre
Place de la Vingeanne
5100 Dave
BELGIUM

Lithuanian Green Movement
Central Post P.O. Box 156
LT–3000 Kaunas
LITHUANIA
atgaja@kauna.omnitel.net

Mouvement Ecologique
6 rue Vauban
Luxembourg
LUXEMBOURG
meco@ci.rech.lu

Moviment Ghall-Ambjent
22E Sister Street
St. Julian's
MALTA
julian@unimt.mt

National Society of Conservationists
Kolto u. 21
1121 Budapest
HUNGARY
ildiko@mtvsz.zpok.hu

Nea Ecologia
Mavromichall 39
10680 Athens
GREECE
ecologia@hol.gr

Nigerian Environmental Study/Action Team (NEST)
27 Aare Avenue, U I P O Box 22025
Bodija, Ibadan
NIGERIA
NEST.NIGERIA@lagosmail.sprint.com

NOAH
Norrebrogade 39 1
DK 2200 Copenhagen
DENMARK
foedenmark@nn.apc.org

Norges Naturvernforbund
Postboks 2113 Grünerlokka
N–0505 Oslo 5
NORWAY
norwaynature@pns.apc.org

Red de Ecología Social (REDES, FoE Uruguay)
Avda. Millan 4113
12900 Montevideo
URUGUAY
redesur@chasque.apc.org

Schweizerischer Bund für Naturschutz
Postfach
CH 4020 Basel
SWITZERLAND
106001.1053@compuserve.com

Society for Sustainable Living
Starotursky Chodnik 1
811 01 Bratislava
SLOVAKIA

Socio-Ecological Union
Krasnoarmeyskaya 25–85
125319 Moscow
RUSSIA
svet@glas.apc.org
soceco@glas.apc.org

Umanotera
Vida Ogorelec Wagner
Resljeva 20
61000 Ljubljana
SLOVENIA
vida@eunet.si

Walhi (FoE Indonesia)
Jl. Mampang Prapatan XV No. 41
Jakarta 12790
INDONESIA
walhi@nusa.or.id

Wuppertal Institute for Climate, Environment and Energy
Postfach 100480
Doppersberg 19, D–421103
Wuppertal
GERMANY
j.spangenberg@mail.wupperinst.org

Zelenyi Svit/ FoE Ukraine
48 Kosiorstreet, apt. 24
320085 Dnipropetzovsk
UKRAINE
eazelenysvit@gluk.apc.org

Index

Page numbers in **bold** refer to tables or figures